Christi @
Plc

MW01616147

Cooperative Learning & Music

Marya Katz
Christi Brown

Kagan

Andrea

Kagan Publishing
981 Calle Amanecer
San Clemente, CA 92673
1 (800) 933-2667
www.KaganOnline.com

ISBN: 978-1-933445-09-0

Table of Contents

Section 1: Let's Learn About Music

Table of Contents (continued)

Section 1: Let's Learn About Music (continued)

Section 2: Let's Talk & Write About Music

Table of Contents (continued)

Section 2: Let's Talk & Write About Music (continued)

Table of Contents (continued)

Section 2: Let's Talk & Write About Music (continued)

Section 3: More Music Resources

Cooperative Learning & Music Introduction

This book is divided into sections: 1) Let's Learn About Music, and 2) Let's Talk and Write About Music. The Kagan Cooperative Learning Structures included offer students the opportunity to do what they love: move around and talk to their peers while guiding them in rich learning experiences through peer tutoring and interaction. After all, musicians know the saying, "If you can SAY it, then you can PLAY it." Students do not retain knowledge by hearing the information. They learn more when they talk about the thinking, respond to higher-level questions, or explain music knowledge to someone else. When writing about music, students are engaged in learning various music concepts through the medium of writing, including traditional music notation. The authors feel that this format will allow teachers both the flexibility in choosing appropriate Cooperative Learning Structures, based on student and curriculum needs, and the ability to manage the structures for maximum student engagement.

Teaching music involves considering both the concepts of music composition (melody, rhythm, harmony, form, tone color, texture, and expression), as well as appropriate activities to assist in the learning of those concepts (singing, playing instruments, reading and notating music, moving, listening, creating, and evaluating music performances). Each of the Structures in this book may be used with various grade levels; knowledgeable teachers will be able to assess the difficulty level and relative usefulness of each structure, depending on their curricular needs and the focus of their lessons.

Assessing student understanding is an ongoing process, and one that many teachers struggle with in the limited time frame of most music classes. These Structures offer yet another tool for engaging students through the activities described, as well as allowing the teacher to check for understanding before continuing on to another musical concept.

When students work in pairs or teams to further their understanding of a concept, they take the responsibility of learning to a higher level than when the teacher simply gives them the information. The principles of Kagan Cooperative Learning are perfectly suited to the music classroom, where students routinely work together to achieve a goal—after all, performing music is most often done in combination with others. Music classrooms in elementary and secondary levels using Kagan Structures allow each student to be more accountable for the learning and performing process. It is more difficult for students to hide in performance (handing the mallets to a stronger student or simply mouthing the words in a choral piece) when the practice includes Kagan Structures. Properly structured Cooperative Learning activities engage all students, and thus boost music smarts for all.

Appreciations

We especially want to thank Miguel Kagan for believing in us and reviewing the manuscript. Thank you to Dr. Spencer and Mrs. Laurie Kagan for creating Kagan Structures, providing meaningful trainings, and allowing the freedom of implementing music content into each structure! Thanks to Heather Malk for making these lessons come alive with her design and illustrations; Alex Core, for the design and cover color; Becky Herrington, for managing the publication; Erin Kant, for her illustrations; and Kim Fields, for copy editing.

Thanks to Samantha Quesenberry and Roselynn Hopkins for encouraging me to pursue the possibility of publishing the manipulatives I had begun to create for my own personal music classroom use with Kagan Cooperative Learning Structures. A huge thanks to my co-author Christi Brown for her insight, good humor, and gentle teaching to help me fully understand what Kagan is all about and how it can be used most effectively—I could never have completed this book on my own!—**Marya Katz**

Thank you to my mother, Phyllis Brown, who gently guided my musical journey all of my life and steered me to the path of becoming a music teacher. A heartfelt thanks to my co-author Marya Katz for her endless patience and creativity in transforming Kagan Structures into any music classroom. Thank you, Marya, for bringing life to our ideas and making it a reality!—**Christi Brown**

About the Authors

Marya Katz describes herself as a musician, an educator, a lover of growing things, and a lifelong learner. She is a National Board Certified Teacher (Early/Middle Childhood Music, 2002), and taught public school vocal music for 33 years (preK through grade 12, with the majority of time spent at the elementary school level). She also conducts the adult choir at her church, which recently celebrated her 25th year in that position. She makes her home in Blacksburg, VA, in the beautiful Blue Ridge mountains. In addition to teaching music, Marya is also a performer and composer. She plays hammered dulcimer and sings with the folk group *Simple Gifts of the Blue Ridge*, teaches and performs at various Dulcimer Festivals along the East Coast, enjoys working with private students, is featured on several recordings, and has published three books of her dulcimer music. Two of her tunes have also been published in *Dulcimer Players News*, a journal devoted to both hammered and Appalachian dulcimers. More information about her hammered dulcimer passion, as well as contact information, can be found on her Web page at http://www.dulcimations.com.

Marya's interest in Kagan Cooperative Learning Structures was born after attending a week-long Kagan institute in 2007. At that time there were very few resources specifically targeted toward music teachers. So, upon her return home, she began to develop many of the ideas and materials found in this book. She considers it a lucky whim when she decided to contact Kagan Publishing Company to test their interest in turning her work into a printed volume, and an even greater benefit to have been paired with Christi Brown as co-author when they agreed to consider the proposal.

A 1975 graduate of Alderson-Broaddus College (Philippi, WV) with a Bachelor of Arts in Music Education, Marya went on to complete her MA in Music Education in 1981 from Marshall University (Huntington, WV). In addition to her National Board Certification, she also holds certifications in Orff and Kodály pedagogies, has been the recipient of several grants (*Arts in the Afternoon*, for at-risk students; *Secret Codes of the Underground Railroad*, a collaborative quilting project with Art and Social Studies; *Chinese Music and Art*), has been a Mentor-Coach for new teachers in her county, and is included in various "Who's Who" editions (*American Women, American Education, American Colleges and Universities, and most recently the Presidential Who's Who*). She has presented workshops in her local area to both music and classroom teachers on integrating music activities with academic classroom studies in social studies, mathematics, science, language arts, and children's literature. She has also devoted several years to mentoring other National Board candidates in her region, and served as the chair for developing the current Music Curriculum for her county.

Marya's professional Web-based publications include "Secret Codes of the Underground Railroad: A Unit of Plans," which was the recipient of the American Music Education Initiative national award in 2001, and "Liberty For All: The Young Republic" (lesson plans to accompany the Liberty For All CD-ROM, a project of the Music Educators National Conference, 2006). She also has several lesson plans published on the MENC Web site under the "My Music Class" link.

Christi Brown was an Orff Music Specialist having spent time in both the Memphis City Schools in Memphis, TN, and at a Kagan demonstration school in Auburndale, FL. While at Berkley School in Auburndale, FL, she was awarded Teacher of the Year in 2001. Christi received a Bachelor of Arts in Music, Master of Arts in Teaching, and Master Class Level of Orff Training from the University of Memphis in Memphis, TN. Her Orff Apprenticeship was completed at Eastman School of Music in Rochester, NY. She has been a presenter and clinician at numerous conferences such as American Orff Schulwerk Association (AOSA), Florida Music Educators Association (FMEA), Association of Supervision and Curriculum Development (ASCD), National Middle School Association (NMSA), and Texas ASCD conferences. Christi is a contributing author of a movement piece called "Bluegrass Stomp," published by MacMillan-McGraw-Hill in the *Share the Music* textbook series, grade 6.

As an Internationally Certified K–12 Kagan Trainer, she has traveled the world. Some of the countries include Germany, England, Malaysia, Newfoundland, Spain, and Singapore. Although Christi regularly teaches many Kagan courses, her specialties include *Cooperative Learning, Multiple Intelligences*, and *Advanced Cooperative Learning*. She is a co-author of the *Music, Movement & More* Kagan training.

Section 1

Let's Learn About Music

Structure 1

Quiz-Quiz-Trade

Structure 1

Quiz-Quiz-Trade

Students quiz a partner using question cards, and answer a question in return from that same partner. The two students trade cards and repeat the process with a new partner.

Steps

Setup: *Each student receives one Quiz-Quiz-Trade card, which has a question for music knowledge building (content mastery).*

1 The teacher tells students to "*Stand up, put a hand up, and pair up.*"
After every student gets a card, they take their cards and do a StandUp–HandUp–PairUp to find a partner.

2 Partner A quizzes B.
In our Word Wizard example, Partner A begins by showing the graphic notation on the card and asking, "*What word do these notes spell?*"

3 Partner B answers.
Partner B silently reads the letter names of the notes in the order shown and then tells Partner A what word was spelled (for example, a card with a note in the 2nd space, the 3rd space, and the bottom line spells, "ACE").

4 Partner A praises or coaches.
After Partner B has answered, Partner A assesses the answer given for correctness. If correct, appropriate praise is given ("*Way to go!*" "*You got it!*" "*You are music smart!*" etc.). If incorrect, Partner A gives a hint to the correct answer and Partner B attempts to identify the note(s) a second time. For example, Partner A might say "*Remember that the note in the 2nd space of the treble clef staff is an 'A'—try again, starting with that note.*"

5 Partners switch roles.
Steps 2–4 are repeated with Partner B quizzing Partner A for the word on his/her card that the letter names of the notes spell.

6 Partners trade cards and thank each other.
The two students then **trade cards with each other**, express thanks to each other for being their partner, and move to find a new partner by repeating the hand up, pair up step of the structure.

7 Repeat steps 1–6 a number of times.
Students continue quizzing and trading until the teacher stops the structure.

Sample Activity

Word Wizard: **Cards are prepared where each card has a music notation pattern that will spell a word when the individual letter name notes are read from left to right.**

Benefits

- All students are actively involved.
- Students receive more learning in less time.
- Students interact with many classmates, which promotes classbuilding.
- Students make connections with partners.
- Students learn and practice social skills: greeting others, tolerance, taking turns, coaching, asking for help, and praising.
- Students rely on each other, rather than on the teacher, to check for accuracy in response to the questions.
- By using different sets of cards, many music concepts can be reinforced.
- Quiz-Quiz-Trade can be used as a pretest, as a review of concepts, or as a check for comprehension.

Hints

- **Model.** When introducing the structure, model each of the steps with a student. Emphasize the importance of trading the cards in Step 6.
- **Watch for Shadows and Magnets.** Encourage students to mix with everyone, not just with their friends, and to seek out partners in close proximity so that the structure proceeds quickly.
- **Open Space/Classroom Climate.** Model how to move safely around the room, pair-up, and move away from other pairs if crowding is an issue. An open space can help manage the movement during Quiz-Quiz-Trade. Keep the activity as free of distraction as possible—no music playing as they are doing the structure.
- **Coaching.** Teach, if needed. Use the model "tip, tip, tell, re-ask"—give up to 2 hints to your partner before telling the answer, then ask the question again for the partner to give the answer back.
- **Creating Cards.** If upper elementary and secondary level students create their own cards for a test review, check for accuracy.

Quiz-Quiz-Trade

Structure 1

Quiz-Quiz-Trade (continued)

Principles

P Positive Interdependence: Students need each other to complete the task.

I Individual Accountability: Students are accountable to a partner. Students are accountable for asking, answering, coaching, and praising.

E Equal Participation: Students are given equal opportunities through turn-taking.

S Simultaneous Interaction: 50% of the students will be quizzing while the other 50% will be responding.

Extension to the Lesson: Mix-N-Match

When question cards have a matching pair floating around the room, Quiz-Quiz-Trade can extend into a whole class review, or as an assessment in checking for understanding, by using the Mix-N-Match structure.

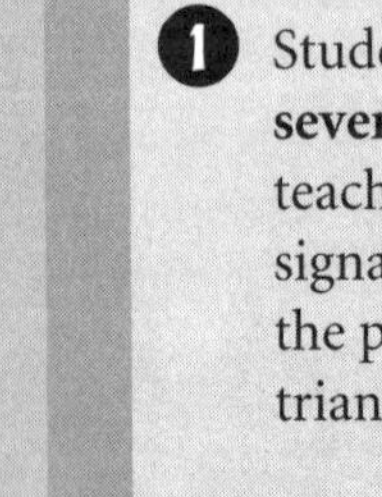

Bass Clef Bonanza: Half of the students are holding cards with a notated tone on the bass clef staff; the other half are holding cards which describe the note placement. For either type of card, the response is letter name identification of the note.

1. Students "mix" around the room **doing all seven steps of Quiz-Quiz-Trade** until the teacher calls "*Stop*" or gives an attention signal (for example, by playing a fanfare on the piano or tapping a rhythm pattern on a triangle).

2. When the teacher stops the action, students "freeze" in place while hiding their cards from each other. The teacher asks students to think about which card will match the one they are holding. During this 3–5 second "think time," no one moves, talks, or shares answers.

3. Teacher calls, "*Find your match.*" Students show their card and say the match they are looking for. (For example, the student with a notated "C" in the 2nd space of the bass clef staff is looking for the student who has "*What note is in the 2nd space of the bass clef staff?*") As pairs are created, students move to the perimeter of the room to create a circle, and the teacher leads the class in a whole-class check.

4. Teacher calls, "*Quiz-Quiz-Trade*" and students resume the original structure. Additional *Mix-N-Match* extensions may be done as desired or needed within the time frame of the lesson.

Quiz-Quiz-Trade
Activities

Word Wizard: Treble Clef 8-16
The cards in these sets display a pattern of notes that spell simple words on the treble clef staff. *The easier cards in the treble clef set are recommended for primary level students; other cards in the treble clef set are recommended for upper elementary students.*

Bass Clef Bonanza 17-23
The cards in this set ask for the letter name of a single pitch on the bass clef staff, either by showing the note in music notation or by describing where it is located on the staff. *Recommended for upper elementary (3rd–6th grade) or secondary level students.*

Dazzling Dynamics 24-34
The symbols and meanings of various dynamics markings are presented on the cards in this set. *Recommended for elementary or secondary level students.*

Enharmonic Enigma 35-42
The cards in this set ask for identification of enharmonic tones, as well as various definitions of symbols that create enharmonics. *Recommended for secondary level students.*

Form Fit 43-48
The cards in this set include graphic representations of form structures and corresponding hints for identifying each form structure. *Recommended for elementary level students.*

Tempo Terms 49-56
The cards in this set ask students to identify the meaning of the various markings found on a metronome to indicate the speed of the beat. *Recommended for upper elementary (3rd–6th grade) and secondary level students.*

Vocabulary Volley 57-105
The cards in this set include questions about various music concepts and music notation terms. Cards are separated into three sets: 1) Elementary, 2) Secondary, and 3) Elementary & Secondary. *Recommended for upper elementary (3rd–6th grade) and secondary level students.*

Blank Card Template 106
Use this blank card template to create your own Quiz-Quiz-Trade cards.

Additional Activities for Quiz-Quiz-Trade Cards

Card sets can also be used for Structure 2: Fan-N-Pick and Structure 3: Showdown.

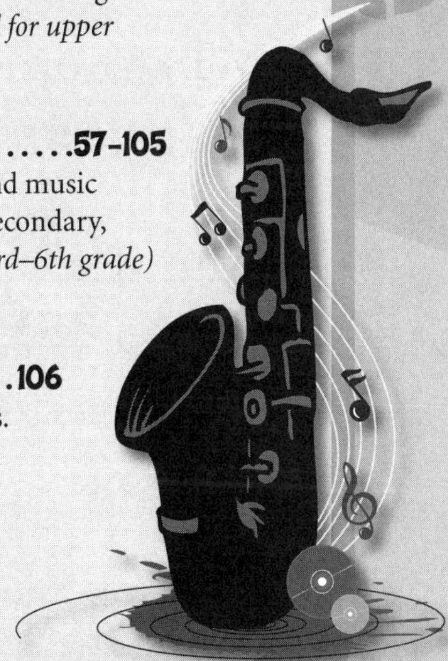

Word Wizard: Treble Clef

Instructions: Cut out each card along the dotted line. Students cover answers while quizzing. Give each student a card to play Quiz-Quiz-Trade.

Word Wizard: Treble Clef 1

What word does this pattern spell?

Answer: BE

Word Wizard: Treble Clef 2

What word does this pattern spell?

Answer: ACE

Word Wizard: Treble Clef 3

What word does this pattern spell?

Answer: ADE

Word Wizard: Treble Clef 4

What word does this pattern spell?

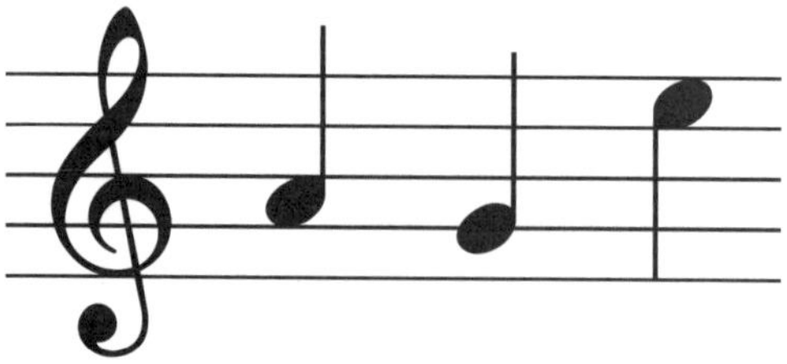

Answer: AGE

Word Wizard: Treble Clef

Instructions: Cut out each card along the dotted line. Students cover answers while quizzing. Give each student a card to play Quiz-Quiz-Trade.

Word Wizard: Treble Clef 5

What word does this pattern spell?

Answer: BAD

Word Wizard: Treble Clef 6

What word does this pattern spell?

Answer: BAG

Word Wizard: Treble Clef 7

What word does this pattern spell?

Answer: BED

Word Wizard: Treble Clef 8

What word does this pattern spell?

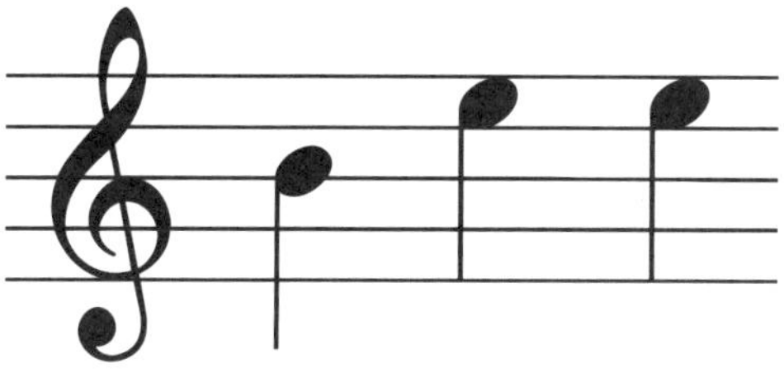

Answer: BEE

Word Wizard: Treble Clef

Instructions: Cut out each card along the dotted line. Students cover answers while quizzing. Give each student a card to play Quiz-Quiz-Trade.

Word Wizard: Treble Clef 9

What word does this pattern spell?

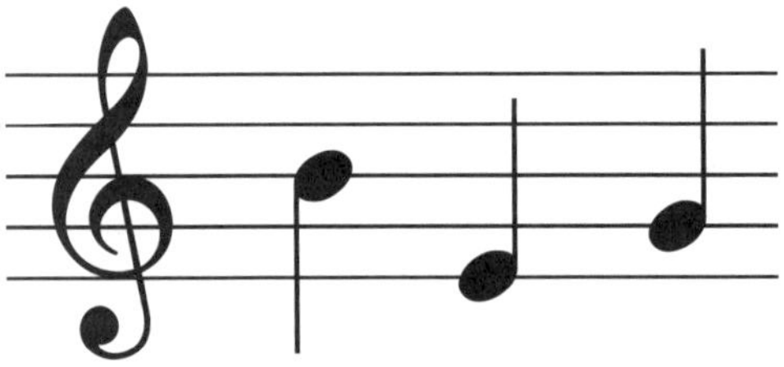

Answer: BEG

Word Wizard: Treble Clef 10

What word does this pattern spell?

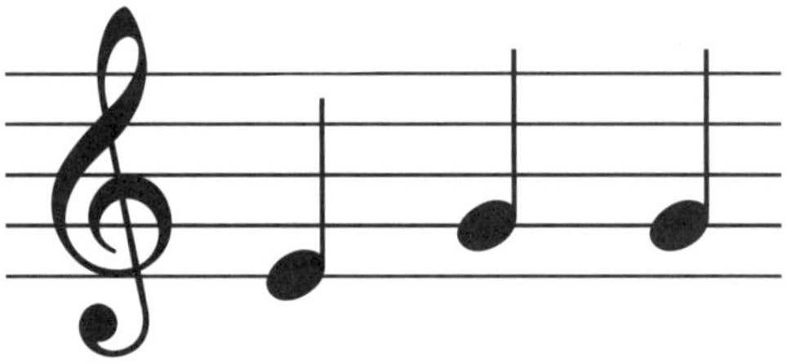

Answer: EGG

Word Wizard: Treble Clef 11

What word does this pattern spell?

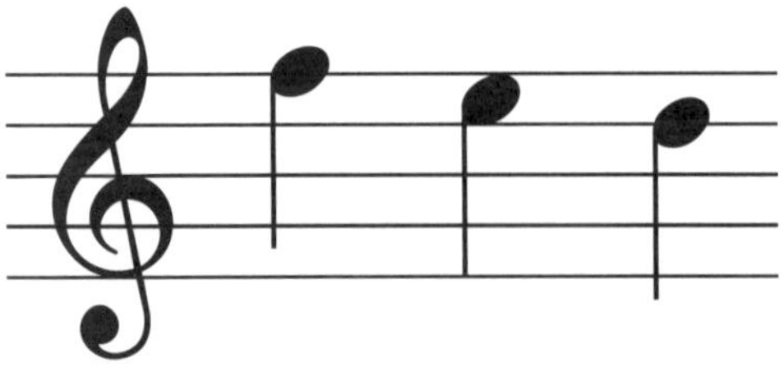

Answer: FED

Word Wizard: Treble Clef 12

What word does this pattern spell?

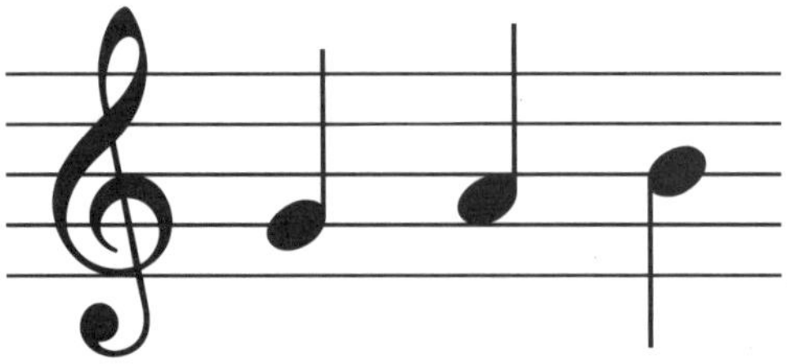

Answer: GAB

Word Wizard: Treble Clef

Instructions: Cut out each card along the dotted line. Students cover answers while quizzing. Give each student a card to play Quiz-Quiz-Trade.

Word Wizard: Treble Clef 13

What word does this pattern spell?

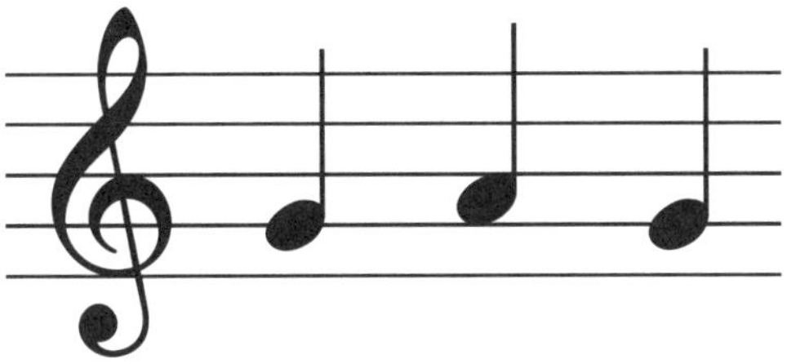

Answer: GAG

Word Wizard: Treble Clef 14

What word does this pattern spell?

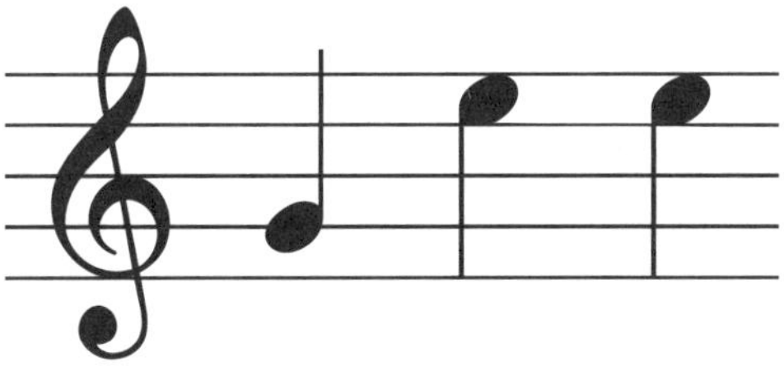

Answer: GEE

Word Wizard: Treble Clef 15

What word does this pattern spell?

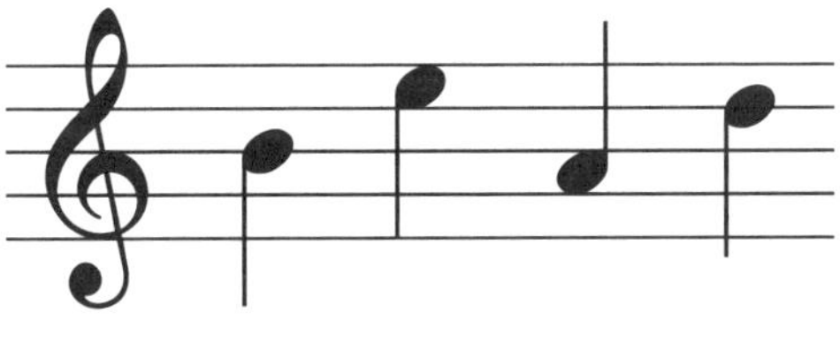

Answer: BEAD

Word Wizard: Treble Clef 16

What word does this pattern spell?

Answer: BEEF

Word Wizard: Treble Clef

Instructions: Cut out each card along the dotted line. Students cover answers while quizzing. Give each student a card to play Quiz-Quiz-Trade.

Word Wizard: Treble Clef 17

What word does this pattern spell?

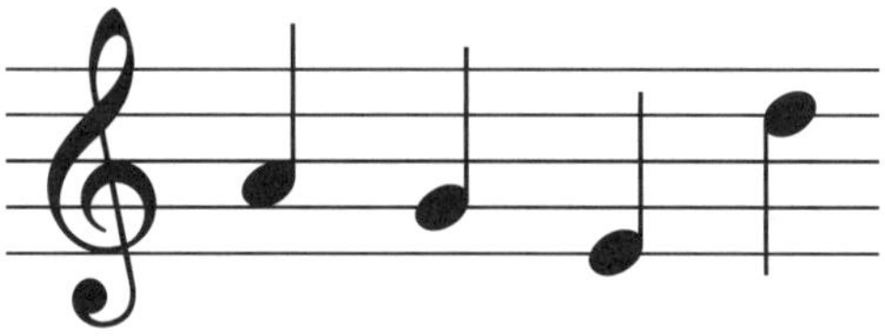

Answer: AGED

Word Wizard: Treble Clef 18

What word does this pattern spell?

Answer: ACED

Word Wizard: Treble Clef 19

What word does this pattern spell?

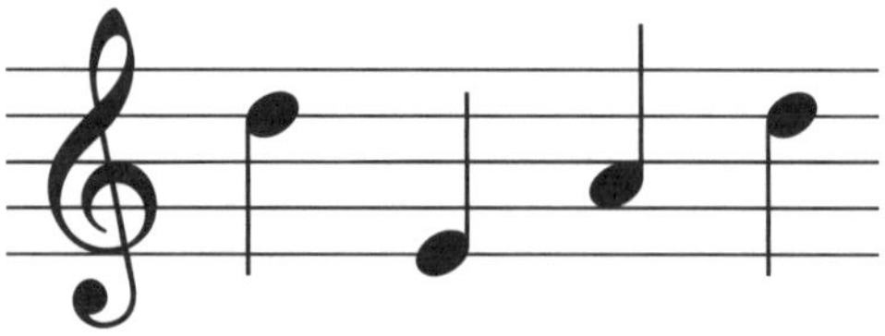

Answer: DEAD

Word Wizard: Treble Clef 20

What word does this pattern spell?

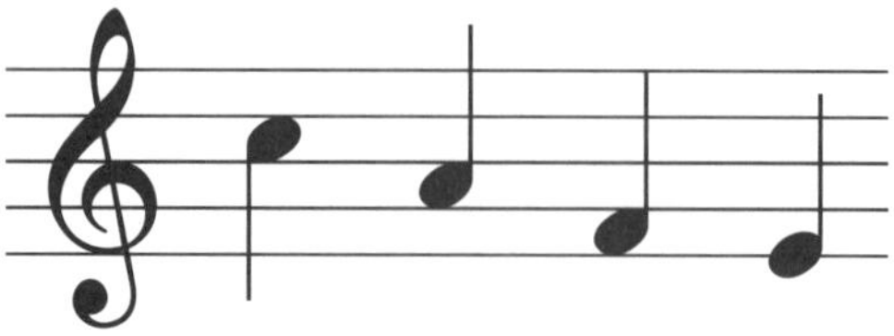

Answer: CAFE

Word Wizard: Treble Clef

Instructions: Cut out each card along the dotted line. Students cover answers while quizzing. Give each student a card to play Quiz-Quiz-Trade.

Word Wizard: Treble Clef 21

What word does this pattern spell?

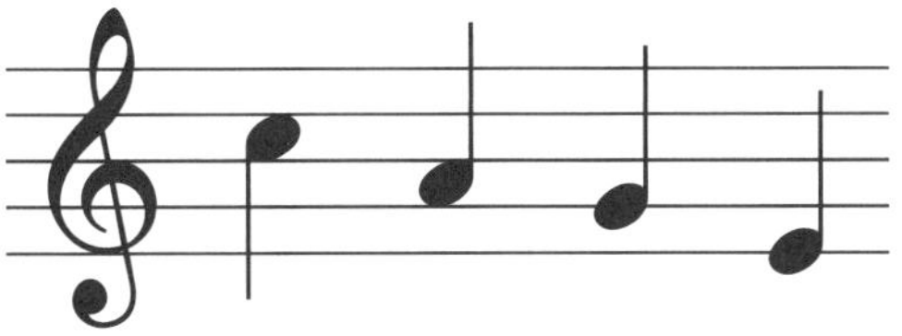

Answer: CAGE

Word Wizard: Treble Clef 22

What word does this pattern spell?

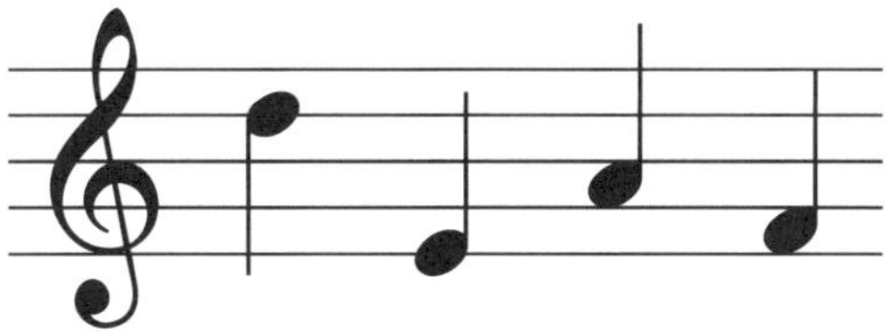

Answer: DEAF

Word Wizard: Treble Clef 23

What word does this pattern spell?

Answer: DEED

Word Wizard: Treble Clef 24

What word does this pattern spell?

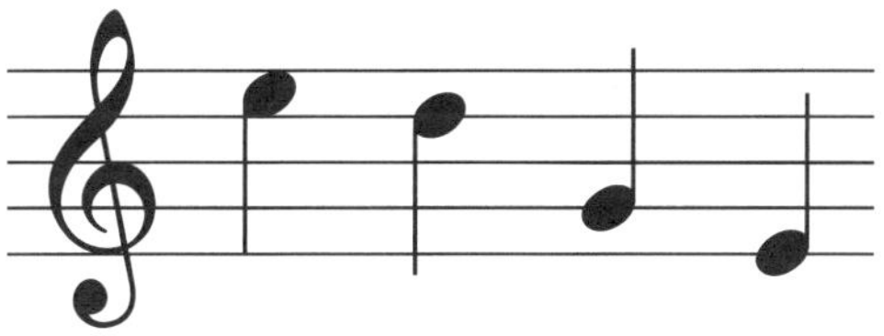

Answer: EDGE

Word Wizard: Treble Clef

Instructions: Cut out each card along the dotted line. Students cover answers while quizzing. Give each student a card to play Quiz-Quiz-Trade.

Word Wizard: Treble Clef 25

What word does this pattern spell?

Answer: FACE

Word Wizard: Treble Clef 26

What word does this pattern spell?

Answer: FADE

Word Wizard: Treble Clef 27

What word does this pattern spell?

Answer: FEED

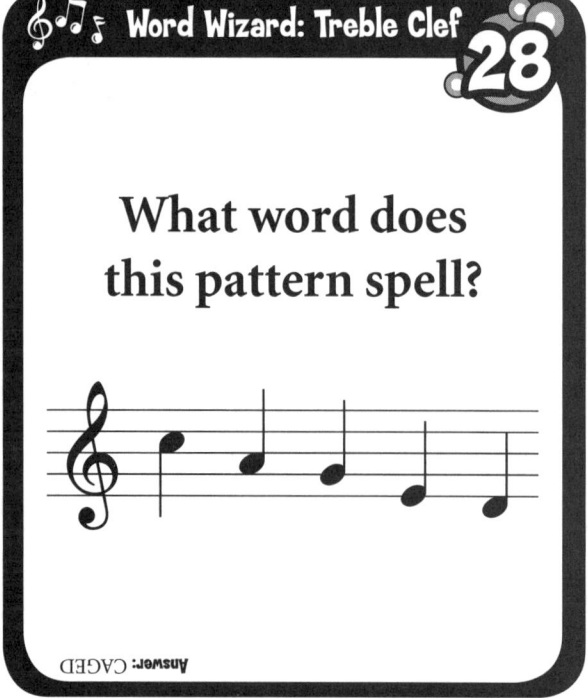

Word Wizard: Treble Clef 28

What word does this pattern spell?

Answer: CAGED

Word Wizard: Treble Clef

Instructions: Cut out each card along the dotted line. Students cover answers while quizzing. Give each student a card to play Quiz-Quiz-Trade.

Word Wizard: Treble Clef — 29

What word does this pattern spell?

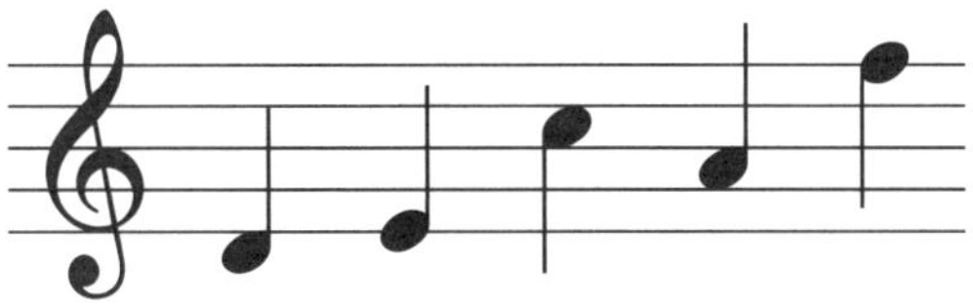

Answer: DECAF

Word Wizard: Treble Clef — 30

What word does this pattern spell?

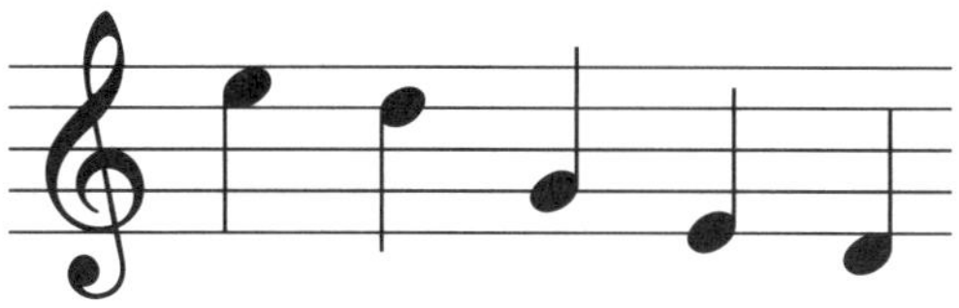

Answer: EDGED

Word Wizard: Treble Clef — 31

What word does this pattern spell?

Answer: FACED

Word Wizard: Treble Clef — 32

What word does this pattern spell?

Answer: FADED

Word Wizard: Treble Clef

Instructions: Cut out each card along the dotted line. Students cover answers while quizzing. Give each student a card to play Quiz-Quiz-Trade.

Word Wizard: Treble Clef 33

What word does this pattern spell?

Answer: BAGGED

Word Wizard: Treble Clef 34

What word does this pattern spell?

Answer: BEADED

Word Wizard: Treble Clef 35

What word does this pattern spell?

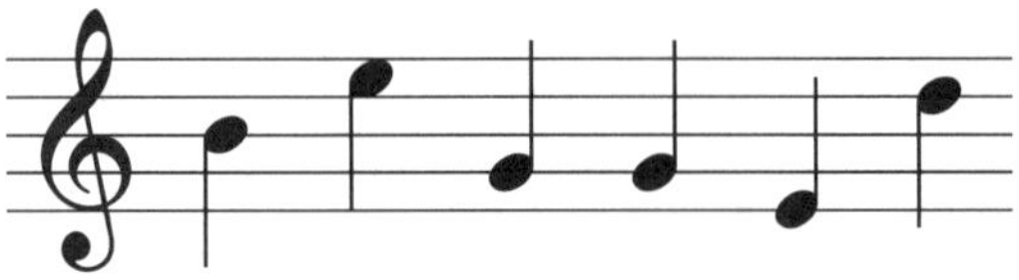

Answer: BEGGED

Word Wizard: Treble Clef 36

What word does this pattern spell?

Answer: GAGGED

Bass Clef Bonanza

Instructions: Cut out each card along the dotted line. Students cover answers while quizzing. Give each student a card to play Quiz-Quiz-Trade. Matching cards may also be used for Mix-N-Match.

Bass Clef Bonanza 1

What note is on the first ledger line above the bass clef staff?

Answer: C

Bass Clef Bonanza 2

What is the letter name of this note?

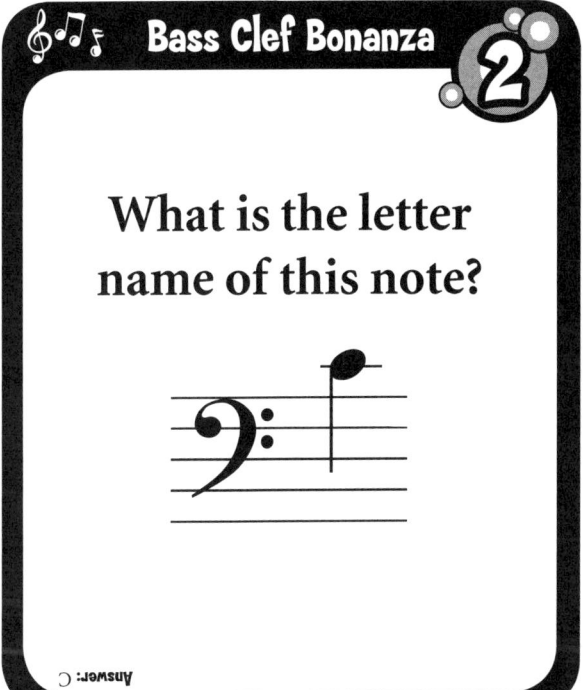

Answer: C

Bass Clef Bonanza 3

What note is in the space above the first ledger line above the bass clef staff?

Answer: D

Bass Clef Bonanza 4

What is the letter name of this note?

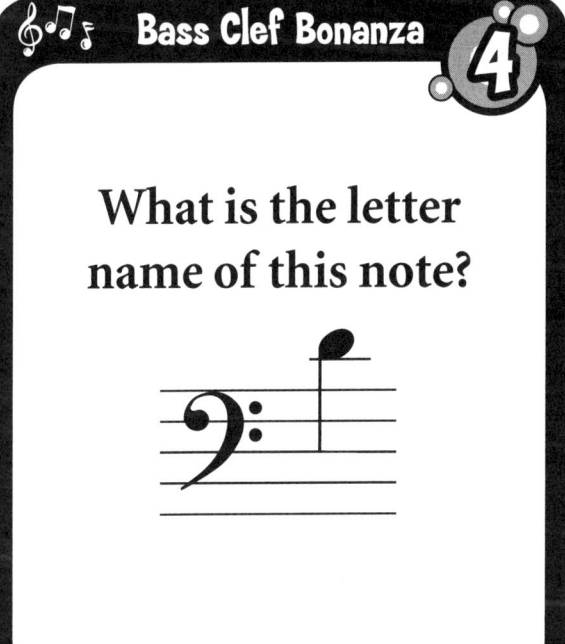

Answer: D

Bass Clef Bonanza

Instructions: Cut out each card along the dotted line. Students cover answers while quizzing. Give each student a card to play Quiz-Quiz-Trade. Matching cards may also be used for Mix-N-Match.

Bass Clef Bonanza — 5

What note is in the space just above the bass clef staff?

Answer: B

Bass Clef Bonanza — 6

What is the letter name of this note?

Answer: B

Bass Clef Bonanza — 7

What note is on the fifth line of the bass clef staff?

Answer: A

Bass Clef Bonanza — 8

What is the letter name of this note?

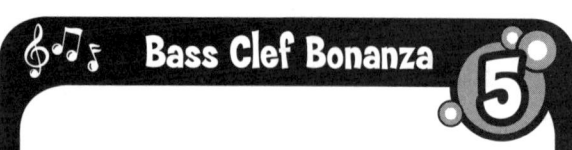

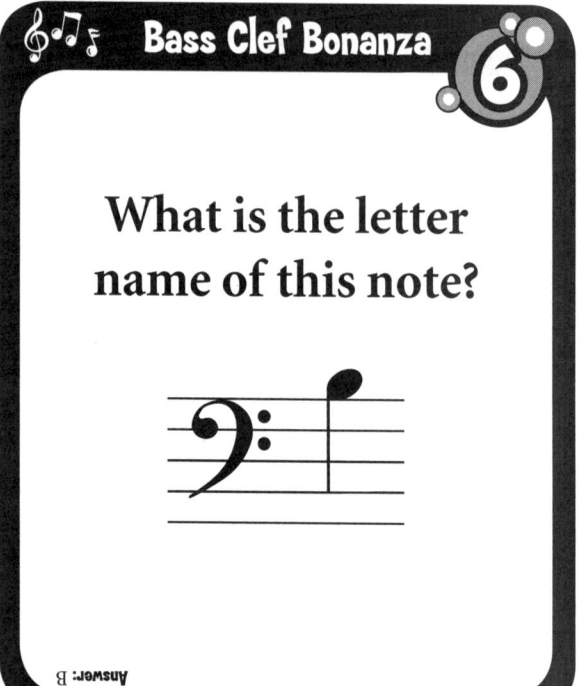

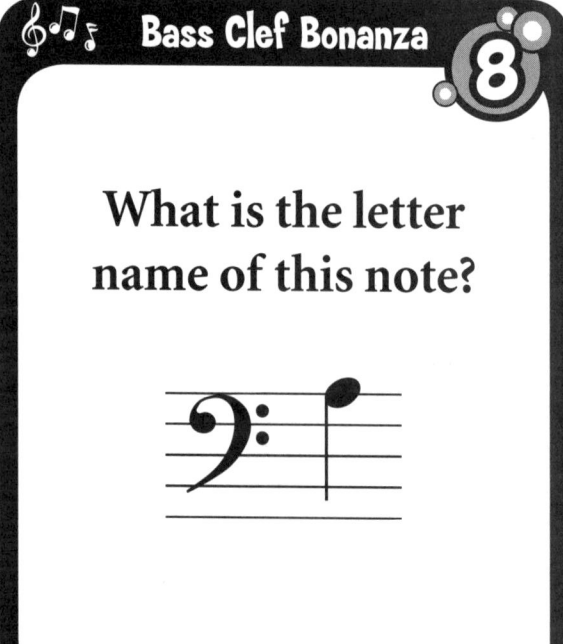

Answer: A

Bass Clef Bonanza

Instructions: Cut out each card along the dotted line. Students cover answers while quizzing. Give each student a card to play Quiz-Quiz-Trade. Matching cards may also be used for Mix-N-Match.

Bass Clef Bonanza 9

What note is in the fourth space of the bass clef staff?

Answer: G

Bass Clef Bonanza 10

What is the letter name of this note?

Answer: G

Bass Clef Bonanza 11

What note is on the fourth line of the bass clef staff?

Answer: F

Bass Clef Bonanza 12

What is the letter name of this note?

Answer: F

Bass Clef Bonanza

Instructions: Cut out each card along the dotted line. Students cover answers while quizzing. Give each student a card to play Quiz-Quiz-Trade. Matching cards may also be used for Mix-N-Match.

Bass Clef Bonanza 13

What note is in the third space of the bass clef staff?

Answer: E

Bass Clef Bonanza 14

What is the letter name of this note?

Answer: E

Bass Clef Bonanza 15

What note is on the third line of the bass clef staff?

Answer: D

Bass Clef Bonanza 16

What is the letter name of this note?

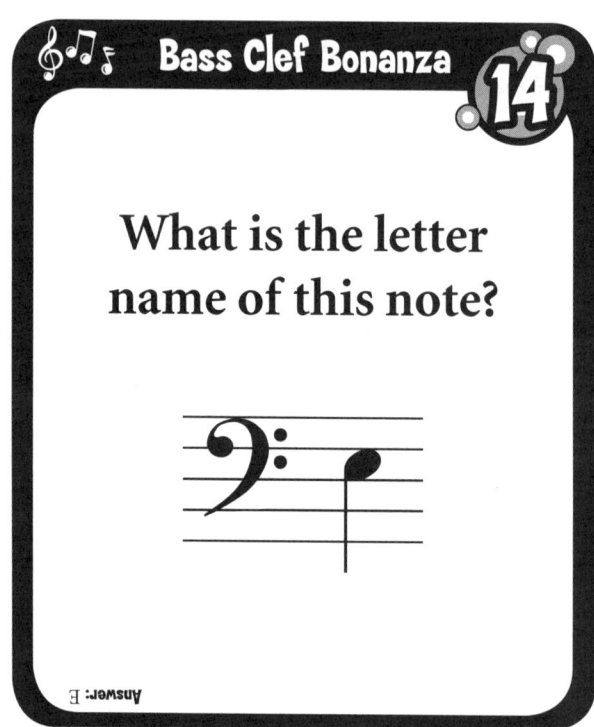

Answer: D

Bass Clef Bonanza

Instructions: Cut out each card along the dotted line. Students cover answers while quizzing. Give each student a card to play Quiz-Quiz-Trade. Matching cards may also be used for Mix-N-Match.

Bass Clef Bonanza 17

What note is in the second space of the bass clef staff?

Answer: C

Bass Clef Bonanza 18

What is the letter name of this note?

Answer: C

Bass Clef Bonanza 19

What note is on the second line of the bass clef staff?

Answer: B

Bass Clef Bonanza 20

What is the letter name of this note?

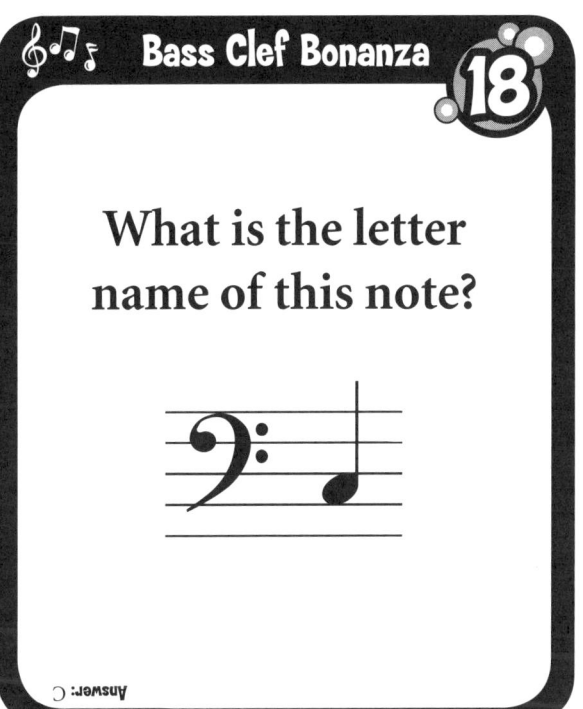

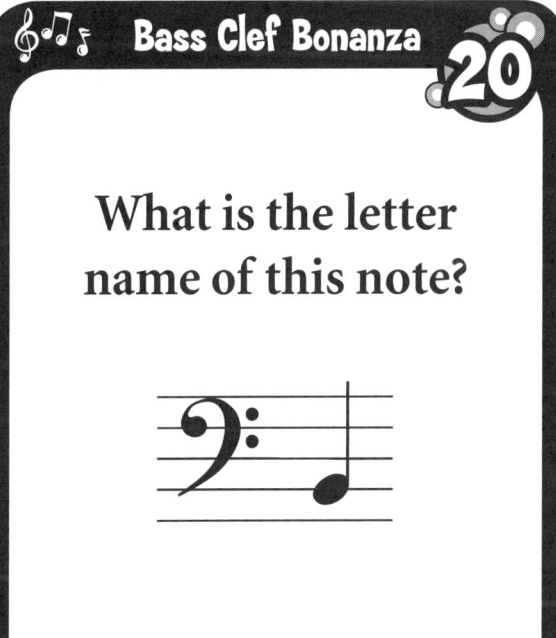

Answer: B

Bass Clef Bonanza

Instructions: Cut out each card along the dotted line. Students cover answers while quizzing. Give each student a card to play Quiz-Quiz-Trade. Matching cards may also be used for Mix-N-Match.

Bass Clef Bonanza 21

What note is in the first space of the bass clef staff?

Answer: A

Bass Clef Bonanza 22

What is the letter name of this note?

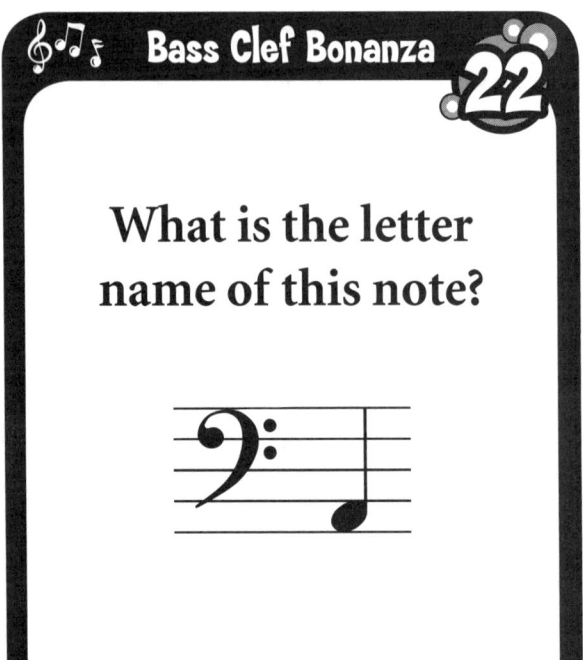

Answer: A

Bass Clef Bonanza 23

What note is on the first line of the bass clef staff?

Answer: G

Bass Clef Bonanza 24

What is the letter name of this note?

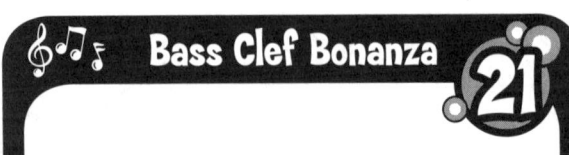

Answer: G

Bass Clef Bonanza

Instructions: Cut out each card along the dotted line. Students cover answers while quizzing. Give each student a card to play Quiz-Quiz-Trade. Matching cards may also be used for Mix-N-Match.

Bass Clef Bonanza 25

What note is in the space just below the bass clef staff?

Answer: F

Bass Clef Bonanza 26

What is the letter name of this note?

Answer: F

Bass Clef Bonanza 27

What note is on the first ledger line below the bass clef staff?

Answer: E

Bass Clef Bonanza 28

What is the letter name of this note?

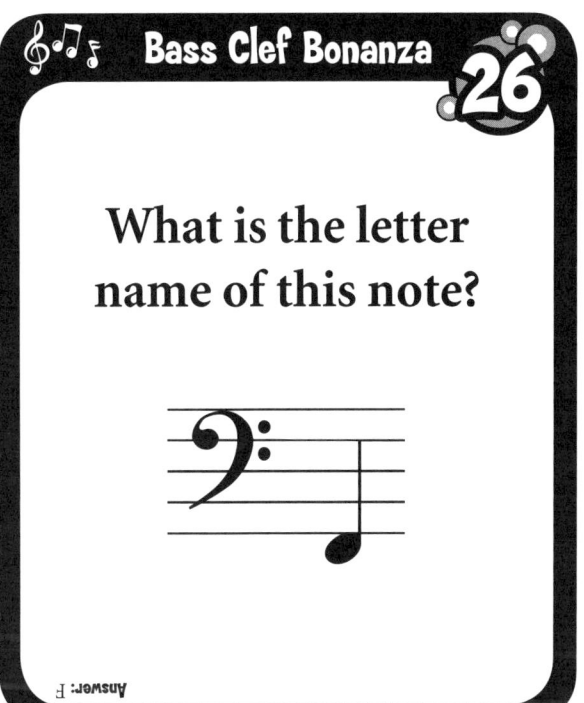

Answer: E

Dazzling Dynamics

Instructions: Cut out each card along the dotted line. Students cover answers while quizzing. Give each student a card to play Quiz-Quiz-Trade. Matching cards may also be used for Mix-N-Match.

Dazzling Dynamics 1

What does the dynamics symbol "*pp*" stand for?

Answer: pianissimo

Dazzling Dynamics 2

What is the dynamics symbol for "pianissimo"?

Answer: *pp*

Dazzling Dynamics 3

What does the dynamics symbol "*p*" stand for?

Answer: piano

Dazzling Dynamics 4

What is the dynamics symbol for "piano"?

Answer: *p*

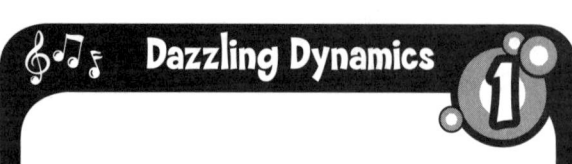

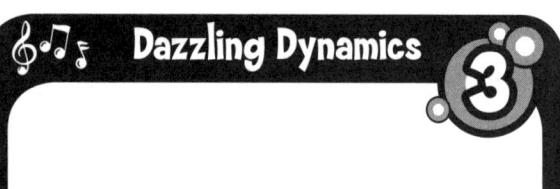

Dazzling Dynamics

Instructions: Cut out each card along the dotted line. Students cover answers while quizzing. Give each student a card to play Quiz-Quiz-Trade. Matching cards may also be used for Mix-N-Match.

Dazzling Dynamics 5

What does the dynamics symbol "*f*" stand for?

Answer: forte

Dazzling Dynamics 6

What is the dynamics symbol for "forte"?

Answer: *f*

Dazzling Dynamics 7

What does the dynamics symbol "*ff*" stand for?

Answer: fortissimo

Dazzling Dynamics 8

What is the dynamics symbol for "fortissimo"?

Answer: *ff*

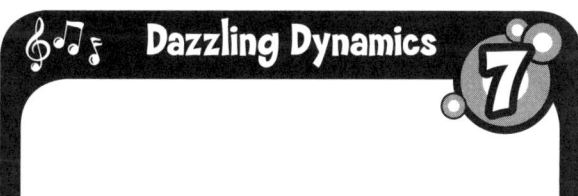

Dazzling Dynamics

Instructions: Cut out each card along the dotted line. Students cover answers while quizzing. Give each student a card to play Quiz-Quiz-Trade. Matching cards may also be used for Mix-N-Match.

Dazzling Dynamics 9

What does the dynamics symbol "*mp*" stand for?

Answer: mezzo-piano

Dazzling Dynamics 10

What is the dynamics symbol for "mezzo-piano"?

Answer: *mp*

Dazzling Dynamics 11

What does the dynamics symbol "*mf*" stand for?

Answer: mezzo-forte

Dazzling Dynamics 12

What is the dynamics symbol for "mezzo-forte"?

Answer: *mf*

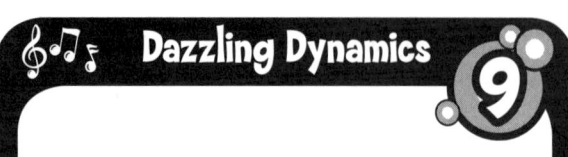

Dazzling Dynamics

Instructions: Cut out each card along the dotted line. Students cover answers while quizzing. Give each student a card to play Quiz-Quiz-Trade. Matching cards may also be used for Mix-N-Match.

Dazzling Dynamics 13

Which dynamics symbol looks like a long sideways "V" with the open end to the right?

Answer: crescendo

Dazzling Dynamics 14

What is the dynamics symbol for "crescendo"?

Answer: long sideways "V" with the open end to the right

Dazzling Dynamics 15

Which dynamics symbol looks like a long sideways "V" with the open end to the left?

Answer: decrescendo or diminuendo

Dazzling Dynamics 16

What is the dynamics symbol for "decrescendo" or "diminuendo"?

Answer: long sideways "V" with the open end to the left

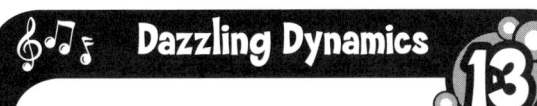

Dazzling Dynamics

Instructions: Cut out each card along the dotted line. Students cover answers while quizzing. Give each student a card to play Quiz-Quiz-Trade. Matching cards may also be used for Mix-N-Match.

Dazzling Dynamics 17

Which dynamics symbol looks like a small sideways "v" above or below a note?

Answer: accent

Dazzling Dynamics 18

What is the dynamics symbol for an "accent?

Answer: small sideways "v" above or below a note

Dazzling Dynamics 19

What does the dynamics symbol "*sfz*" stand for?

Answer: sforzando

Dazzling Dynamics 20

What is the dynamics symbol for "sforzando"?

Answer: *sfz*

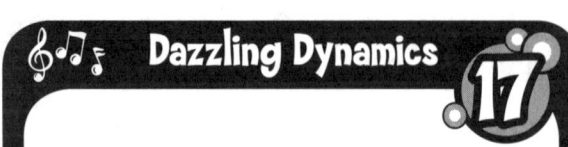

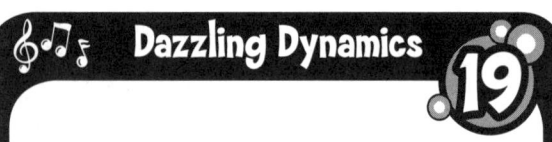

Dazzling Dynamics

Instructions: Cut out each card along the dotted line. Students cover answers while quizzing. Give each student a card to play Quiz-Quiz-Trade. Matching cards may also be used for Mix-N-Match.

Dazzling Dynamics 21

What does the abbreviation "*cresc*" stand for?

Answer: crescendo

Dazzling Dynamics 22

What is the abbreviation for "crescendo"?

Answer: *cresc*

Dazzling Dynamics 23

What does the abbreviation "*dim*" stand for?

Answer: diminuendo

Dazzling Dynamics 24

What is the abbreviation for "diminuendo"?

Answer: *dim*

Dazzling Dynamics

Instructions: Cut out each card along the dotted line. Students cover answers while quizzing. Give each student a card to play Quiz-Quiz-Trade. Matching cards may also be used for Mix-N-Match.

Dazzling Dynamics 25

What does "crescendo" mean?

Answer: start softly and gradually get louder

Dazzling Dynamics 26

What is the dynamics term that means to start softly and gradually get louder?

Answer: crescendo

Dazzling Dynamics 27

What does "descrescendo" or "diminuendo" mean?

Answer: start softly and gradually get softer

Dazzling Dynamics 28

What is the dynamics term that means to start softly and gradually get softer?

Answer: descrescendo or diminuendo

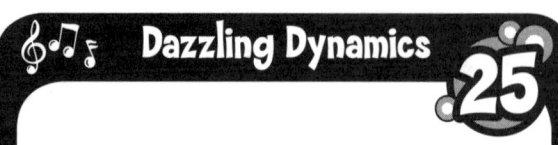

Dazzling Dynamics

Instructions: Cut out each card along the dotted line. Students cover answers while quizzing. Give each student a card to play Quiz-Quiz-Trade. Matching cards may also be used for Mix-N-Match.

Dazzling Dynamics 29

What does the Italian word *pianissimo* mean?

Answer: perform the music very softly

Dazzling Dynamics 30

What is the Italian word that means to perform the music very softly?

Answer: pianissimo

Dazzling Dynamics 31

What does the Italian word *piano* mean?

Answer: perform the music softly

Dazzling Dynamics 32

What is the Italian word that means to perform the music softly?

Answer: piano

Dazzling Dynamics

Instructions: Cut out each card along the dotted line. Students cover answers while quizzing. Give each student a card to play Quiz-Quiz-Trade. Matching cards may also be used for Mix-N-Match.

Dazzling Dynamics 33

What does the Italian word *mezzo-piano* mean?

Answer: perform the music at a medium-soft level

Dazzling Dynamics 34

What is the Italian word that means to perform the music at a medium-soft level?

Answer: mezzo-piano

Dazzling Dynamics 35

What does the Italian word *mezzo-forte* mean?

Answer: perform the music at a medium-loud level

Dazzling Dynamics 36

What is the Italian word that means to perform the music at a medium-loud level?

Answer: mezzo-forte

Dazzling Dynamics

Instructions: Cut out each card along the dotted line. Students cover answers while quizzing. Give each student a card to play Quiz-Quiz-Trade. Matching cards may also be used for Mix-N-Match.

Dazzling Dynamics 37

What does the Italian word *forte* mean?

Answer: perform the music loudly

Dazzling Dynamics 38

What is the Italian word that means to perform the music loudly?

Answer: forte

Dazzling Dynamics 39

What does the Italian word *fortissimo* mean?

Answer: perform the music very loudly

Dazzling Dynamics 40

What is the Italian word that means to perform the music very loudly?

Answer: fortissimo

Dazzling Dynamics

Instructions: Cut out each card along the dotted line. Students cover answers while quizzing. Give each student a card to play Quiz-Quiz-Trade. Matching cards may also be used for Mix-N-Match.

Dazzling Dynamics 41

What does the Italian word *sforzando* mean?

Answer: start the sound loudly, suddenly change to a soft sound, and then gradually get louder again

Dazzling Dynamics 42

What is the Italian word that means to start the sound loudly, suddenly change to a soft sound, and then gradually get louder again?

Answer: sforzando

Dazzling Dynamics 43

What does the Italian word *subito* mean?

Answer: change dynamic levels suddenly

Dazzling Dynamics 44

What is the Italian word that means to change dynamic levels suddenly?

Answer: subito

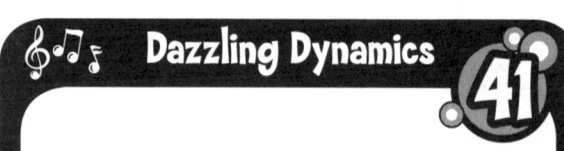

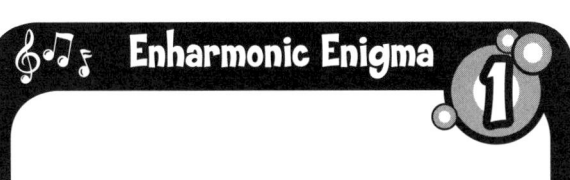

Enharmonic Enigma

Instructions: Cut out each card along the dotted line. Students cover answers while quizzing. Give each student a card to play Quiz-Quiz-Trade. Matching cards may also be used for Mix-N-Match.

Enharmonic Enigma 1

How does a sharp sign change the pitch?

Answer: makes the pitch change by moving it up one half-step

Enharmonic Enigma 2

What marking makes the pitch change by moving it up one half-step?

Answer: sharp sign

Enharmonic Enigma 3

How does a flat sign change the pitch?

Answer: makes the pitch change by moving it down one half-step

Enharmonic Enigma 4

What marking makes the pitch change by moving it down one half-step?

Answer: flat sign

Enharmonic Enigma

Instructions: Cut out each card along the dotted line. Students cover answers while quizzing. Give each student a card to play Quiz-Quiz-Trade. Matching cards may also be used for Mix-N-Match.

Enharmonic Enigma 5

How does a natural sign change the pitch?

Answer: cancels a sharp or flat in the music

Enharmonic Enigma 6

What marking cancels a sharp or flat in the music?

Answer: natural sign

Enharmonic Enigma 7

What is an "accidental"?

Answer: sharp, flat, or natural sign found in the score that is not indicated in the key signature

Enharmonic Enigma 8

What do you call a sharp, flat, or natural sign found in the score that is not indicated in the key signature?

Answer: accidental

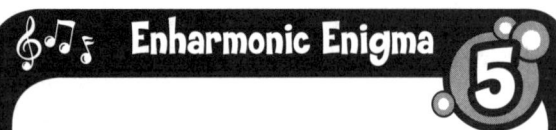

Enharmonic Enigma

Instructions: Cut out each card along the dotted line. Students cover answers while quizzing. Give each student a card to play Quiz-Quiz-Trade. Matching cards may also be used for Mix-N-Match.

Enharmonic Enigma 9

How many steps does a double-sharp move the pitch?

Answer: one whole step up

Enharmonic Enigma 10

What marking makes the pitch change one whole step up?

Answer: double-sharp

Enharmonic Enigma 11

How many steps does a double-flat move the pitch?

Answer: one whole step down

Enharmonic Enigma 12

What marking makes the pitch change one whole step down?

Answer: double-flat

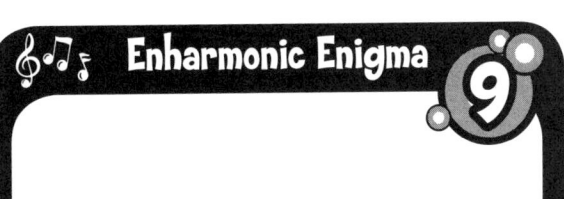

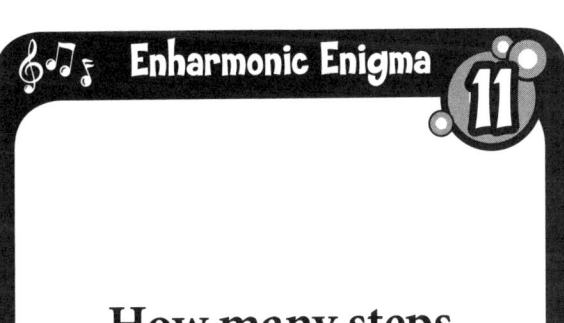

Enharmonic Enigma

Instructions: Cut out each card along the dotted line. Students cover answers while quizzing. Give each student a card to play Quiz-Quiz-Trade. Matching cards may also be used for Mix-N-Match.

Enharmonic Enigma 13

What does "enharmonic" mean?

Answer: two tones which sound the same pitch but are notated differently

Enharmonic Enigma 14

What is the word that means two tones which sound the same pitch but are notated differently?

Answer: enharmonic

Enharmonic Enigma 15

What is the letter name of the enharmonic pitch for C-sharp?

=?

Answer: D-flat

Enharmonic Enigma 16

What is the letter name of the enharmonic pitch for D-flat?

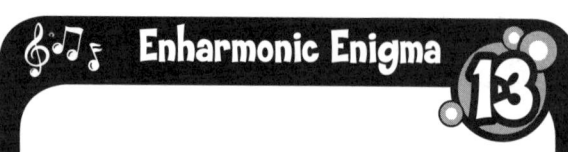

=?

Answer: C-sharp

Enharmonic Enigma

Instructions: Cut out each card along the dotted line. Students cover answers while quizzing. Give each student a card to play Quiz-Quiz-Trade. Matching cards may also be used for Mix-N-Match.

Enharmonic Enigma 17

What is the letter name of the enharmonic pitch for D-sharp?

=?

Answer: E-flat

Enharmonic Enigma 18

What is the letter name of the enharmonic pitch for E-flat?

=?

Answer: D-sharp

Enharmonic Enigma 19

What is the letter name of the enharmonic pitch for E?

=?

Answer: F-flat

Enharmonic Enigma 20

What is the letter name of the enharmonic pitch for F-flat?

=?

Answer: E

Enharmonic Enigma

Instructions: Cut out each card along the dotted line. Students cover answers while quizzing. Give each student a card to play Quiz-Quiz-Trade. Matching cards may also be used for Mix-N-Match.

Enharmonic Enigma 21

What is the letter name of the enharmonic pitch for F-sharp?

Answer: G-flat

Enharmonic Enigma 22

What is the letter name of the enharmonic pitch for G-flat?

Answer: F-sharp

Enharmonic Enigma 23

What is the letter name of the enharmonic pitch for G-sharp?

Answer: A-flat

Enharmonic Enigma 24

What is the letter name of the enharmonic pitch for A-flat?

Answer: G-sharp

Enharmonic Enigma

Instructions: Cut out each card along the dotted line. Students cover answers while quizzing. Give each student a card to play Quiz-Quiz-Trade. Matching cards may also be used for Mix-N-Match.

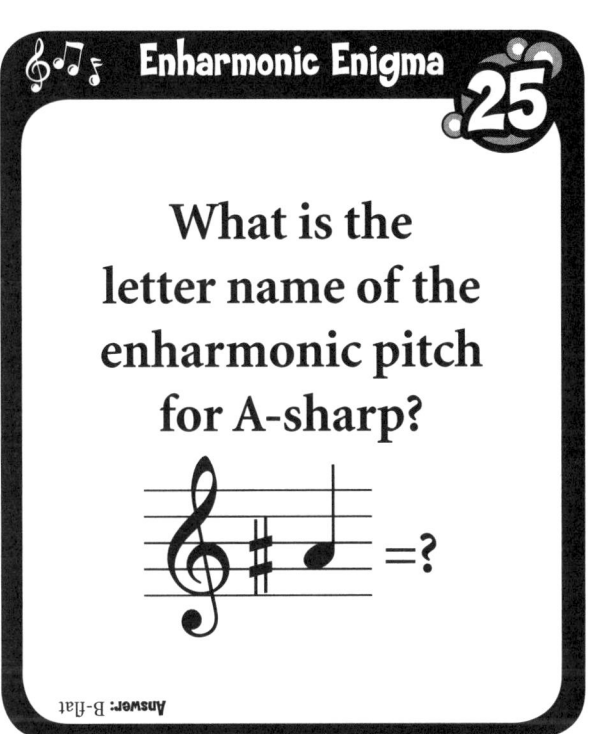

Enharmonic Enigma 25

What is the letter name of the enharmonic pitch for A-sharp?

Answer: B-flat

Enharmonic Enigma 26

What is the letter name of the enharmonic pitch for B-flat?

Answer: A-sharp

Enharmonic Enigma 27

What is the letter name of the enharmonic pitch for B-sharp?

Answer: C

Enharmonic Enigma 28

What is the letter name of the enharmonic pitch for C?

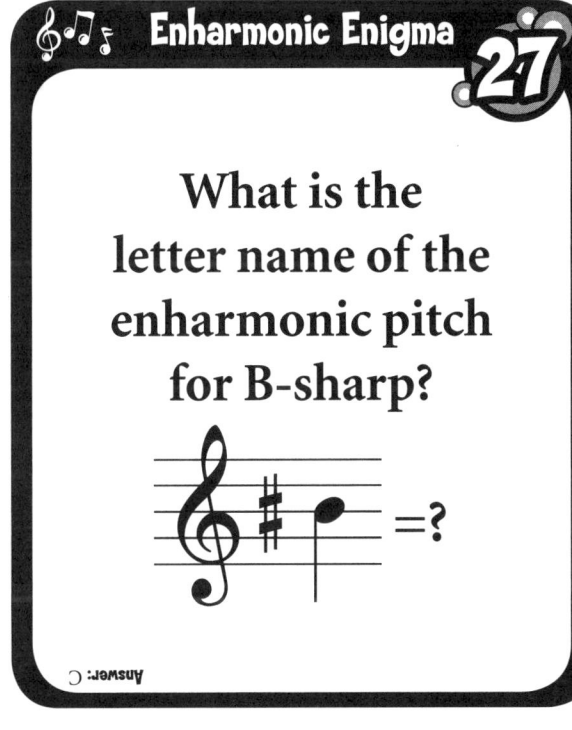

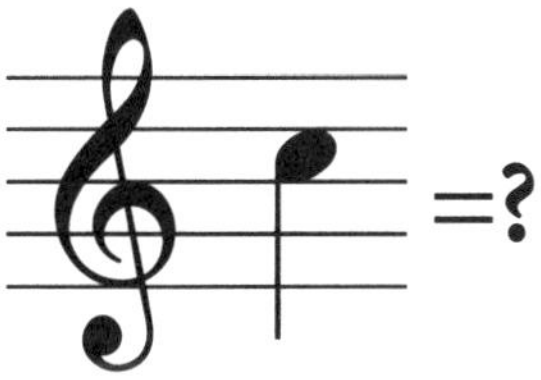

Answer: B-sharp

Enharmonic Enigma

Instructions: Cut out each card along the dotted line. Students cover answers while quizzing. Give each student a card to play Quiz-Quiz-Trade. Matching cards may also be used for Mix-N-Match.

Enharmonic Enigma 29

What is the letter name of the enharmonic pitch for E-sharp?

Answer: F

Enharmonic Enigma 30

What is the letter name of the enharmonic pitch for F?

Answer: E-sharp

Enharmonic Enigma 31

What is the letter name of the enharmonic pitch for C-flat?

Answer: B

Enharmonic Enigma 32

What is the letter name of the enharmonic pitch for B?

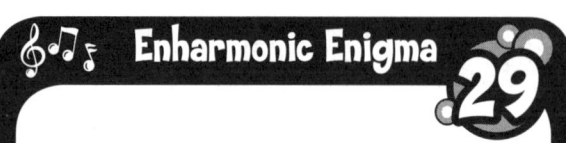

Answer: C-flat

Form Fit

Instructions: Cut out each card along the dotted line. Students cover answers while quizzing. Give each student a card to play Quiz-Quiz-Trade. Matching cards may also be used for Mix-N-Match.

Form Fit 1

What is this Form Structure?

Answer: AB

Form Fit 2

What letters represent a Form Structure that has 2 different parts or sections?

Answer: AB

Form Fit 3

What is this Form Structure?

Answer: ABA

Form Fit 4

What letters represent a 3-part Form Structure where the 1st and 3rd sections are alike, and the 2nd is different?

Answer: ABA

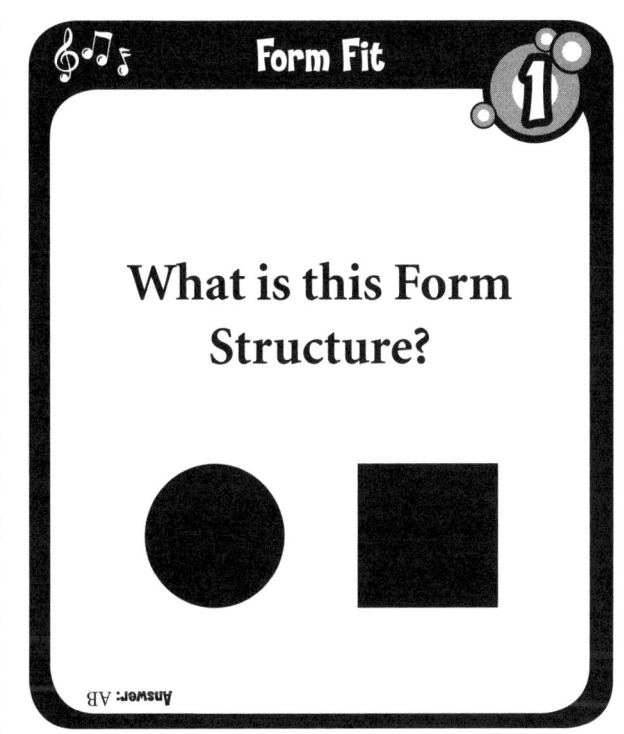

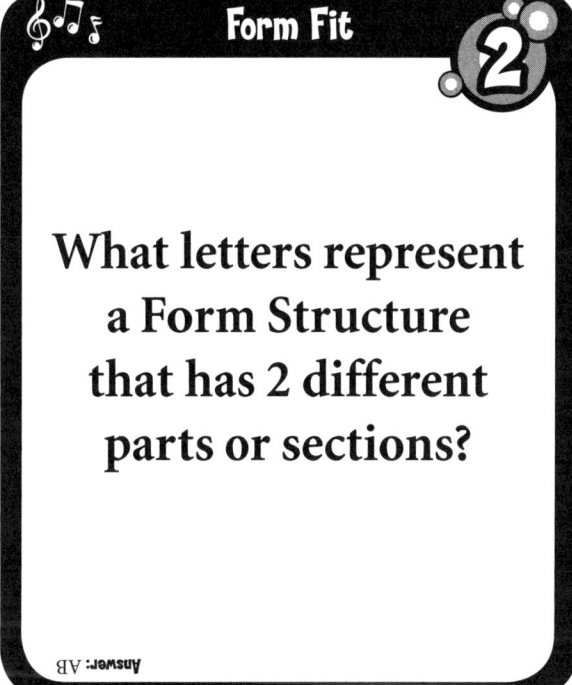

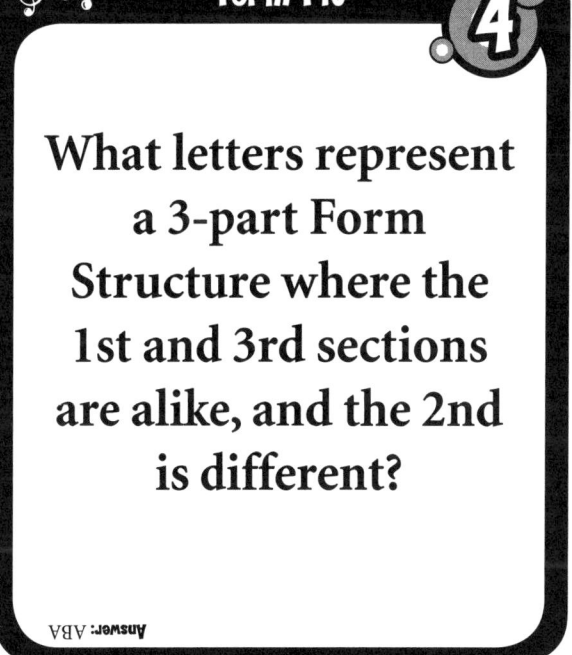

Form Fit

Instructions: Cut out each card along the dotted line. Students cover answers while quizzing. Give each student a card to play Quiz-Quiz-Trade. Matching cards may also be used for Mix-N-Match.

Form Fit 5

What is this Form Structure?

Answer: ABACA

Form Fit 6

What letters would describe a 5-part "Rondo" that has 3 different sections?

Answer: ABACA

Form Fit 7

What is this Form Structure?

Answer: ABABA

Form Fit 8

What letters would describe a 5-part "Rondo" that has only 2 different sections?

Answer: ABABA

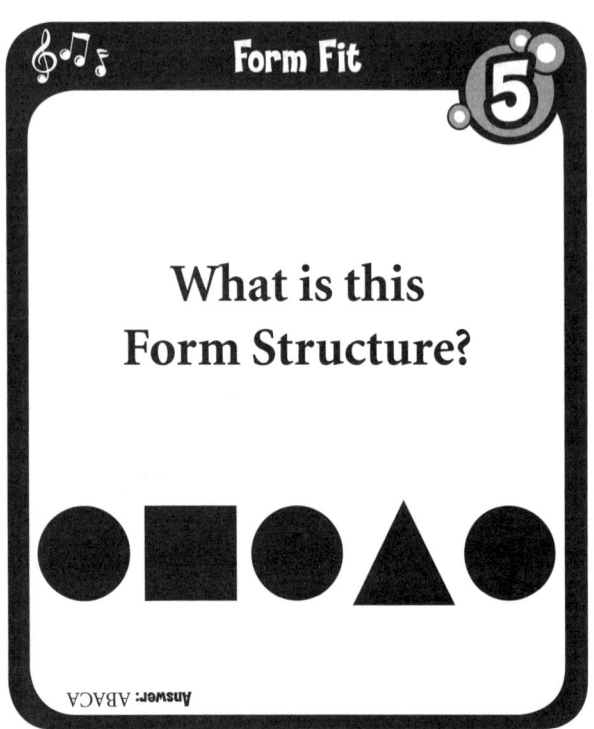

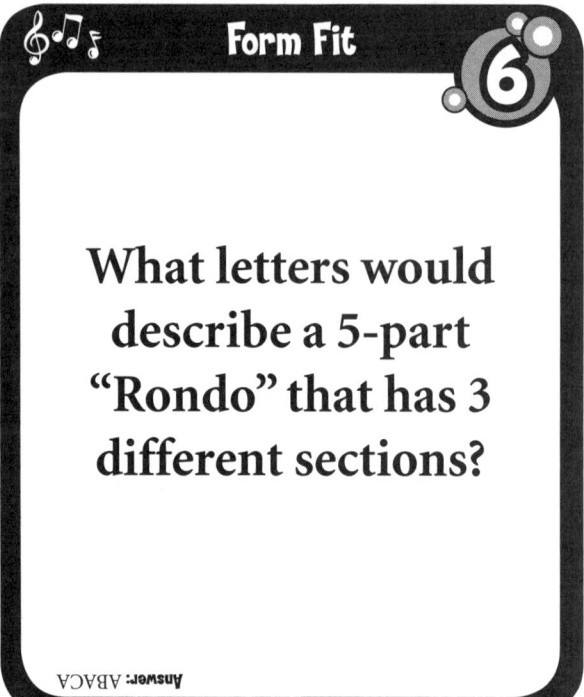

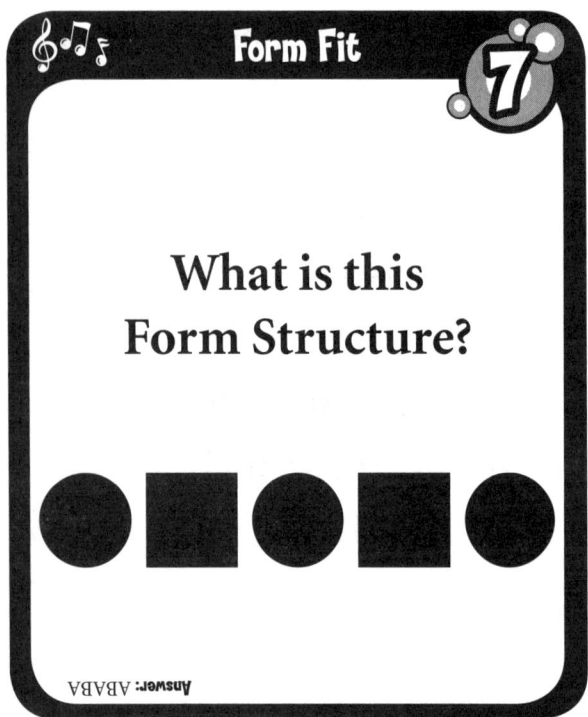

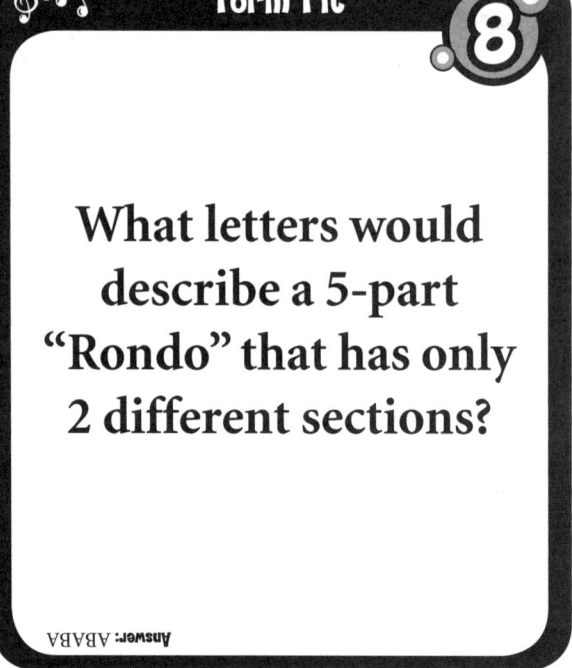

Form Fit

Instructions: Cut out each card along the dotted line. Students cover answers while quizzing. Give each student a card to play Quiz-Quiz-Trade. Matching cards may also be used for Mix-N-Match.

Form Fit 9

What is this Form Structure?

Answer: ABBA

Form Fit 10

What letters represent the Form Structure that has 4 phrases, where the 1st and last are alike, and the 2nd and 3rd are alike (but not the same as the 1st and last)?

Answer: ABBA

Form Fit 11

What is this Form Structure?

Answer: AABA

Form Fit 12

What letters represent the Form Structure that has 4 phrases, where the 1st, 2nd, and last are all alike, and the 3rd is different?

Answer: AABA

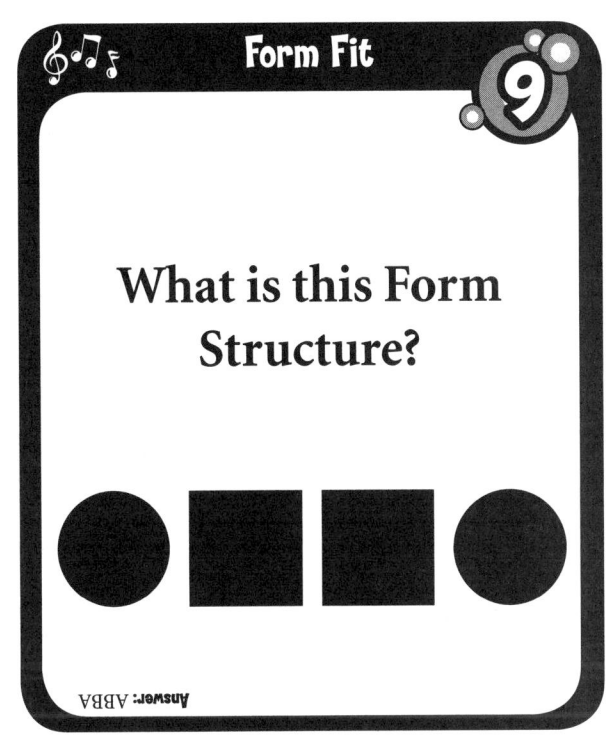

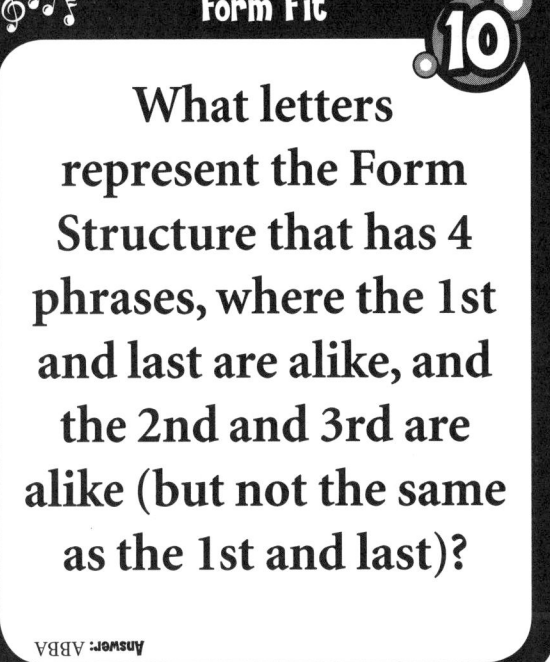

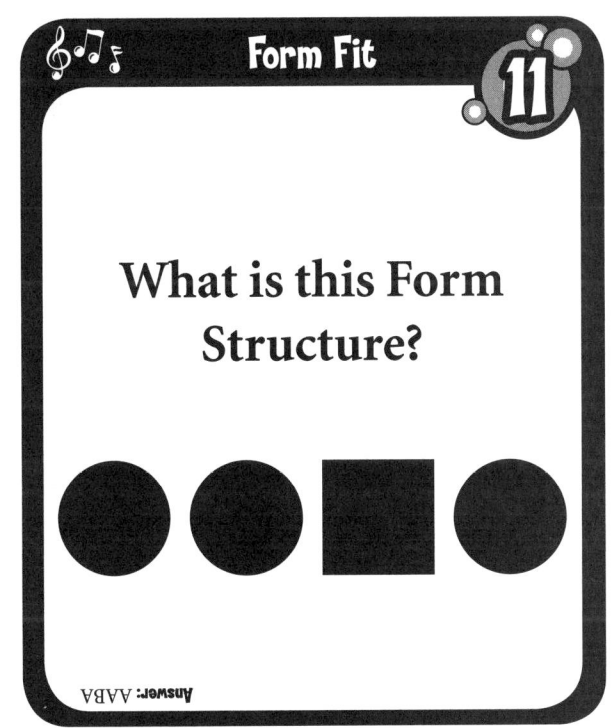

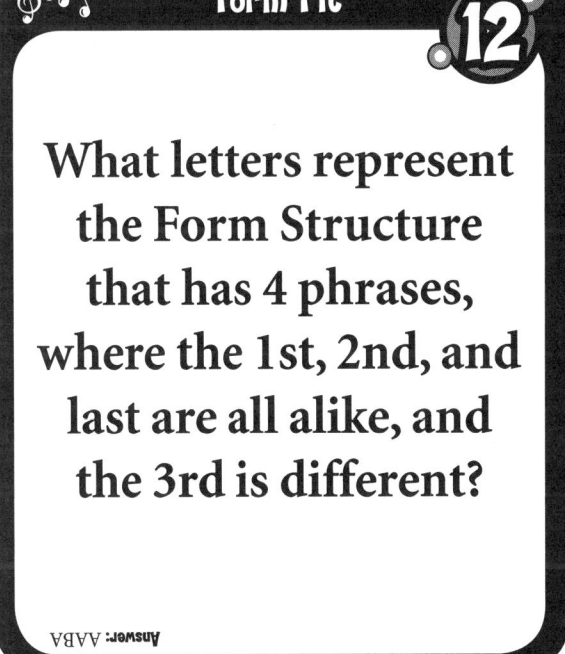

Form Fit

Instructions: Cut out each card along the dotted line. Students cover answers while quizzing. Give each student a card to play Quiz-Quiz-Trade. Matching cards may also be used for Mix-N-Match.

Form Fit 13

What is this Form Structure?

Answer: AAB

Form Fit 14

What letters represent the Form Structure that has 3 phrases, where the first two are alike and the 3rd is different (also called "Blues Form")?

Answer: AAB

Form Fit 15

What is this Form Structure?

Answer: ABAB

Form Fit 16

What letters represent the Form Structure that has 4 phrases, where the 1st and 3rd are alike, and the 2nd and 4th are alike (but different from the 1st and 3rd)?

Answer: ABAB

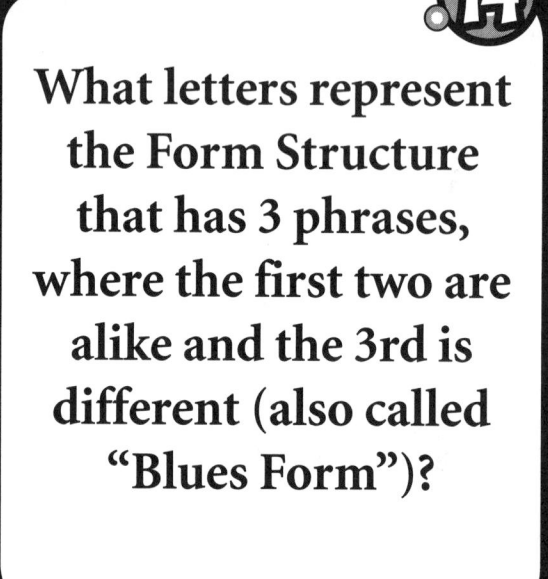

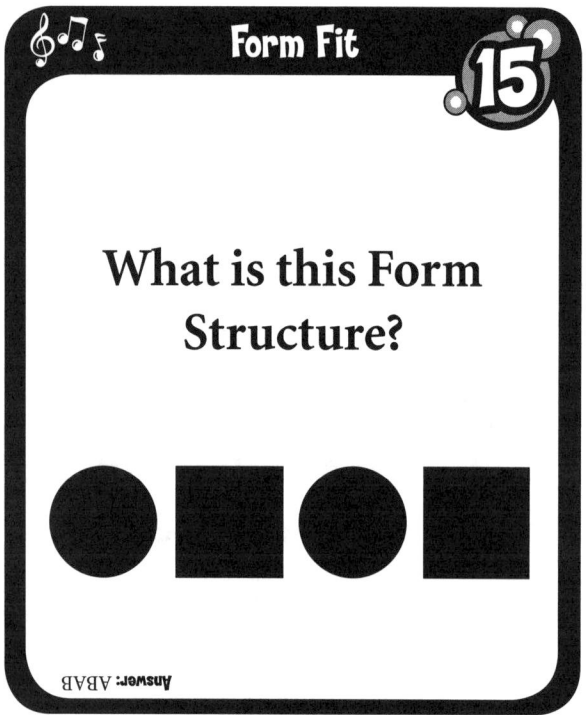

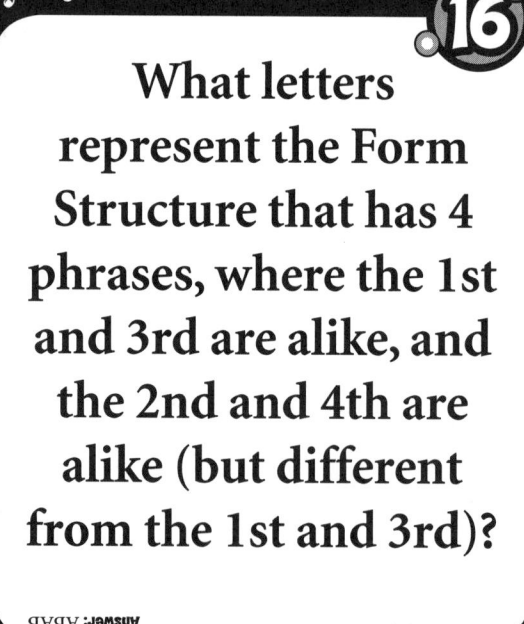

Form Fit

Instructions: Cut out each card along the dotted line. Students cover answers while quizzing. Give each student a card to play Quiz-Quiz-Trade. Matching cards may also be used for Mix-N-Match.

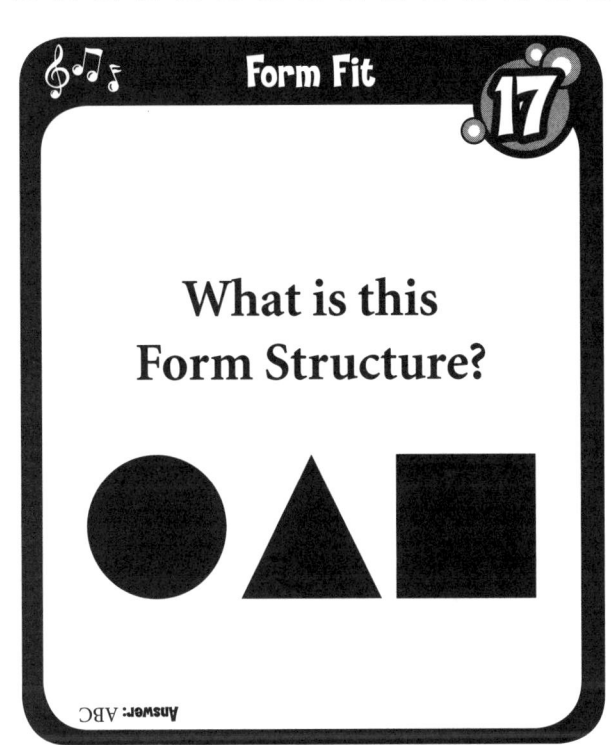

Form Fit 17

What is this Form Structure?

Answer: ABC

Form Fit 18

What letters represent the Form Structure where there are 3 different sections to the music?

Answer: ABC

Form Fit 19

What is this Form Structure?

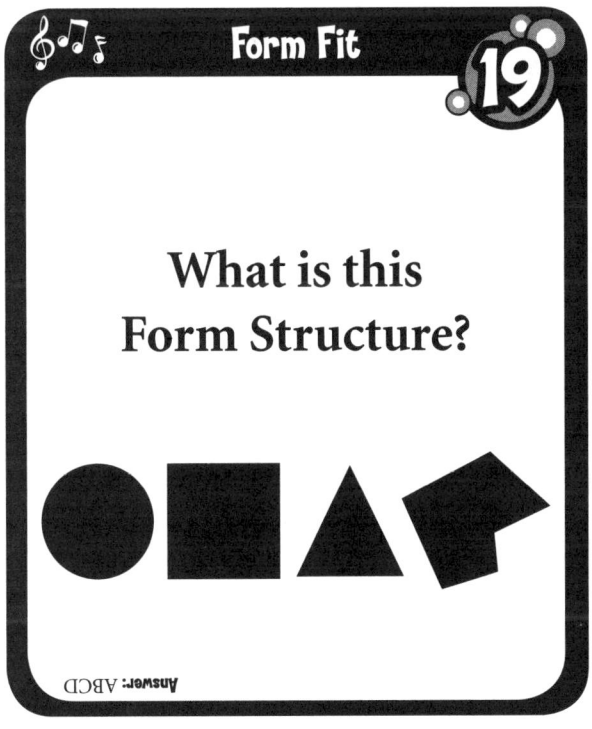

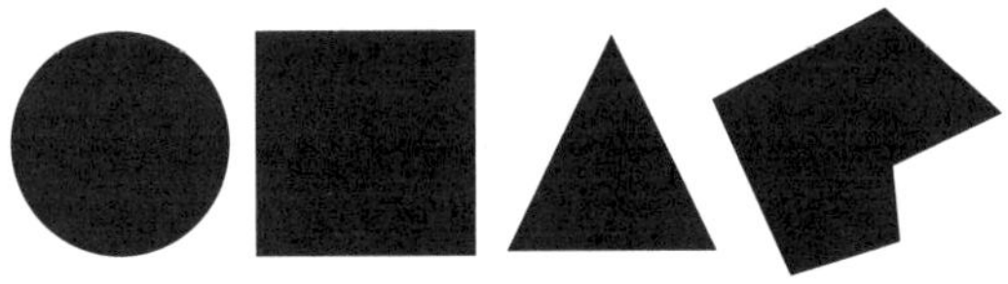

Answer: ABCD

Form Fit 20

What letters represent the Form Structure where there are 4 different phrases to the music (sometimes called "through-composed")?

Answer: ABCD

Form Fit

Instructions: Cut out each card along the dotted line. Students cover answers while quizzing. Give each student a card to play Quiz-Quiz-Trade. Matching cards may also be used for Mix-N-Match.

Form Fit 21

What is this Form Structure?

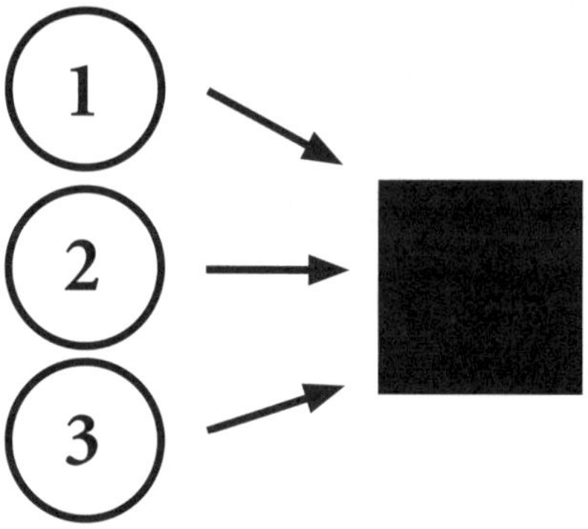

Answer: Verse Refrain

Form Fit 22

What is the name of the 2-section Form Structure where the lyrics in one section keep changing while the second section stays the same after each time the first section is sung?

Answer: Verse Refrain

Form Fit 23

What is this Form Structure?

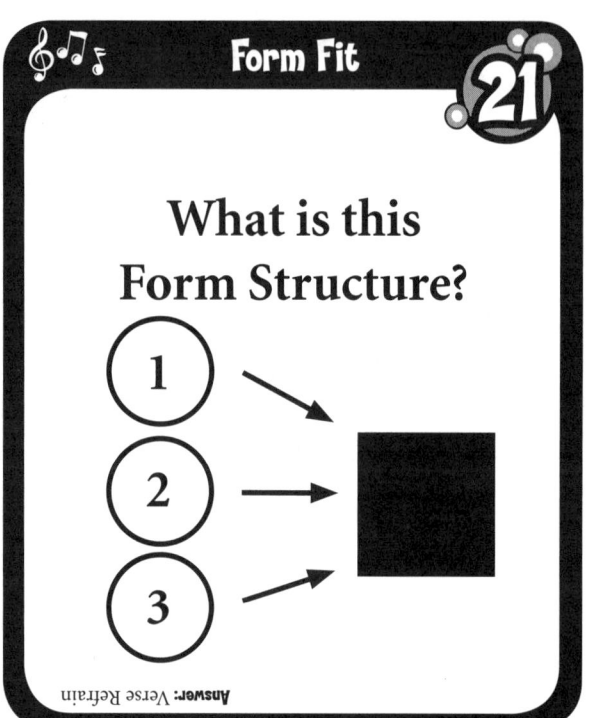

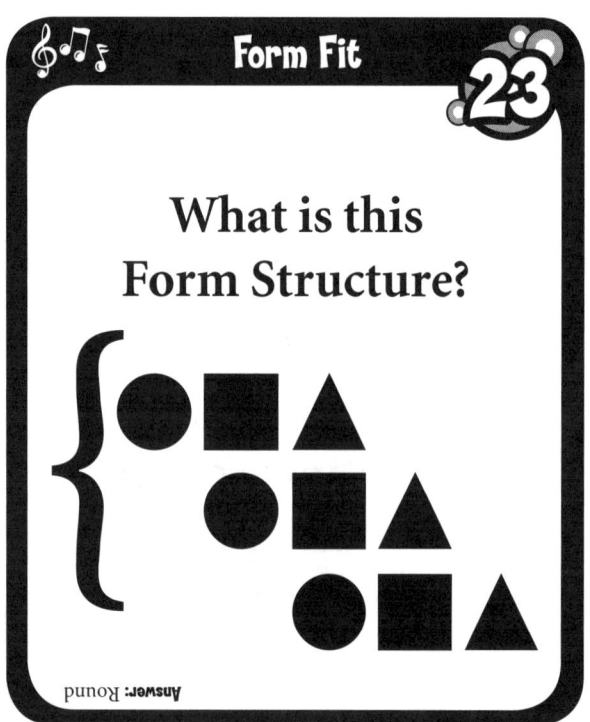

Answer: Round

Form Fit 24

What is the name of the Form Structure where one part begins a song, and other parts begin the same song a little bit later?

Answer: Round

Tempo Terms

Instructions: Cut out each card along the dotted line. Students cover answers while quizzing. Give each student a card to play Quiz-Quiz-Trade. Matching cards may also be used for Mix-N-Match.

Tempo Terms — 1

What is a "metronome" (met'-roh-nome)?

Answer: device used for setting the tempo of the steady beat

Tempo Terms — 2

What is the name of the device used for setting the tempo of the steady beat?

Answer: metronome

Tempo Terms — 3

How fast is the tempo called "Grave" (grah'-vay)?

Answer: slowest tempo

Tempo Terms — 4

What is the name for the slowest tempo?

Answer: Grave

Tempo Terms

Instructions: Cut out each card along the dotted line. Students cover answers while quizzing. Give each student a card to play Quiz-Quiz-Trade. Matching cards may also be used for Mix-N-Match.

Tempo Terms 5

How fast is the tempo called "Largo"?

Answer: very slow tempo

Tempo Terms 6

What is the name for a very slow tempo?

Answer: Largo

Tempo Terms 7

How fast is the tempo called "Lento" (len'-toh)?

Answer: slow tempo

Tempo Terms 8

What is the name for a slow tempo?

Answer: Lento

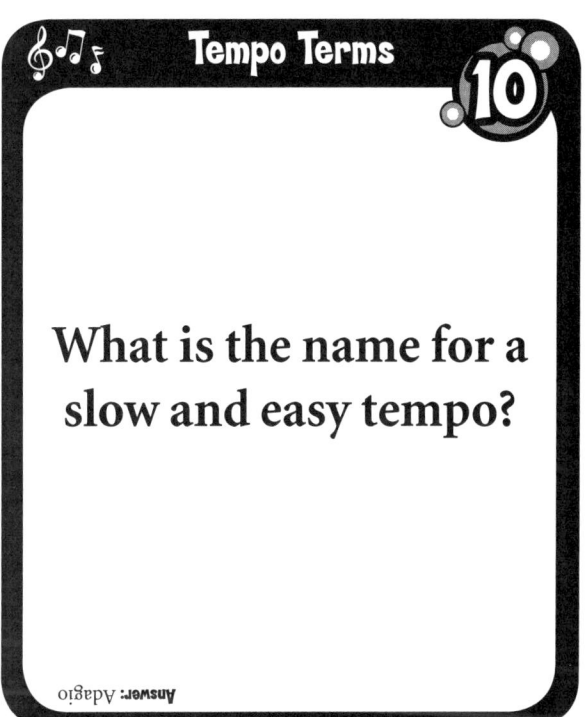

Tempo Terms

Instructions: Cut out each card along the dotted line. Students cover answers while quizzing. Give each student a card to play Quiz-Quiz-Trade. Matching cards may also be used for Mix-N-Match.

Tempo Terms 9

How fast is the tempo called "Adagio" (ah-dah'-zhee-oh)?

Answer: slow and easy tempo

Tempo Terms 10

What is the name for a slow and easy tempo?

Answer: Adagio

Tempo Terms 11

How fast is the tempo called "Andante" (ahn-dahn'-tay)?

Answer: medium-paced walking speed tempo

Tempo Terms 12

What is the name for a medium paced, walking speed tempo?

Answer: Andante

Tempo Terms

Instructions: Cut out each card along the dotted line. Students cover answers while quizzing. Give each student a card to play Quiz-Quiz-Trade. Matching cards may also be used for Mix-N-Match.

Tempo Terms 13

How fast is the tempo called "Andantino" (ahn-dahn-tee'-noh)?

Answer: tempo that is slightly faster than Andante

Tempo Terms 14

What is the name for a tempo that is slightly faster than Andante?

Answer: Andantino

Tempo Terms 15

How fast is the tempo called "Moderato" (mod-er-ah'-toh)?

Answer: medium tempo

Tempo Terms 16

What is the name for a medium tempo?

Answer: Moderato

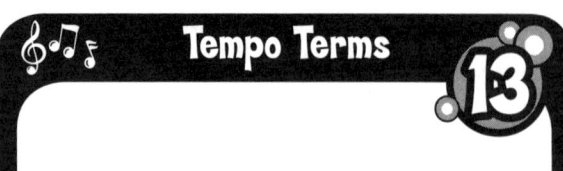

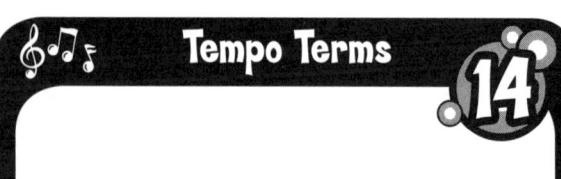

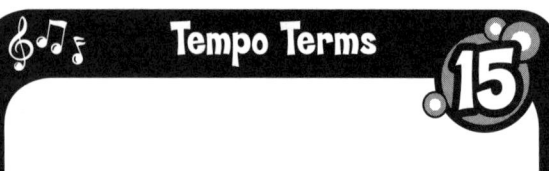

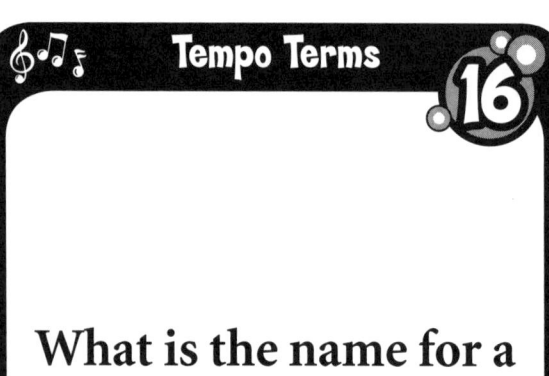

Tempo Terms

Instructions: Cut out each card along the dotted line. Students cover answers while quizzing. Give each student a card to play Quiz-Quiz-Trade. Matching cards may also be used for Mix-N-Match.

Tempo Terms 17

How fast is the tempo called "Allegretto" (ah-leh-gret'-toh)?

Answer: light and cheerful tempo, not as fast as "Allegro"

Tempo Terms 18

What is the name for a light and cheerful tempo, not as fast as "Allegro"?

Answer: Allegretto

Tempo Terms 19

How fast is the tempo called "Allegro" (ah-leh'-groh)?

Answer: quick and lively fast tempo

Tempo Terms 20

What is the name for a quick and lively fast tempo?

Answer: Allegro

Tempo Terms

Instructions: Cut out each card along the dotted line. Students cover answers while quizzing. Give each student a card to play Quiz-Quiz-Trade. Matching cards may also be used for Mix-N-Match.

Tempo Terms 21

How fast is the tempo called "Vivace" (vee-vah'-chay)?

Answer: tempo that is rather fast and spirited

Tempo Terms 22

What is the name for a tempo that is rather fast and spirited?

Answer: Vivace

Tempo Terms 23

How fast is the tempo called "Presto" (press'-toh)?

Answer: very fast tempo

Tempo Terms 24

What is the name for a very fast tempo?

Answer: Presto

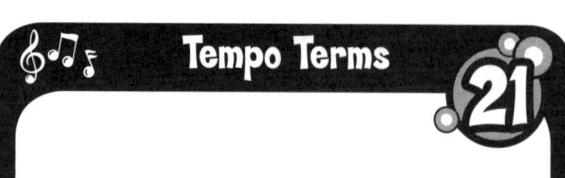

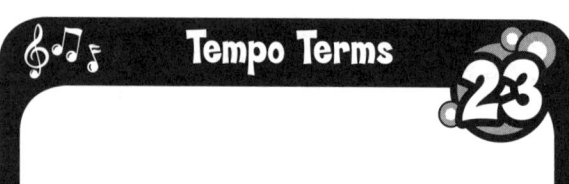

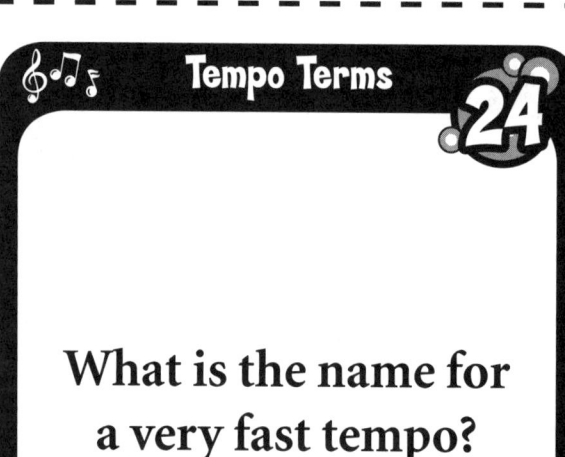

Tempo Terms

Instructions: Cut out each card along the dotted line. Students cover answers while quizzing. Give each student a card to play Quiz-Quiz-Trade. Matching cards may also be used for Mix-N-Match.

Tempo Terms 25

How fast is the tempo called "Prestissimo" (press-ti'-sim-oh)?

Answer: the fastest tempo

Tempo Terms 26

What is the name for the fastest tempo?

Answer: Prestissimo

Tempo Terms 27

What does "A tempo" (ah tem-po) mean to do?

Answer: go back to the original tempo after there has been a change

Tempo Terms 28

What is the tempo marking that tells you to go back to the original tempo after there has been a change?

Answer: a tempo

Tempo Terms

Instructions: Cut out each card along the dotted line. Students cover answers while quizzing. Give each student a card to play Quiz-Quiz-Trade. Matching cards may also be used for Mix-N-Match.

Tempo Terms 29

What happens to the tempo if there is an "Accelerando" (ah-chel-er-ahn'-doh)?

Answer: gradually gets faster and faster

Tempo Terms 30

What is the tempo marking that tells you to gradually get faster and faster?

Answer: Accelerando

Tempo Terms 31

What happens to the tempo if there is a "Ritardando" (ree-tar-dahn'-doh)?

Answer: gradually gets slower and slower

Tempo Terms 32

What is the tempo marking that tells you to gradually get slower and slower?

Answer: Ritardando

Vocabulary Volley

Set 1: Elementary

Instructions: Cut out each card along the dotted line. Students cover answers while quizzing. Give each student a card to play Quiz-Quiz-Trade. Matching cards may also be used for Mix-N-Match.

Vocabulary Volley Set 1 — **1**

What is "melody"?

Answer: single line of pitches that move upward, downward, or stay on the same pitch

Vocabulary Volley Set 1 — **2**

What is the term for a single line of pitches that move upward, downward, or stay on the same pitch?

Answer: Melody

Vocabulary Volley Set 1 — **3**

What is "rhythm"?

Answer: series of long sounds, short sounds, or silences arranged to create patterns in music

Vocabulary Volley Set 1 — **4**

What is the term for a series of long sounds, short sounds, or silences that are arranged to create patterns in music?

Answer: rhythm

Vocabulary Volley

Set 1: Elementary

Instructions: Cut out each card along the dotted line. Students cover answers while quizzing. Give each student a card to play Quiz-Quiz-Trade. Matching cards may also be used for Mix-N-Match.

Vocabulary Volley Set 1 — **5**

What is "harmony"?

Answer: two or more different pitches sounded at the same time

Vocabulary Volley Set 1 — **6**

What is the term for two or more different pitches that are sounded at the same time?

Answer: harmony

Vocabulary Volley Set 1 — **7**

What is "texture"?

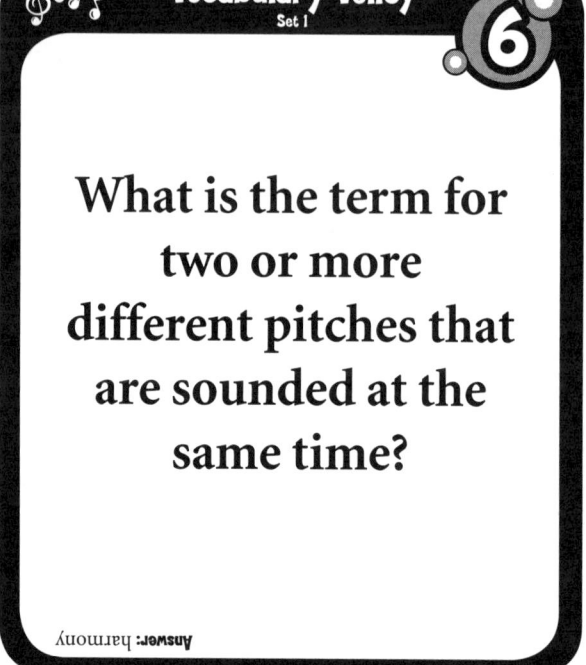

Answer: sound quality created by the layering of melodies and harmony parts in a composition

Vocabulary Volley Set 1 — **8**

What is the term for the sound quality created by the layering of melodies and harmony parts in a composition?

Answer: texture

Vocabulary Volley

Set 1: Elementary

Instructions: Cut out each card along the dotted line. Students cover answers while quizzing. Give each student a card to play Quiz-Quiz-Trade. Matching cards may also be used for Mix-N-Match.

Vocabulary Volley Set 1 — **9**

What is an "introduction"?

Answer: instrumental part at the beginning of a composition that is played before the main theme or before voices enter

Vocabulary Volley Set 1 — **10**

What is the term for the instrumental part at the beginning of a composition that is played before the main theme or before voices enter?

Answer: introduction

Vocabulary Volley Set 1 — **11**

What is a "coda"?

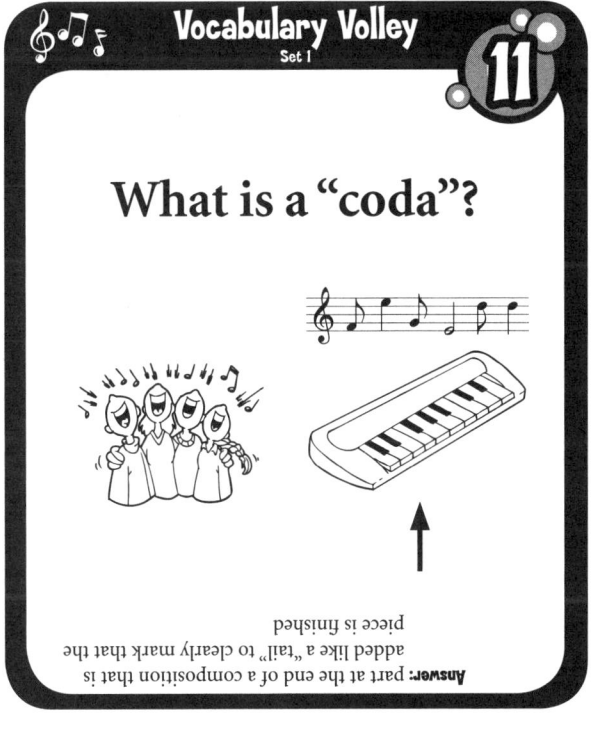

Answer: part at the end of a composition that is added like a "tail" to clearly mark that the piece is finished

Vocabulary Volley Set 1 — **12**

What is the term for the part at the end of a composition that is added like a "tail" to clearly mark that the piece is finished?

Answer: coda

Vocabulary Volley

Set 1: Elementary

Instructions: Cut out each card along the dotted line. Students cover answers while quizzing. Give each student a card to play Quiz-Quiz-Trade. Matching cards may also be used for Mix-N-Match.

Vocabulary Volley Set 1 — 13

What is an "interlude"?

Answer: instrumental music that is played in between sections or verses of a composition

Vocabulary Volley Set 1 — 14

What is the term for instrumental music that is played in between sections or verses of a composition?

Answer: interlude

Vocabulary Volley Set 1 — 15

What is "Form Structure" in music?

Answer: music organized by phrases or contrasting sections

Vocabulary Volley Set 1 — 16

What is the term for the way that music is organized by phrases or contrasting sections?

Answer: Form Structure

Vocabulary Volley

Set 1: Elementary

Instructions: Cut out each card along the dotted line. Students cover answers while quizzing. Give each student a card to play Quiz-Quiz-Trade. Matching cards may also be used for Mix-N-Match.

Vocabulary Volley Set 1 — **17**

What is "call and response" form?

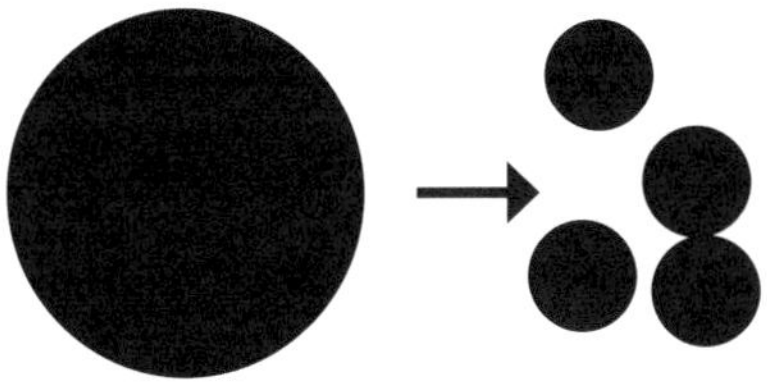

Answer: form structure where one part sings or plays a phrase and other parts sing or play an answering phrase

Vocabulary Volley Set 1 — **18**

What is the name of the form structure where one part sings or plays a phrase and other parts sing or play an answering phrase?

Answer: call and response

Vocabulary Volley Set 1 — **19**

What is a "round"?

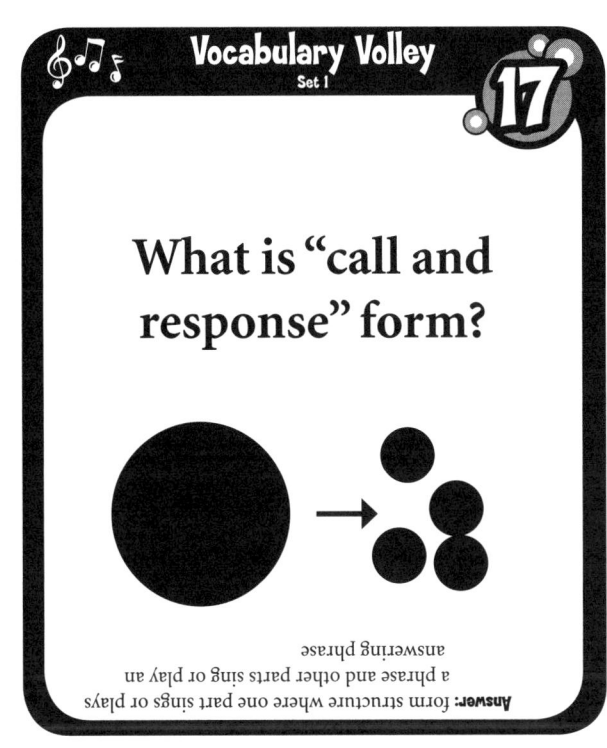

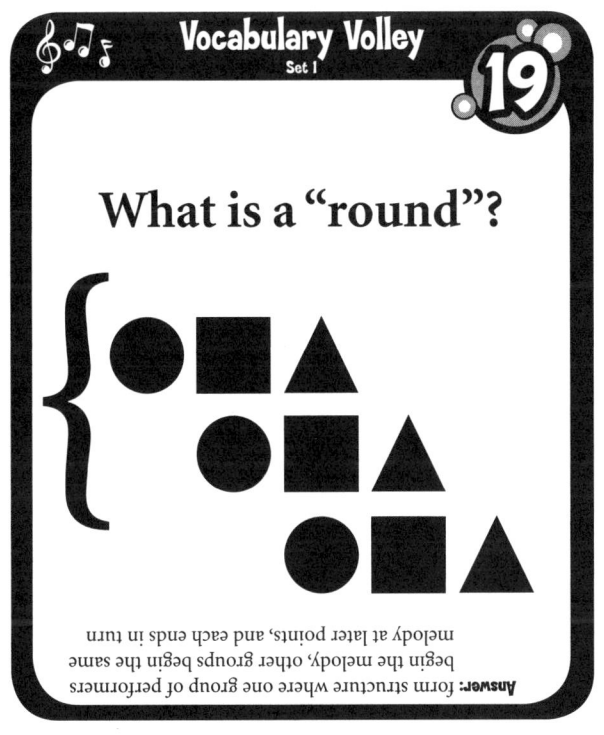

Answer: form structure where one group of performers begin the melody, other groups begin the same melody at later points, and each ends in turn

Vocabulary Volley Set 1 — **20**

What is the name of the form structure where one group of performers begin the melody, other groups begin the same melody at later points, and each ends in turn?

Answer: round

Vocabulary Volley

Set 1: Elementary

Instructions: Cut out each card along the dotted line. Students cover answers while quizzing. Give each student a card to play Quiz-Quiz-Trade. Matching cards may also be used for Mix-N-Match.

Vocabulary Volley
Set 1
21

What is a "canon"?

Answer: vocal or instrumental piece where the same melody is begun by different groups one after the other, but all end together

Vocabulary Volley
Set 1
22

What is the term for a vocal or instrumental piece where the same melody is begun by different groups one after the other, but all end together?

Answer: canon

Vocabulary Volley
Set 1
23

What are "partner songs"?

Answer: term for two or more different songs that can be performed at the same time to create harmony

Vocabulary Volley
Set 1
24

What is the term for two or more different songs that can be performed at the same time to create harmony?

Answer: partner songs

Vocabulary Volley

Set 1: Elementary

Instructions: Cut out each card along the dotted line. Students cover answers while quizzing. Give each student a card to play Quiz-Quiz-Trade. Matching cards may also be used for Mix-N-Match.

Vocabulary Volley Set 1 — **25**

What is a "step" in the melody?

Answer: two tones that are right next to each other in the scale and are sung or played one after the other in the melody

Vocabulary Volley Set 1 — **26**

What is the term for two tones that are right next to each other in the scale, and are sung or played one after the other in the melody?

Answer: step

Vocabulary Volley Set 1 — **27**

What are "repeated tones" in the melody?

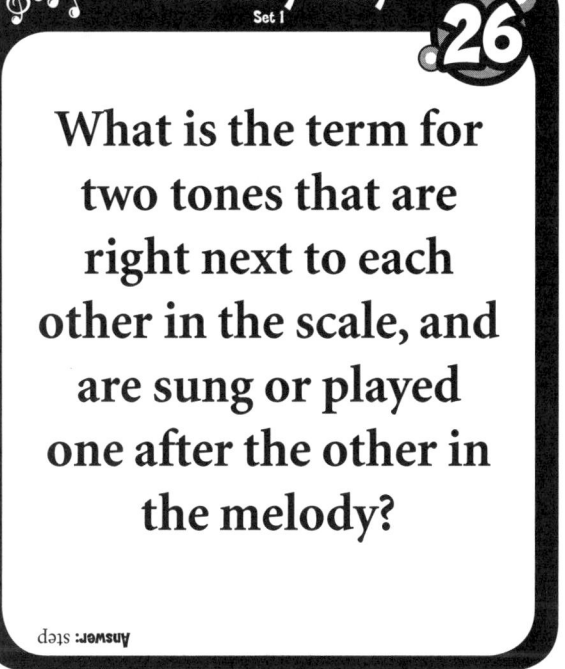

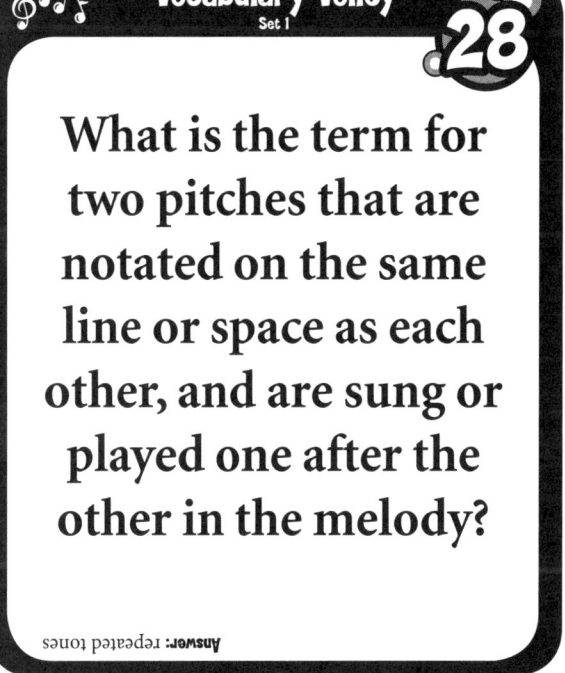

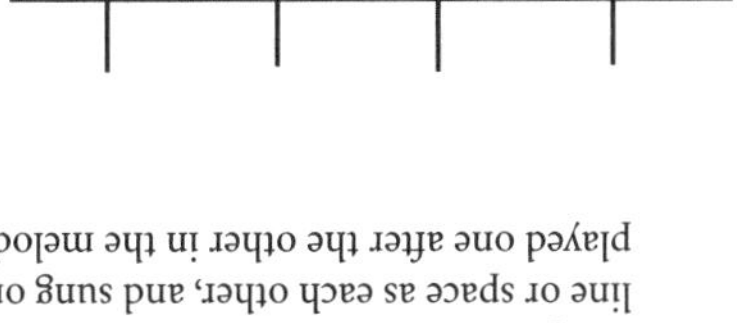

Answer: two pitches that are notated on the same line or space as each other, and sung or played one after the other in the melody

Vocabulary Volley Set 1 — **28**

What is the term for two pitches that are notated on the same line or space as each other, and are sung or played one after the other in the melody?

Answer: repeated tones

Vocabulary Volley

Set 1: Elementary

Instructions: Cut out each card along the dotted line. Students cover answers while quizzing. Give each student a card to play Quiz-Quiz-Trade. Matching cards may also be used for Mix-N-Match.

Vocabulary Volley Set 1 — **29**

What is a "leap" or "skip" in the melody?

Answer: two tones not right next to each other in the scale, and sung or played one after the other in the melody

Vocabulary Volley Set 1 — **30**

What is the term for two tones that are not right next to each other in the scale, and are sung or played one after the other in the melody?

Answer: leap or skip

Vocabulary Volley Set 1 — **31**

What is a melodic "interval"?

Answer: relationship between two pitches that are notated next to each other, and are measured in distance from one to the other

Vocabulary Volley Set 1 — **32**

What is the term for the relationship between two pitches that are notated next to each other, and are measured in distance from one to the other?

Answer: interval

Vocabulary Volley

Set 1: Elementary

Instructions: Cut out each card along the dotted line. Students cover answers while quizzing. Give each student a card to play Quiz-Quiz-Trade. Matching cards may also be used for Mix-N-Match.

Vocabulary Volley
Set 1
33

What does "major" sound like?

Answer: bright musical sound that is centered on the home tone of DO in the diatonic scale

Vocabulary Volley
Set 1
34

What is the term for a bright musical sound that is centered on the home tone of DO in the diatonic scale?

Answer: major

Vocabulary Volley
Set 1
35

What does "minor" sound like?

Answer: dark musical sound that is centered on the tone of LA in the diatonic scale

Vocabulary Volley
Set 1
36

What is the term for a dark musical sound that is centered on the tone of LA in the diatonic scale?

Answer: minor

Vocabulary Volley

Set 1: Elementary

Instructions: Cut out each card along the dotted line. Students cover answers while quizzing. Give each student a card to play Quiz-Quiz-Trade. Matching cards may also be used for Mix-N-Match.

Vocabulary Volley Set 1 — **37**

What is "tone color" or "timbre"?

Answer: particular sound that each instrument or voice makes

Vocabulary Volley Set 1 — **38**

What is the term for the particular sound that each instrument or voice makes?

Answer: tone color or timbre

Vocabulary Volley Set 1 — **39**

What are "dynamics"?

mp ***ff***

$>$

Answer: how loud or soft music sounds, indicated by markings in the score

---

Vocabulary Volley Set 1 — **40**

What is the term for how loud or soft the music sounds, indicated by markings in the score?

Answer: dynamics

Vocabulary Volley

Set 1: Elementary

Instructions: Cut out each card along the dotted line. Students cover answers while quizzing. Give each student a card to play Quiz-Quiz-Trade. Matching cards may also be used for Mix-N-Match.

Vocabulary Volley Set 1 — **41**

What is a "staff"?

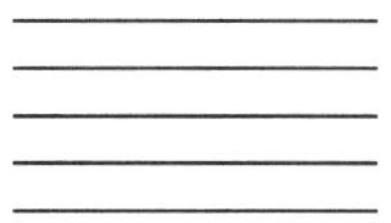

Answer: set of lines and spaces where music notation is written

Vocabulary Volley Set 1 — **42**

What is the term for the set of lines and spaces where music notation is written?

Answer: staff

Vocabulary Volley Set 1 — **43**

What is a "clef" sign?

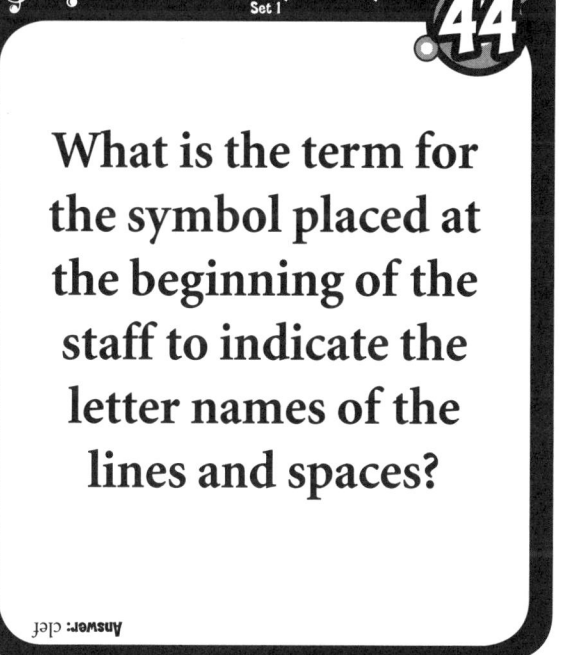

Answer: the symbol placed at the beginning of the staff to indicate the letter names of the lines and spaces

Vocabulary Volley Set 1 — **44**

What is the term for the symbol placed at the beginning of the staff to indicate the letter names of the lines and spaces?

Answer: clef

Vocabulary Volley

Set 1: Elementary

Instructions: Cut out each card along the dotted line. Students cover answers while quizzing. Give each student a card to play Quiz-Quiz-Trade. Matching cards may also be used for Mix-N-Match.

Vocabulary Volley
Set 1
45

What are "bar lines"?

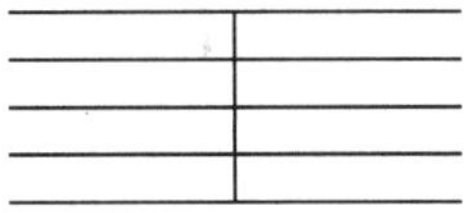

Answer: vertical lines in the music notation that divide groups of beats into measures

Vocabulary Volley
Set 1
46

What is the term for the vertical lines in the music notation that divide groups of beats into measures?

Answer: bar lines

Vocabulary Volley
Set 1
47

What is a "measure"?

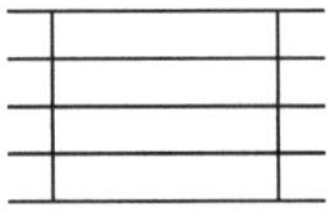

Answer: grouping of beats according to the meter signature, set apart with bar lines on each side

Vocabulary Volley
Set 1
48

What is the term for a grouping of beats according to the meter signature, set apart with bar lines on each side?

Answer: measure

Vocabulary Volley

Set 1: Elementary

Instructions: Cut out each card along the dotted line. Students cover answers while quizzing. Give each student a card to play Quiz-Quiz-Trade. Matching cards may also be used for Mix-N-Match.

Vocabulary Volley Set 1 — 49

What is "melody contour"?

Answer: shape of the melody (upward, downward, by steps, by leaps, or by repeated tones)

Vocabulary Volley Set 1 — 50

What is the term for the shape of the melody (upward, downward, by steps, by leaps, or by repeated tones)?

Answer: melody contour

Vocabulary Volley Set 1 — 51

What is a "sequence"?

Answer: melody form where a theme is repeated at a higher or lower pitch two or more times in a row

Vocabulary Volley Set 1 — 52

What is the term for a melody form where a theme is repeated at a higher or lower pitch two or more times in a row?

Answer: sequence

Vocabulary Volley

Set 1: Elementary

Instructions: Cut out each card along the dotted line. Students cover answers while quizzing. Give each student a card to play Quiz-Quiz-Trade. Matching cards may also be used for Mix-N-Match.

Vocabulary Volley Set 1 **53**

What are "repeat signs"?

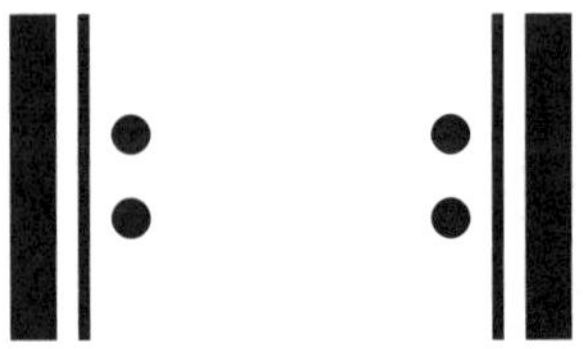

Answer: notation symbols that indicate a section is to be played or sung again right away

Vocabulary Volley Set 1 **54**

What is the term for notation symbols that indicate a section is to be played or sung again right away?

Answer: repeat signs

Vocabulary Volley Set 1 **55**

What is a "double bar line"?

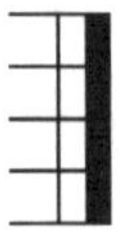

Answer: marking in the music notation that indicates the end of a piece

Vocabulary Volley Set 1 **56**

What is the term for the marking in the music notation that indicates the end of a piece?

Answer: double bar line

Vocabulary Volley

Set 1: Elementary

Instructions: Cut out each card along the dotted line. Students cover answers while quizzing. Give each student a card to play Quiz-Quiz-Trade. Matching cards may also be used for Mix-N-Match.

Vocabulary Volley Set 1 — **57**

What is a "verse"?

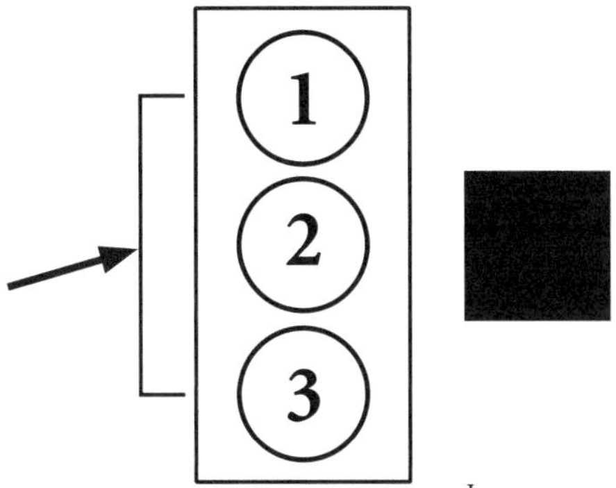

Answer: part of a song where the melody always stays the same but the lyrics change each time it is repeated

---

Vocabulary Volley Set 1 — **58**

What is the term for the part of a song where the melody always stays the same but the lyrics change each time it is repeated?

Answer: verse

Vocabulary Volley Set 1 — **59**

What is a "refrain"?

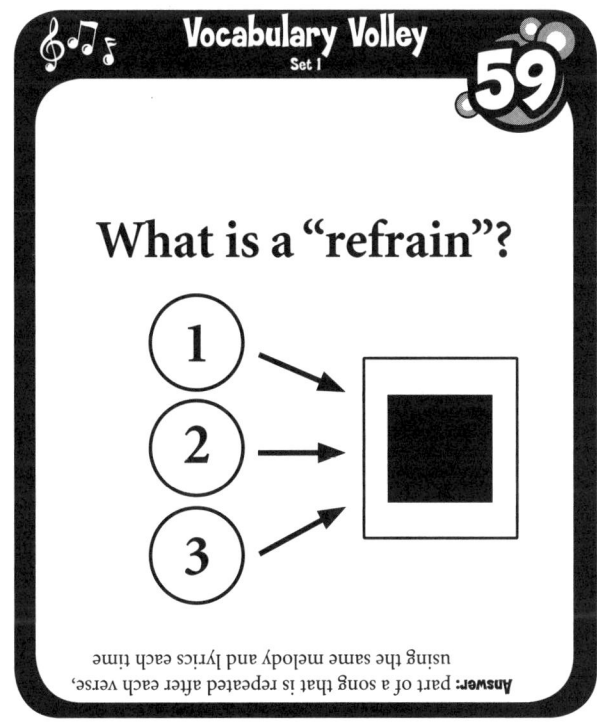

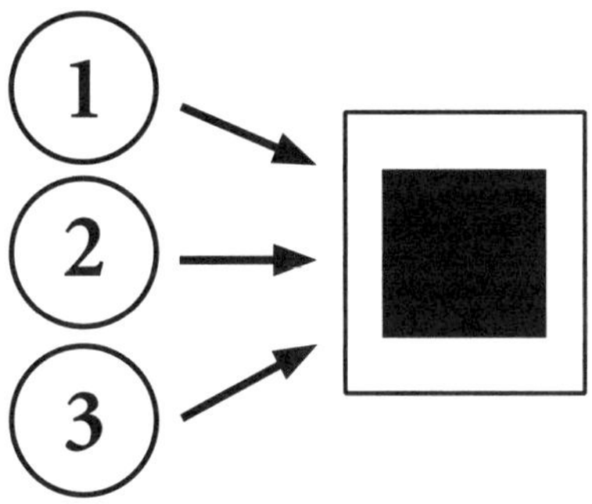

Answer: part of a song that is repeated after each verse, using the same melody and lyrics each time

---

Vocabulary Volley Set 1 — **60**

What is the term for the part of a song that is repeated after each verse, using the same melody and lyrics each time?

Answer: refrain

Vocabulary Volley

Set 1: Elementary

Instructions: Cut out each card along the dotted line. Students cover answers while quizzing. Give each student a card to play Quiz-Quiz-Trade. Matching cards may also be used for Mix-N-Match.

Vocabulary Volley
Set 1
61

What are "lyrics"?

Answer: words of a song

Vocabulary Volley
Set 1
62

What is the term for the words of a song?

Answer: lyrics

Vocabulary Volley
Set 1
63

What is "Theme and Variation"?

Answer: form structure where the melody is at first performed simply, and then repeated several times with one or more of the musical elements changed

Vocabulary Volley
Set 1
64

What is the term for a form structure where the melody is at first performed simply, and then repeated several times with one or more of the musical elements changed?

Answer: Theme and Variation

Vocabulary Volley

Set 1: Elementary

Instructions: Cut out each card along the dotted line. Students cover answers while quizzing. Give each student a card to play Quiz-Quiz-Trade. Matching cards may also be used for Mix-N-Match.

Vocabulary Volley Set 1 — **65**

What is an "accent"?

>

Answer: marking in the music indicating that the note it is attached to should be performed more strongly

Vocabulary Volley Set 1 — **66**

What is the term for a marking in the music indicating that the note it is attached to should be performed more strongly?

Answer: accent

Vocabulary Volley Set 1 — **67**

What is "beat"?

Answer: steady pulse of music

Vocabulary Volley Set 1 — **68**

What is the term for the steady pulse of music?

Answer: beat

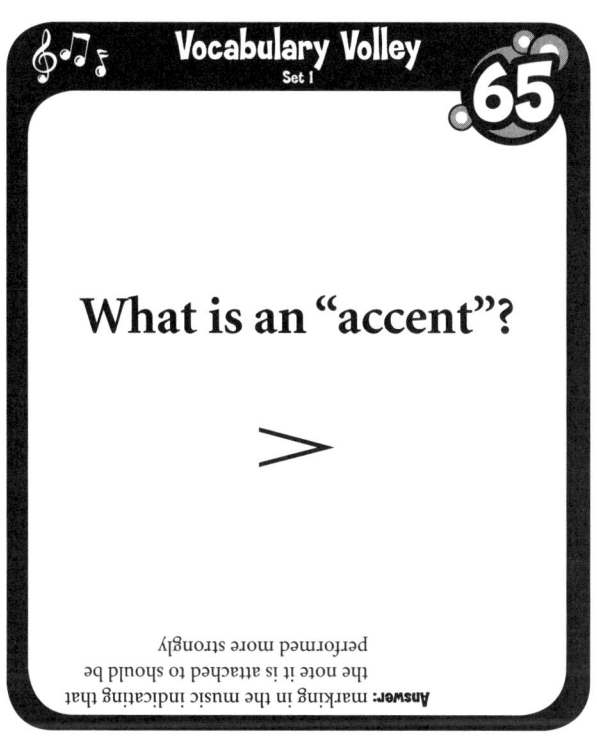

Vocabulary Volley

Set 1: Elementary

Instructions: Cut out each card along the dotted line. Students cover answers while quizzing. Give each student a card to play Quiz-Quiz-Trade. Matching cards may also be used for Mix-N-Match.

Vocabulary Volley Set 1 — **69**

What is a "phrase"?

Answer: group of notes in the melody, like a musical sentence,which has a definite beginning and ending

Vocabulary Volley Set 1 — **70**

What is the term for a group of notes in the melody, like a musical sentence, which has a definite beginning and ending?

Answer: phrase

Vocabulary Volley Set 1 — **71**

What is "syncopation"?

Answer: rhythmic pattern where emphasis or accent is shifted to a beat that is not normally a strong one

Vocabulary Volley Set 1 — **72**

What is the term for a rhythmic pattern where the emphasis or accent is shifted to a beat that is not normally a strong one?

Answer: syncopation

Vocabulary Volley

Set 1: Elementary

Instructions: Cut out each card along the dotted line. Students cover answers while quizzing. Give each student a card to play Quiz-Quiz-Trade. Matching cards may also be used for Mix-N-Match.

Vocabulary Volley Set 1 — 73

What is "accompaniment"?

Answer: vocal or instrumental part that supports a solo part, or music that is played to back up singers

Vocabulary Volley Set 1 — 74

What is the term for a vocal or instrumental part that supports a solo part, or the music that is played to back up singers?

Answer: accompaniment

Vocabulary Volley Set 1 — 75

What is a "rondo"?

Answer: form structure where a theme or section returns repeatedly after each contrasting theme or section is performed

Vocabulary Volley Set 1 — 76

What is the term for a form structure where a theme or section returns repeatedly after each contrasting theme or section is performed?

Answer: rondo

Vocabulary Volley

Set 2: Secondary

Instructions: Cut out each card along the dotted line. Students cover answers while quizzing. Give each student a card to play Quiz-Quiz-Trade. Matching cards may also be used for Mix-N-Match.

Vocabulary Volley Set 2 — **1**

How does a "complete cadence" end?

Answer: on the home tone of the scale, for example on "DO"

Vocabulary Volley Set 2 — **2**

What is the term for the kind of melodic cadence that ends on the home tone of the scale, for example on "DO"?

Answer: complete cadence

Vocabulary Volley Set 2 — **3**

How does an "incomplete cadence" end?

Answer: often on the 5th tone of the scale ("SOL"), but never on the home tone ("DO")

Vocabulary Volley Set 2 — **4**

What is the term for the kind of melodic cadence that often ends on the 5th tone of the scale ("SOL"), but never on the home tone ("DO")?

Answer: incomplete cadence

Vocabulary Volley

Set 2: Secondary

Instructions: Cut out each card along the dotted line. Students cover answers while quizzing. Give each student a card to play Quiz-Quiz-Trade. Matching cards may also be used for Mix-N-Match.

Vocabulary Volley
Set 2
5

What does "atonal" mean?

Answer: sound or pattern of pitches that seem to have no feeling of a home key

Vocabulary Volley
Set 2
6

What is the term for a sound or pattern of pitches that seem to have no feeling of a home key?

Answer: atonal

Vocabulary Volley
Set 2
7

What does "chromatic" mean?

Answer: musical sound that uses all 12 tones of the scale

Vocabulary Volley
Set 2
8

What is the term for a musical sound that uses all 12 tones of the scale?

Answer: chromatic

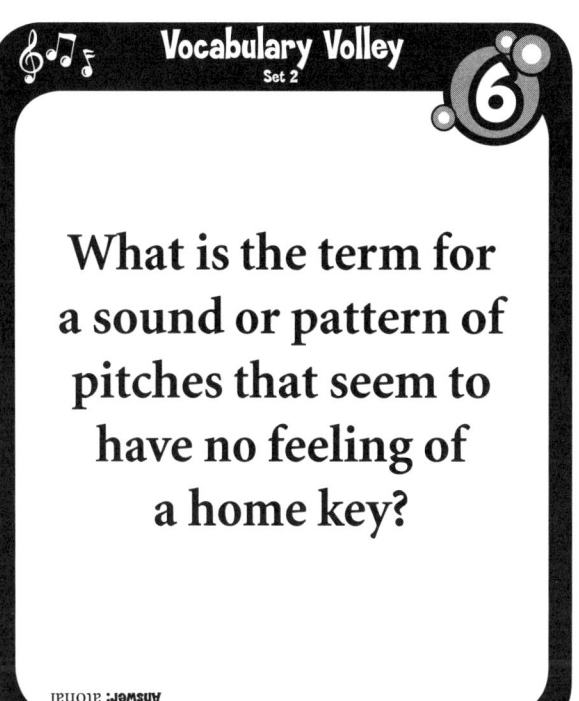

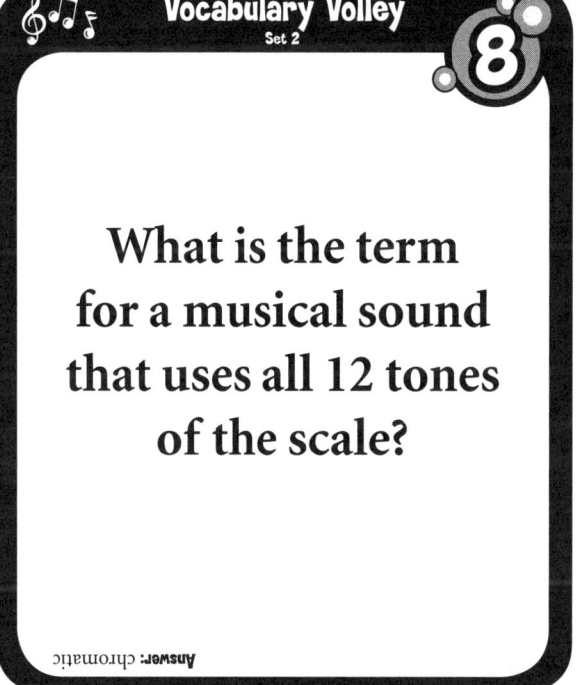

Vocabulary Volley

Set 2: Secondary

Instructions: Cut out each card along the dotted line. Students cover answers while quizzing. Give each student a card to play Quiz-Quiz-Trade. Matching cards may also be used for Mix-N-Match.

Vocabulary Volley
Set 2

9

What does "legato" mean?

Answer: performing a series of melody notes smoothly, without any break between them, often indicated by a slur

Vocabulary Volley
Set 2

10

What is the term for performing a series of melody notes smoothly, without any break between them, often indicated by a slur?

Answer: legato

Vocabulary Volley
Set 2

11

What does "staccato" mean?

Answer: performing a series of melody notes with a separation between them by stopping each tone in a quick choppy sound, indicated by small dots above or below the note heads

Vocabulary Volley
Set 2

12

What is the term for performing a series of melody notes with a separation between them by stopping each tone in a quick choppy sound, indicated by small dots above or below the note heads?

Answer: staccato

Vocabulary Volley

Set 2: Secondary

Instructions: Cut out each card along the dotted line. Students cover answers while quizzing. Give each student a card to play Quiz-Quiz-Trade. Matching cards may also be used for Mix-N-Match.

Vocabulary Volley Set 2 — 13

What is "meter" in music?

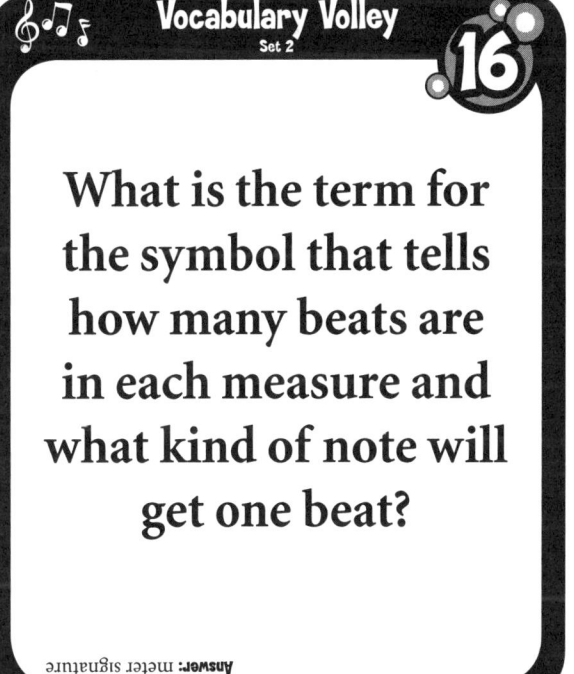

Answer: pattern of rhythmic pulses, usually in 2s or 3s, or a combination of 2s and 3s

Vocabulary Volley Set 2 — 14

What is the term for the pattern of rhythmic pulses, usually in 2s or 3s, or a combination of 2s and 3s?

Answer: meter

Vocabulary Volley Set 2 — 15

What is a "meter signature"?

$\begin{matrix}2\\4\end{matrix}$

Answer: symbol that tells how many beats are in each measure and what kind of note will get one beat

Vocabulary Volley Set 2 — 16

What is the term for the symbol that tells how many beats are in each measure and what kind of note will get one beat?

Answer: meter signature

Vocabulary Volley

Set 2: Secondary

Instructions: Cut out each card along the dotted line. Students cover answers while quizzing. Give each student a card to play Quiz-Quiz-Trade. Matching cards may also be used for Mix-N-Match.

Vocabulary Volley
Set 2
17

What is "duple meter"?

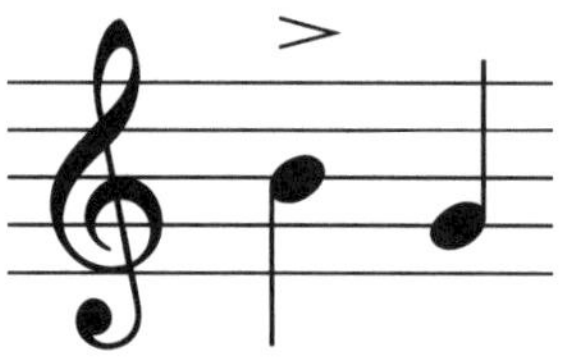

Answer: sets of beats that are grouped in 2s, where beat number one is strong and beat number two has a weaker sound

Vocabulary Volley
Set 2
18

What is the term for sets of beats that are grouped in 2s, where beat number one is strong and beat number two has a weaker sound?

Answer: duple meter

Vocabulary Volley
Set 2
19

What does "triple meter" mean?

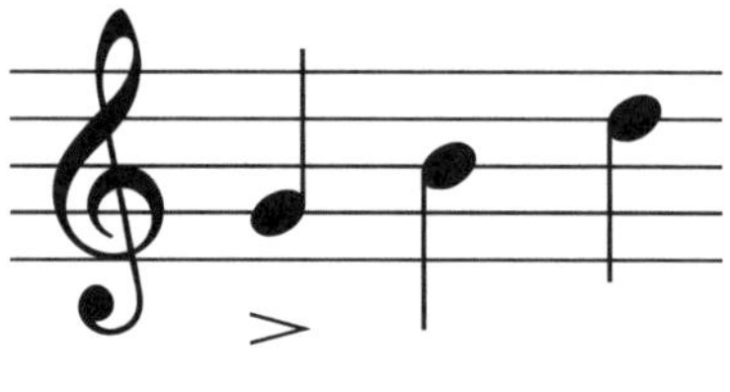

Answer: sets of beats that are grouped in 3s, where beat number one is strong and beats two and three have a weaker sound

Vocabulary Volley
Set 2
20

What is the term for sets of beats that are grouped in 3s, where beat number one is strong and beats two and three have a weaker sound?

Answer: triple meter

Vocabulary Volley

Set 2: Secondary

Instructions: Cut out each card along the dotted line. Students cover answers while quizzing. Give each student a card to play Quiz-Quiz-Trade. Matching cards may also be used for Mix-N-Match.

Vocabulary Volley Set 2 — **21**

What is a "chord"?

Answer: 3 or more pitches sung or played at the same time, where the pitches are usually stacked in intervals of a third

Vocabulary Volley Set 2 — **22**

What is the term for 3 or more pitches sung or played at the same time, where the pitches are usually stacked in intervals of a third?

Answer: chord

Vocabulary Volley Set 2 — **23**

What is a "chord root"?

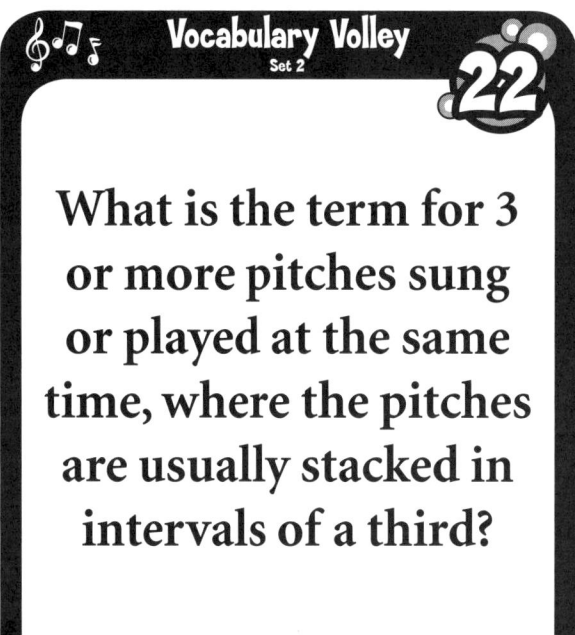

Answer: letter name of the home tone of a chord; also tone that the chord is built upon

Vocabulary Volley Set 2 — **24**

What is the term for the letter name of the home tone of a chord? This is also the tone that the chord is built upon.

Answer: chord root

Vocabulary Volley

Set 2: Secondary

Instructions: Cut out each card along the dotted line. Students cover answers while quizzing. Give each student a card to play Quiz-Quiz-Trade. Matching cards may also be used for Mix-N-Match.

Vocabulary Volley
Set 2
25

What is a "descant"?

Answer: harmony part that is usually higher in pitch than the melody

Vocabulary Volley
Set 2
26

What is the term for a harmony part that is usually higher in pitch than the melody?

Answer: descant

Vocabulary Volley
Set 2
27

What is a "countermelody"?

Answer: additional melody part that harmonizes with and accompanies the melody of a piece

Vocabulary Volley
Set 2
28

What is the term for an additional melody part that harmonizes with and accompanies the melody of a piece?

Answer: countermelody

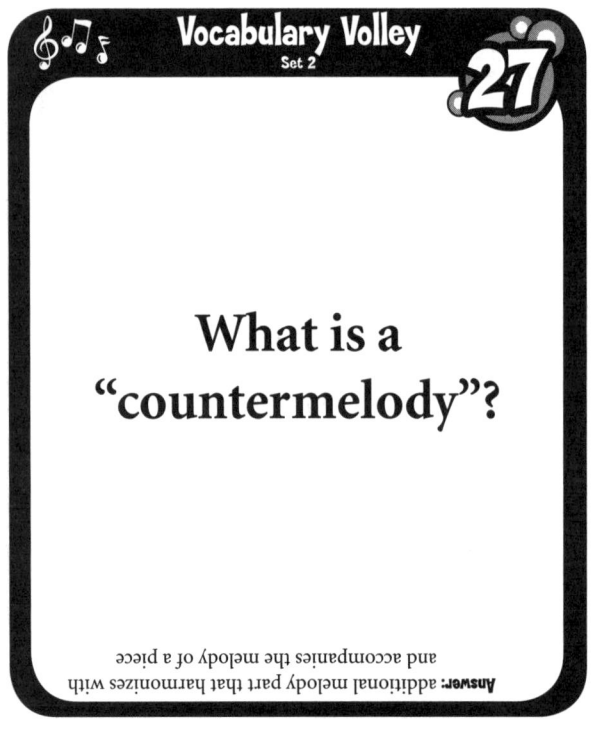

Vocabulary Volley

Set 2: Secondary

Instructions: Cut out each card along the dotted line. Students cover answers while quizzing. Give each student a card to play Quiz-Quiz-Trade. Matching cards may also be used for Mix-N-Match.

Vocabulary Volley
Set 2
29

What does "Nationalism" mean?

Answer: composition that reflects the sound and style of a composer's native country

Vocabulary Volley
Set 2
30

What is the term for a composition that reflects the sound and style of a composer's native country?

Answer: Nationalism

Vocabulary Volley
Set 2
31

What is "program music"?

Answer: instrumental music that tells a story, illustrates a scene, or describes an event

Vocabulary Volley
Set 2
32

What is the term for instrumental music that tells a story, illustrates a scene, or describes an event?

Answer: program music

Vocabulary Volley

Set 2: Secondary

Instructions: Cut out each card along the dotted line. Students cover answers while quizzing. Give each student a card to play Quiz-Quiz-Trade. Matching cards may also be used for Mix-N-Match.

Vocabulary Volley
Set 2
33

What is a "bordun"?

Answer: repetitive 2-tone pattern used as accompaniment, usually performed on barred instruments

Vocabulary Volley
Set 2
34

What is the term for a repetitive 2-tone pattern used as accompaniment, usually performed on barred instruments?

Answer: bordun

Vocabulary Volley
Set 2
35

What are "terraced dynamics"?

Answer: style of dynamic contrast where the loudness or softness of the sound suddenly changes from one level to another

Vocabulary Volley
Set 2
36

What is the term for the style of dynamic contrast where the loudness or softness of the sound suddenly changes from one level to another?

Answer: terraced dynamics

Vocabulary Volley

Set 2: Secondary

Instructions: Cut out each card along the dotted line. Students cover answers while quizzing. Give each student a card to play Quiz-Quiz-Trade. Matching cards may also be used for Mix-N-Match.

Vocabulary Volley Set 2 — **37**

What is an "upbeat" or "anacrusis"?

Answer: weaker or unaccented beats that come before the first full measure of a composition

Vocabulary Volley Set 2 — **38**

What is the term for the weaker or unaccented beats that come before the first full measure of a composition?

Answer: upbeat or anacrusis

Vocabulary Volley Set 2 — **39**

What is a "parallel harmony"?

Answer: harmony part that moves in equal intervals to the melody of the piece, often in thirds or sixths

Vocabulary Volley Set 2 — **40**

What is the term for a harmony part that moves in equal intervals to the melody of the piece, often in thirds or sixths?

Answer: parallel harmony

Vocabulary Volley

Set 2: Secondary

Instructions: Cut out each card along the dotted line. Students cover answers while quizzing. Give each student a card to play Quiz-Quiz-Trade. Matching cards may also be used for Mix-N-Match.

Vocabulary Volley Set 2 — 41

What is an "ensemble"?

Answer: group of two or more musicians performing together

Vocabulary Volley Set 2 — 42

What is the term for a group of two or more musicians performing together?

Answer: ensemble

Vocabulary Volley Set 2 — 43

What does "unison" mean?

Answer: singing or playing with others all on the same pitch, without harmony

Vocabulary Volley Set 2 — 44

What is the term for singing or playing with others all on the same pitch, without harmony?

Answer: unison

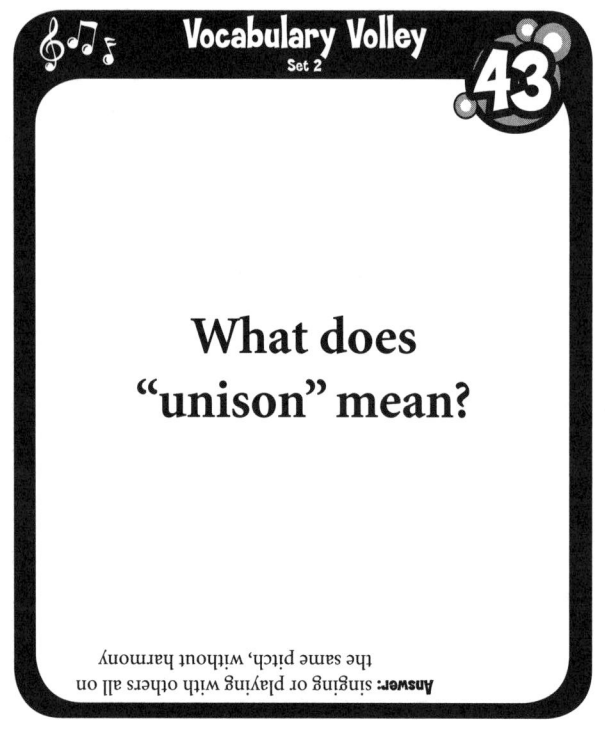

Vocabulary Volley

Set 2: Secondary

Instructions: Cut out each card along the dotted line. Students cover answers while quizzing. Give each student a card to play Quiz-Quiz-Trade. Matching cards may also be used for Mix-N-Match.

Vocabulary Volley Set 2 — **45**

What is a "duet"?

Answer: instrumental or vocal ensemble with 2 performers

Vocabulary Volley Set 2 — **46**

What is the term for an instrumental or vocal ensemble with 2 performers?

Answer: duet

Vocabulary Volley Set 2 — **47**

What is a "trio"?

Answer: instrumental or vocal ensemble with 3 performers

Vocabulary Volley Set 2 — **48**

What is the term for an instrumental or vocal ensemble with 3 performers?

Answer: trio

Vocabulary Volley

Set 2: Secondary

Instructions: Cut out each card along the dotted line. Students cover answers while quizzing. Give each student a card to play Quiz-Quiz-Trade. Matching cards may also be used for Mix-N-Match.

Vocabulary Volley
Set 2
49

What is a "quartet"?

Answer: instrumental or vocal ensemble with 4 performers

Vocabulary Volley
Set 2
50

What is the term for an instrumental or vocal ensemble with 4 performers?

Answer: quartet

Vocabulary Volley
Set 2
51

What is a "quintet"?

Answer: instrumental or vocal ensemble with 5 performers

Vocabulary Volley
Set 2
52

What is the term for an instrumental or vocal ensemble with 5 performers?

Answer: quintet

Vocabulary Volley

Set 2: Secondary

Instructions: Cut out each card along the dotted line. Students cover answers while quizzing. Give each student a card to play Quiz-Quiz-Trade. Matching cards may also be used for Mix-N-Match.

Vocabulary Volley Set 2 — **53**

What is a "cantata"?

Answer: vocal composition with choruses, solos, and recitatives

Vocabulary Volley Set 2 — **54**

What is the term for a vocal composition with choruses, solos, and recitatives?

Answer: cantata

Vocabulary Volley Set 2 — **55**

What is a "concerto"?

Answer: orchestral composition that includes one or more solo instruments

Vocabulary Volley Set 2 — **56**

What is the term for an orchestral composition that includes one or more solo instruments?

Answer: concerto

Vocabulary Volley

Set 2: Secondary

Instructions: Cut out each card along the dotted line. Students cover answers while quizzing. Give each student a card to play Quiz-Quiz-Trade. Matching cards may also be used for Mix-N-Match.

Vocabulary Volley
Set 2
57

What is a "symphony"?

Answer: orchestral composition that is usually arranged in four related movements

Vocabulary Volley
Set 2
58

What is the term for an orchestral composition that is usually arranged in four related movements?

Answer: symphony

Vocabulary Volley
Set 2
59

What is a "suite"?

Answer: set of dance tunes in same or related keys

Vocabulary Volley
Set 2
60

What is the term for a set of dance tunes in the same or related keys?

Answer: suite

Vocabulary Volley

Set 2: Secondary

Instructions: Cut out each card along the dotted line. Students cover answers while quizzing. Give each student a card to play Quiz-Quiz-Trade. Matching cards may also be used for Mix-N-Match.

Vocabulary Volley Set 2 — **61**

What is a "cadenza"?

Answer: extended improvisational section near end of a concerto where soloist shows technical brilliance

Vocabulary Volley Set 2 — **62**

What is the term for an extended improvisational section near the end of a concerto, where the soloist shows technical brilliance?

Answer: cadenza

Vocabulary Volley Set 2 — **63**

What is an "overture"?

Answer: instrumental composition heard as an introduction to an opera, a play, or other extended musical piece

Vocabulary Volley Set 2 — **64**

What is the term for an instrumental composition heard as an introduction to an opera, a play, or other extended musical piece?

Answer: overture

Vocabulary Volley

Set 2: Secondary

Instructions: Cut out each card along the dotted line. Students cover answers while quizzing. Give each student a card to play Quiz-Quiz-Trade. Matching cards may also be used for Mix-N-Match.

Vocabulary Volley Set 2 — **65**

What is a "madrigal"?

Answer: secular polyphonic part song, often sung unaccompanied

Vocabulary Volley Set 2 — **66**

What is the term for a **secular** polyphonic part song, often sung unaccompanied?

Answer: madrigal

Vocabulary Volley Set 2 — **67**

What is a "motet"?

Answer: sacred polyphonic part song, often sung unaccompanied

Vocabulary Volley Set 2 — **68**

What is the term for a **sacred** polyphonic part song, often sung unaccompanied?

Answer: motet

Vocabulary Volley

Set 2: Secondary

Instructions: Cut out each card along the dotted line. Students cover answers while quizzing. Give each student a card to play Quiz-Quiz-Trade. Matching cards may also be used for Mix-N-Match.

Vocabulary Volley Set 2 — 69

What is a "sonata"?

Answer: instrumental composition in 3 or 4 independent movements that may vary in key, mood, or tempo

Vocabulary Volley Set 2 — 70

What is the term for an instrumental composition in 3 or 4 independent movements that may vary in key, mood, or tempo?

Answer: sonata

Vocabulary Volley Set 2 — 71

What is a "toccata"?

Answer: composition written in a free style for organ or other keyboard instruments

Vocabulary Volley Set 2 — 72

What is the term for a composition written in a free style for organ or other keyboard instruments?

Answer: toccata

Vocabulary Volley

Set 2: Secondary

Instructions: Cut out each card along the dotted line. Students cover answers while quizzing. Give each student a card to play Quiz-Quiz-Trade. Matching cards may also be used for Mix-N-Match.

Vocabulary Volley Set 2 — 73

What is a "motif"?

Answer: melody that is used to represent a person, place, or thing and is often a recurring theme in a composition

Vocabulary Volley Set 2 — 74

What is the term for a melody that is used to represent a person, place, or thing, and is often a recurring theme in a composition?

Answer: motif

Vocabulary Volley Set 2 — 75

What does "a cappella" mean?

Answer: performing a song without any instrumental accompaniment

Vocabulary Volley Set 2 — 76

What is the term for performing a song without any instrumental accompaniment?

Answer: a cappella

Vocabulary Volley

Set 3: Elementary & Secondary

Instructions: Cut out each card along the dotted line. Students cover answers while quizzing. Give each student a card to play Quiz-Quiz-Trade. Matching cards may also be used for Mix-N-Match.

Vocabulary Volley Set 3 — **1**

What is a melodic "cadence"?

Answer: the way the melody of a phrase or section of a composition ends

Vocabulary Volley Set 3 — **2**

What is the term for the way the melody of a phrase or section of a composition ends?

Answer: cadence

Vocabulary Volley Set 3 — **3**

What is a "scale"?

Answer: stepwise progression of pitches arranged in order from lowest to highest (or highest to lowest), beginning with the home tone, or keynote

Vocabulary Volley Set 3 — **4**

What is the term for a stepwise progression of pitches arranged in order from lowest to highest (or highest to lowest), beginning with the home tone, or keynote?

Answer: scale

Vocabulary Volley

Set 3: Elementary & Secondary

Instructions: Cut out each card along the dotted line. Students cover answers while quizzing. Give each student a card to play Quiz-Quiz-Trade. Matching cards may also be used for Mix-N-Match.

Vocabulary Volley — Set 3 — 5

What does "diatonic" mean?

Answer: musical sound that uses only the 7 unaltered tones of the scale

Vocabulary Volley — Set 3 — 6

What is the term for a musical sound that uses only the 7 unaltered tones of the scale?

Answer: diatonic

Vocabulary Volley — Set 3 — 7

What does "pentatonic" mean?

Answer: musical sound that uses only 5 tones of the scale, usually DO, RE, MI, SOL, and LA

Vocabulary Volley — Set 3 — 8

What is the term for a musical sound that uses only 5 tones of the scale, usually DO, RE, MI, SOL, and LA?

Answer: pentatonic

Vocabulary Volley

Set 3: Elementary & Secondary

Instructions: Cut out each card along the dotted line. Students cover answers while quizzing. Give each student a card to play Quiz-Quiz-Trade. Matching cards may also be used for Mix-N-Match.

Vocabulary Volley Set 3 — **9**

What does "improvisation" mean?

Answer: creating music while in the process of performing it

Vocabulary Volley Set 3 — **10**

What is the term for creating music while in the process of performing it?

Answer: improvisation

Vocabulary Volley Set 3 — **11**

What does "composition" mean?

Answer: creating original music and notating it for others to read and perform

Vocabulary Volley Set 3 — **12**

What is the term for creating original music and notating it for others to read and perform?

Answer: composition

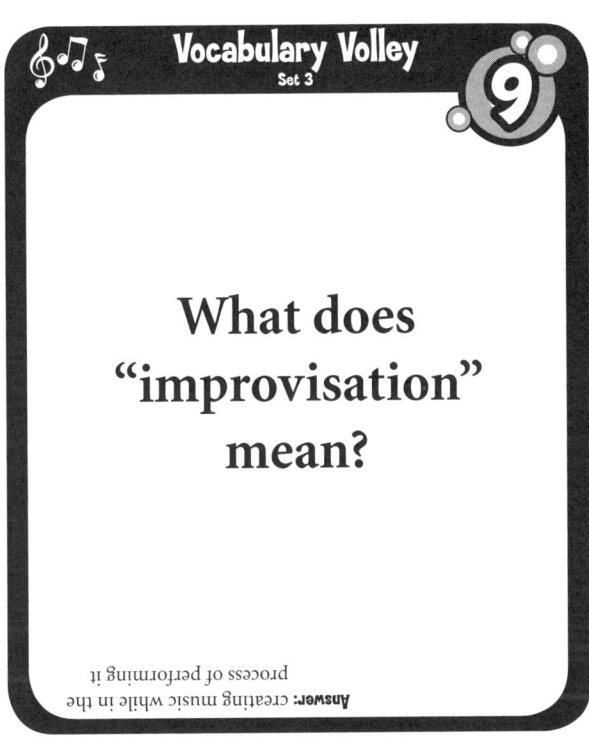

Vocabulary Volley

Set 3: Elementary & Secondary

Instructions: Cut out each card along the dotted line. Students cover answers while quizzing. Give each student a card to play Quiz-Quiz-Trade. Matching cards may also be used for Mix-N-Match.

Vocabulary Volley
Set 3
13

What voice part is "soprano"?

Answer: highest voice part, usually sung by the highest female voices in a choir

Vocabulary Volley
Set 3
14

What is the name of the highest voice part, usually sung by the highest female voices in a choir?

Answer: soprano

Vocabulary Volley
Set 3
15

What voice part is "alto"?

Answer: second highest voice part, usually sung by the lowest female voices in a choir

Vocabulary Volley
Set 3
16

What is the name of the second-highest voice part, usually sung by the lowest female voices in a choir?

Answer: alto

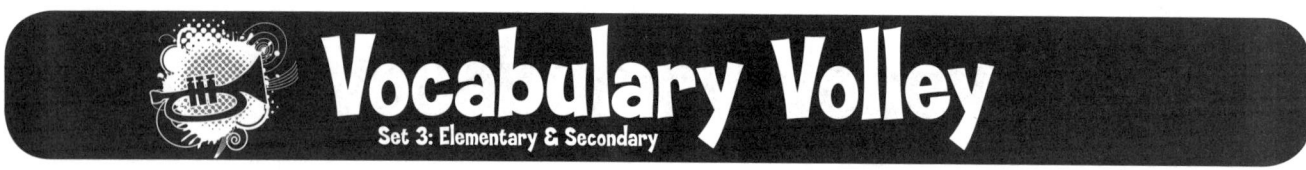

Vocabulary Volley

Set 3: Elementary & Secondary

Instructions: Cut out each card along the dotted line. Students cover answers while quizzing. Give each student a card to play Quiz-Quiz-Trade. Matching cards may also be used for Mix-N-Match.

Vocabulary Volley Set 3 — **17**

What voice part is "tenor"?

Answer: second-lowest voice part, usually sung by the highest male voices in a choir

Vocabulary Volley Set 3 — **18**

What is the name of the second-lowest voice part, usually sung by the highest male voices in a choir?

Answer: tenor

Vocabulary Volley Set 3 — **19**

What voice part is "bass"?

Answer: lowest voice part, usually sung by the lowest male voices in a choir

Vocabulary Volley Set 3 — **20**

What is the name of the lowest voice part, usually sung by the lowest male voices in a choir?

Answer: bass

Vocabulary Volley

Set 3: Elementary & Secondary

Instructions: Cut out each card along the dotted line. Students cover answers while quizzing. Give each student a card to play Quiz-Quiz-Trade. Matching cards may also be used for Mix-N-Match.

Vocabulary Volley Set 3 — **21**

What is musical "style"?

Answer: characteristic way that music sounds, (referring to composer, time period, or culture)

Vocabulary Volley Set 3 — **22**

What is the term for the characteristic way that music sounds? (It may refer to a composer, a time period, or a culture.)

Answer: style

Vocabulary Volley Set 3 — **23**

What is "tempo"?

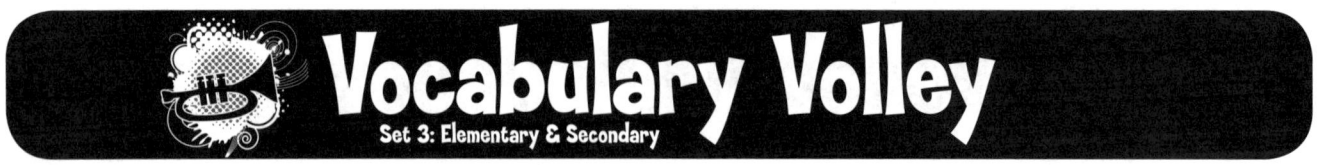

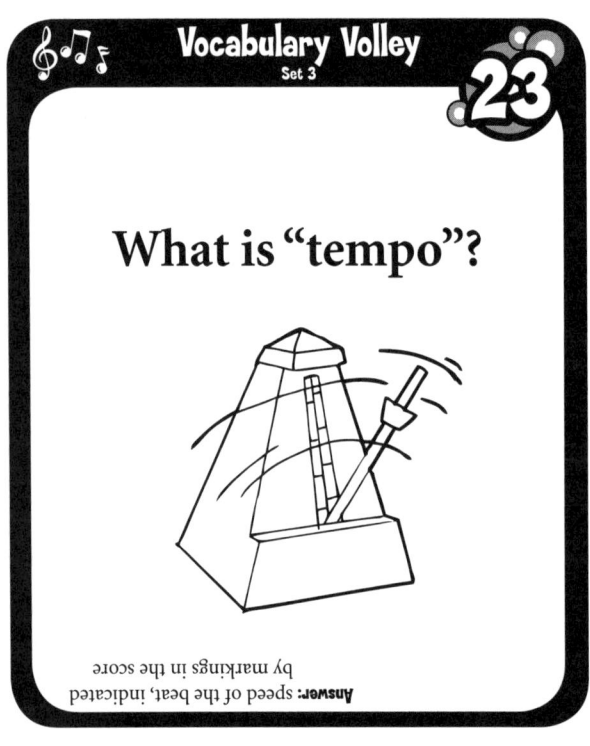

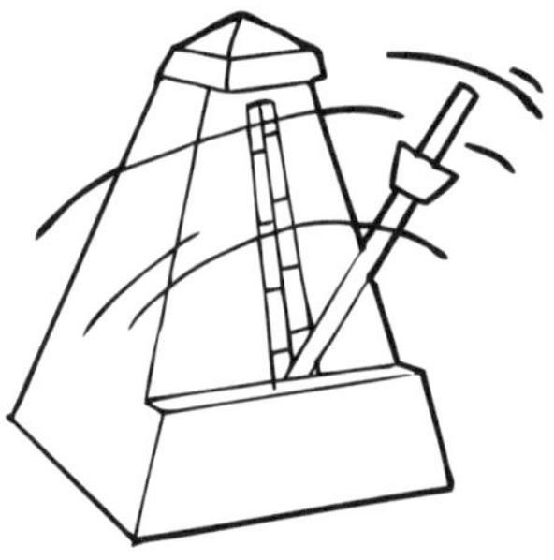

Answer: speed of the beat, indicated by markings in the score

Vocabulary Volley Set 3 — **24**

What is the term for the speed of the beat, indicated by markings in the score?

Answer: tempo

Vocabulary Volley

Set 3: Elementary & Secondary

Instructions: Cut out each card along the dotted line. Students cover answers while quizzing. Give each student a card to play Quiz-Quiz-Trade. Matching cards may also be used for Mix-N-Match.

Vocabulary Volley Set 3 — **25**

What is "expression" in music?

Answer: performing a piece of music with appropriate tempo, dynamics, phrasing, and style

Vocabulary Volley Set 3 — **26**

What is the term for performing a piece of music with appropriate tempo, dynamics, phrasing, and style?

Answer: expression

Vocabulary Volley Set 3 — **27**

What is a "slur"?

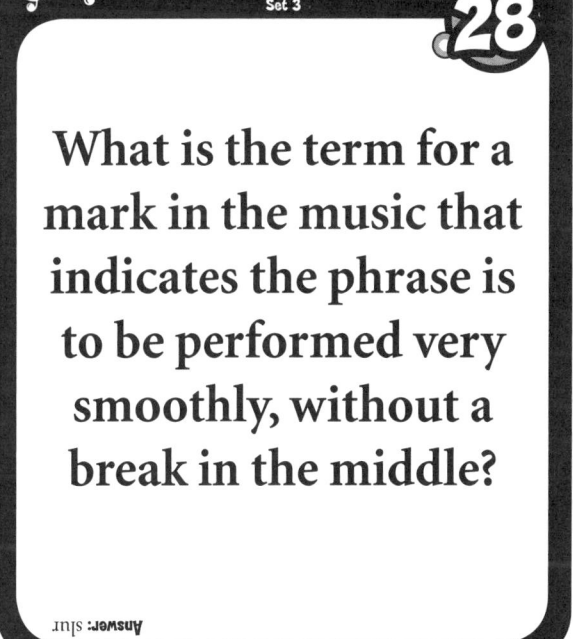

Answer: mark in the music that indicates phrase is to be performed very smoothly, without a break in the middle

Vocabulary Volley Set 3 — **28**

What is the term for a mark in the music that indicates the phrase is to be performed very smoothly, without a break in the middle?

Answer: slur

Vocabulary Volley

Set 3: Elementary & Secondary

Instructions: Cut out each card along the dotted line. Students cover answers while quizzing. Give each student a card to play Quiz-Quiz-Trade. Matching cards may also be used for Mix-N-Match.

Vocabulary Volley Set 3 — **29**

What is musical "register"?

Answer: relative location of a group of tones or pitches in the melody (either mostly high or mostly low)

Vocabulary Volley Set 3 — **30**

What is the term for the relative location of a group of tones or pitches in the melody (either mostly high or mostly low)?

Answer: register

Vocabulary Volley Set 3 — **31**

What is an "octave"?

Answer: interval in the music of 8 steps

Vocabulary Volley Set 3 — **32**

What is the term for an interval in the music of 8 steps, for example moving directly from one DO to the next DO (either going up or going down)?

Answer: octave

Vocabulary Volley

Set 3: Elementary & Secondary

Instructions: Cut out each card along the dotted line. Students cover answers while quizzing. Give each student a card to play Quiz-Quiz-Trade. Matching cards may also be used for Mix-N-Match.

Vocabulary Volley Set 3 — **33**

What is music "notation"?

Answer: system of writing music to show the rhythm, melody, harmony, dynamics, tempo, and tone color of a piece of music

Vocabulary Volley Set 3 — **34**

What is the term for a system of writing music to show the rhythm, melody, harmony, dynamics, tempo, and tone color of a piece of music?

Answer: notation

Vocabulary Volley Set 3 — **35**

What is "orchestration"?

Answer: arranging and writing music for a group of instruments to play together

Vocabulary Volley Set 3 — **36**

What is the term for arranging and writing music for a group of instruments to play together?

Answer: orchestration

Vocabulary Volley

Set 3: Elementary & Secondary

Instructions: Cut out each card along the dotted line. Students cover answers while quizzing. Give each student a card to play Quiz-Quiz-Trade. Matching cards may also be used for Mix-N-Match.

Vocabulary Volley Set 3 — **37**

What does "*D.C. al Fine*" mean?

Answer: symbol that tells the performer to repeat from the beginning of the piece and then stop where the word *Fine* appears

---

Vocabulary Volley Set 3 — **38**

What is the term for the symbol that tells the performer to repeat from the beginning of the piece and then stop where the word *Fine* appears?

Answer: D.C. al Fine

Vocabulary Volley Set 3 — **39**

What does "*D.S. al Fine*" mean?

Answer: tells the performer to repeat from a "sign" found earlier in the piece and then stop where the word *Fine* appears

---

Vocabulary Volley Set 3 — **40**

What is the term for the symbol that tells the performer to repeat from a "sign" found earlier in the piece and then stop where the word *Fine* appears?

Answer: D.S. al Fine

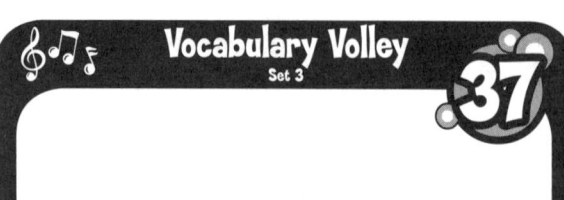

Vocabulary Volley

Set 3: Elementary & Secondary

Instructions: Cut out each card along the dotted line. Students cover answers while quizzing. Give each student a card to play Quiz-Quiz-Trade. Matching cards may also be used for Mix-N-Match.

Vocabulary Volley Set 3 — 41

What is a "fermata"?

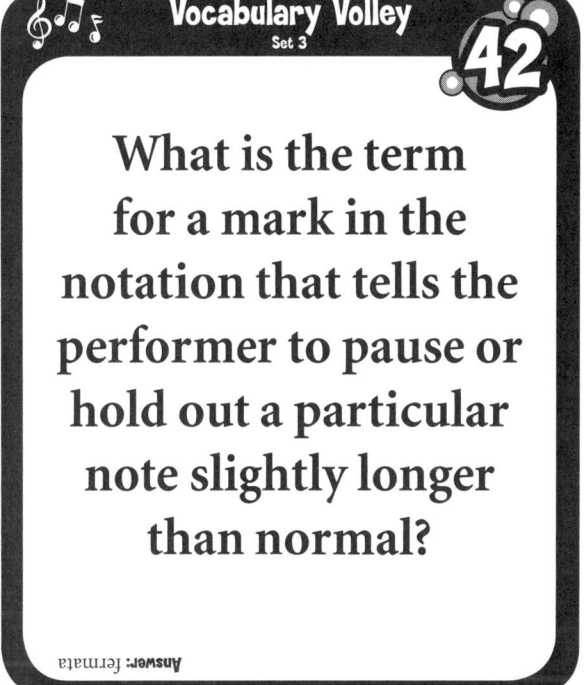

Answer: mark in the notation that tells the performer to pause or hold out a particular note slightly longer than normal

Vocabulary Volley Set 3 — 42

What is the term for a mark in the notation that tells the performer to pause or hold out a particular note slightly longer than normal?

Answer: fermata

Vocabulary Volley Set 3 — 43

What is an "ostinato"?

Answer: short rhythmic or melodic pattern that is repeated over and over as an accompaniment

Vocabulary Volley Set 3 — 44

What is the term for a short rhythmic or melodic pattern that is repeated over and over as an accompaniment?

Answer: ostinato

Blank Card Template

Instructions: Use this blank card template to create your own Quiz-Quiz-Trade cards.

Structure 2

Fan-N-Pick

Structure 2

Fan-N-Pick

Students quiz team members using sets of questions printed on cards, and are quizzed in return by other team members.

Setup: *Students are grouped in teams of 4. Each team receives a set of question cards. Each student has a job to perform during the structure. Jobs are rotated among team members so that everyone has the opportunity to be responsible for each part of the structure. Fan-N-Pick can be used to reinforce a variety of music concepts, including knowledge building (content mastery).*

Steps

1 Student #1 holds question cards in a fan and says, "*Pick a card, any card!*"
Student #1 is careful to display only the back sides of the cards so that no one can see which question will be chosen.

2 Student #2 picks a card, reads the question aloud, and allows five seconds of think time.
In our Road Map Ramble example, student #2 then shows the graphic to Student #3 and asks, "*Can you read this pattern?*" If no answer is given after 5 seconds, Student #4 may begin to coach.

3 Student #3 answers the question.
Student #3 responds by reading or chanting the notation on the card. There are 3 types: rhythm patterns with repeat signs, short poems for 1st/2nd endings, and picture icons for *D.C. al Fine* (for example, the correct answer for one of the *D.C. al Fine* cards would be "*circle, star, triangle, square, circle*").

4 Student #4 responds to the answer.
Student #4 listens and checks the answer given, then either praises or coaches (using the model tip, tip, tell, re-ask to help Student #3 arrive at the correct answer). For example, Student #4 may say "*Bravo*" for a correct response or "*Did you notice where the 'Fine' is?*" to give a hint about correcting a wrong answer.

5 Students rotate roles, one person clockwise, for each new round.
Student #2 becomes the next one to fan the cards out; Student #3 picks one to show to Student #4 while asking, "*Can you read this pattern?*" and Student #1 is now the one to praise or coach.

Sample Activity

Road Map Ramble: **Students use Fan-N-Pick to read examples of music notation that include repeat signs, 1st/2nd endings, or *D.C. al Fine.***

Benefits

- All students are actively involved.
- Students interact with their teammates.
- Students learn and practice social skills: patience, tolerance, taking turns, listening, coaching, praising, and paraphrasing.
- Students rely on each other, rather than on the teacher, to check for accuracy in responses to the questions.
- By using different sets of cards, many music concepts can be reinforced.
- Fan-N-Pick can be used as a pretest, as a review of concepts or vocabulary, as a check for comprehension, or as a teambuilding structure by asking fun musical facts with teammates.

Hints

- **Model.** When introducing the structure, model with a team how to fan the cards, how to quiz (ask the type of question appropriate for the particular set of cards being used), and how to coach. Remind everyone to use "team voices" so that all can participate in the structure simultaneously without interfering with other teams.
- **Visual Assists for Trading Roles.**
  - **Job Mat:** Place the mat in the middle of the team (like a placemat) to remind everyone of their role. As the structure progresses, rotate the mat.
  - **Job Tents:** Each student places one tent in front of them (like a name card). As the roles are rotated, the tents are passed clockwise.
- **Card Sets.** Identical sets may be given to each team, or the entire set may be divided among the teams. Teams may then trade their cards for another team's cards to prolong the activity when they are finished with their set.
- **Creating Cards.** For a test review, upper elementary or secondary level students can make their own cards based on review sheets, or the teacher may simply cut up the actual test and do a Fan-N-Pick review just prior to administering the test itself.
- **Higher-Level Thinking.** For open-ended questions that have no right or wrong answer, the 4th student paraphrases ("*So, you said that…*"), then praises the response given by Student #3 for additional affirmation and clarification.

Fan-N-Pick

Structure 2

Fan-N-Pick (continued)

Variation

Fan-N-Pick Pairs. Fan-N-Pick can be played in pairs. Student #1 fans; Student #2 picks and reads; Student #1 answers; Student #2 coaches or praises; students switch roles.

Principles

P Positive Interdependence: Every student needs one another to do the structure.

I Individual Accountability: Students are each accountable for performing their role.

E Equal Participation: Students participate equally through turns.

S Simultaneous Interaction: 25% active engagement through jobs and turns.

Fan-N-Pick Activities

Additional Activities for Fan-N-Pick Cards
Card sets can also be used for Structure 1: Quiz-Quiz-Trade and Structure 3: Showdown.

Fan-N-Pick

Road Map Ramble

Instructions: Copy one set of cards for each team. Cut out each card along the dotted line. Give each team a set of cards to play Fan-N-Pick.

Road Map Ramble 1

Can you read this pattern?

Road Map Ramble 2

Can you read this pattern?

Road Map Ramble

Instructions: Copy one set of cards for each team. Cut out each card along the dotted line. Give each team a set of cards to play Fan-N-Pick.

Road Map Ramble

3

Can you read this pattern?

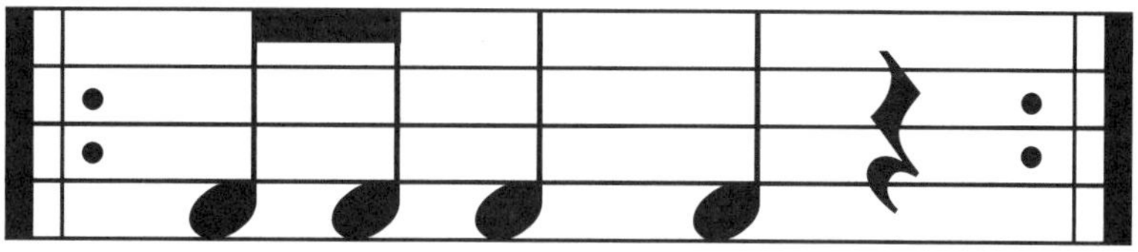

Road Map Ramble

4

Can you read this pattern?

Road Map Ramble

Instructions: Copy one set of cards for each team. Cut out each card along the dotted line. Give each team a set of cards to play Fan-N-Pick.

Road Map Ramble

5

Can you read this pattern?

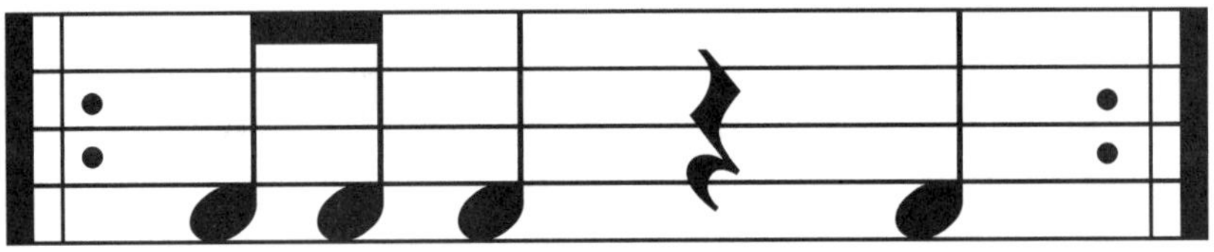

Road Map Ramble

6

Can you read this pattern?

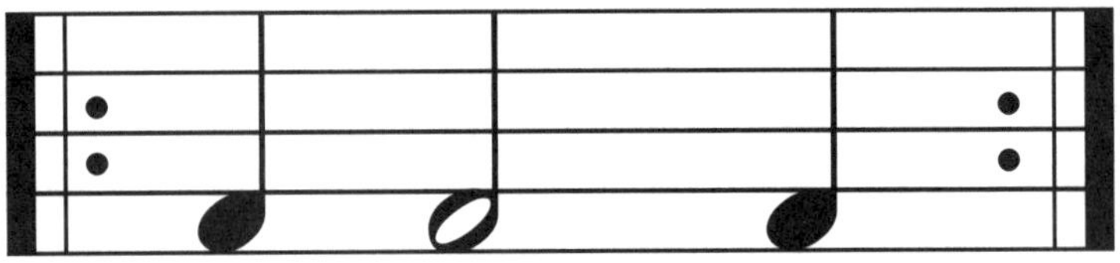

Road Map Ramble

Instructions: Copy one set of cards for each team. Cut out each card along the dotted line. Give each team a set of cards to play Fan-N-Pick.

Road Map Ramble

7

Can you read this pattern?

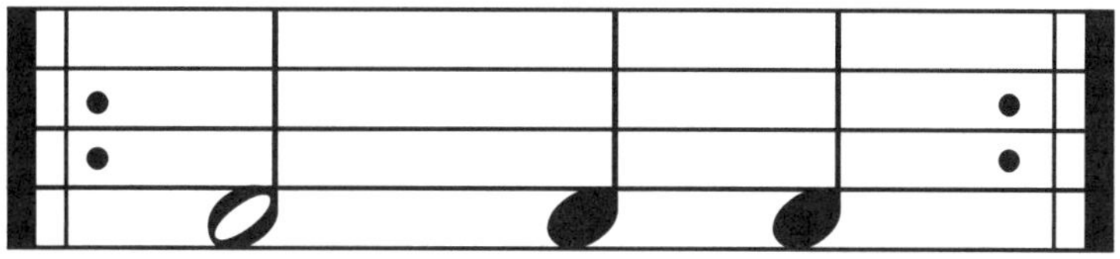

Road Map Ramble

8

Can you read this pattern?

Road Map Ramble

Instructions: Copy one set of cards for each team. Cut out each card along the dotted line. Give each team a set of cards to play Fan-N-Pick.

Road Map Ramble

9

Can you read this pattern?

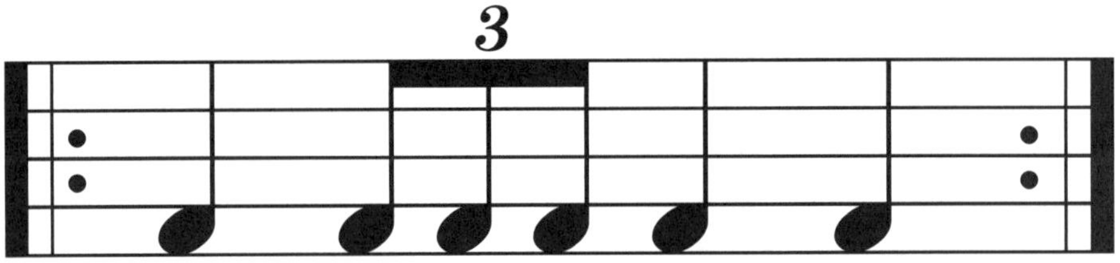

Road Map Ramble

10

Can you read this pattern?

Road Map Ramble

Instructions: Copy one set of cards for each team. Cut out each card along the dotted line. Give each team a set of cards to play Fan-N-Pick.

Road Map Ramble

11

Can you read this pattern?

Road Map Ramble

12

Can you read this pattern?

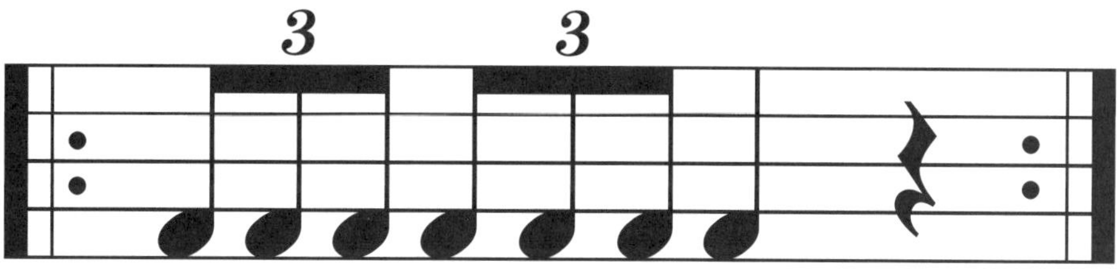

Road Map Ramble

Instructions: Copy one set of cards for each team. Cut out each card along the dotted line. Give each team a set of cards to play Fan-N-Pick.

Road Map Ramble

13

Can you read this poem?

1.	2.

Dog and cat | in a house :|| chased a mouse ||

Road Map Ramble

14

Can you read this poem?

1.	2.

Pretty flower | in a vase :|| full of grace ||

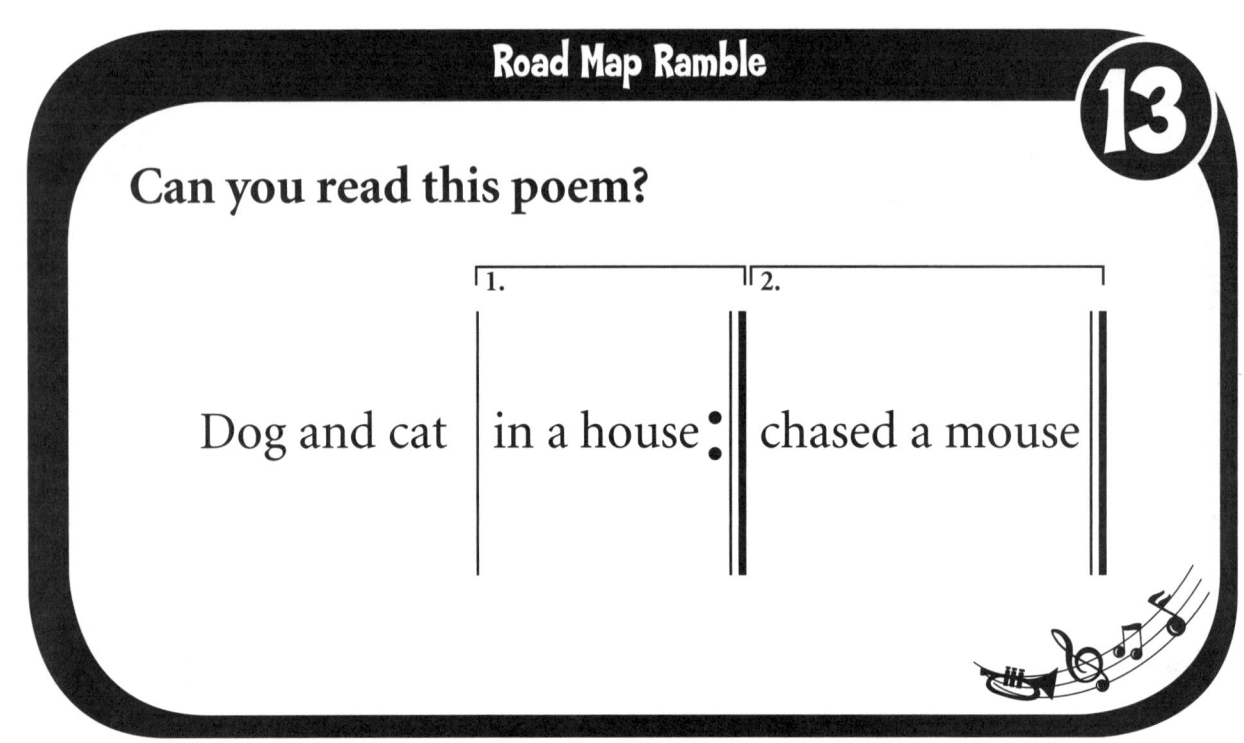

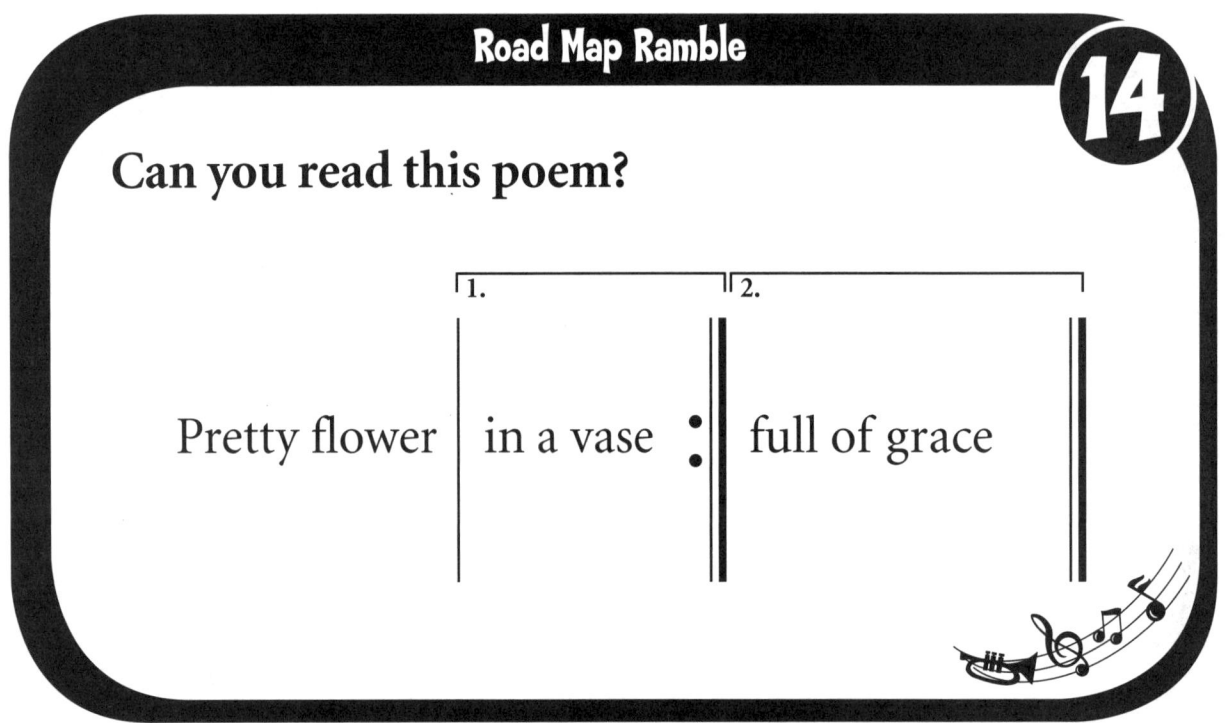

Road Map Ramble

Instructions: Copy one set of cards for each team. Cut out each card along the dotted line. Give each team a set of cards to play Fan-N-Pick.

Road Map Ramble

15

Can you read this poem?

	1.	2.
Kangaroo	hop hop hops :‖	never stops ‖

Road Map Ramble

16

Can you read this poem?

	1.	2.
See the rain	pouring down :‖	all over town ‖

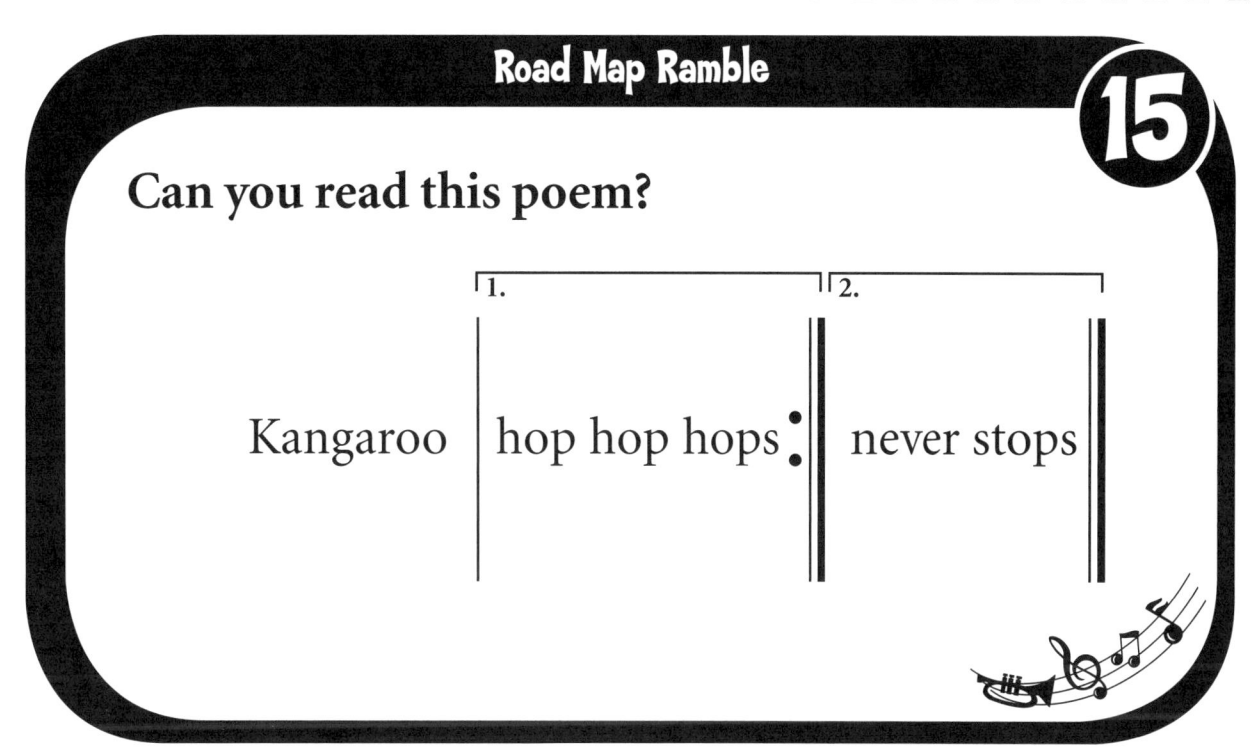

Road Map Ramble

Instructions: Copy one set of cards for each team. Cut out each card along the dotted line. Give each team a set of cards to play Fan-N-Pick.

Road Map Ramble — 17

Can you read this poem?

	1.	2.
When we sing we	sit up tall :	have a ball

Road Map Ramble — 18

Can you read this poem?

	1.	2.
Eat some soup	from a bowl :	with a troll

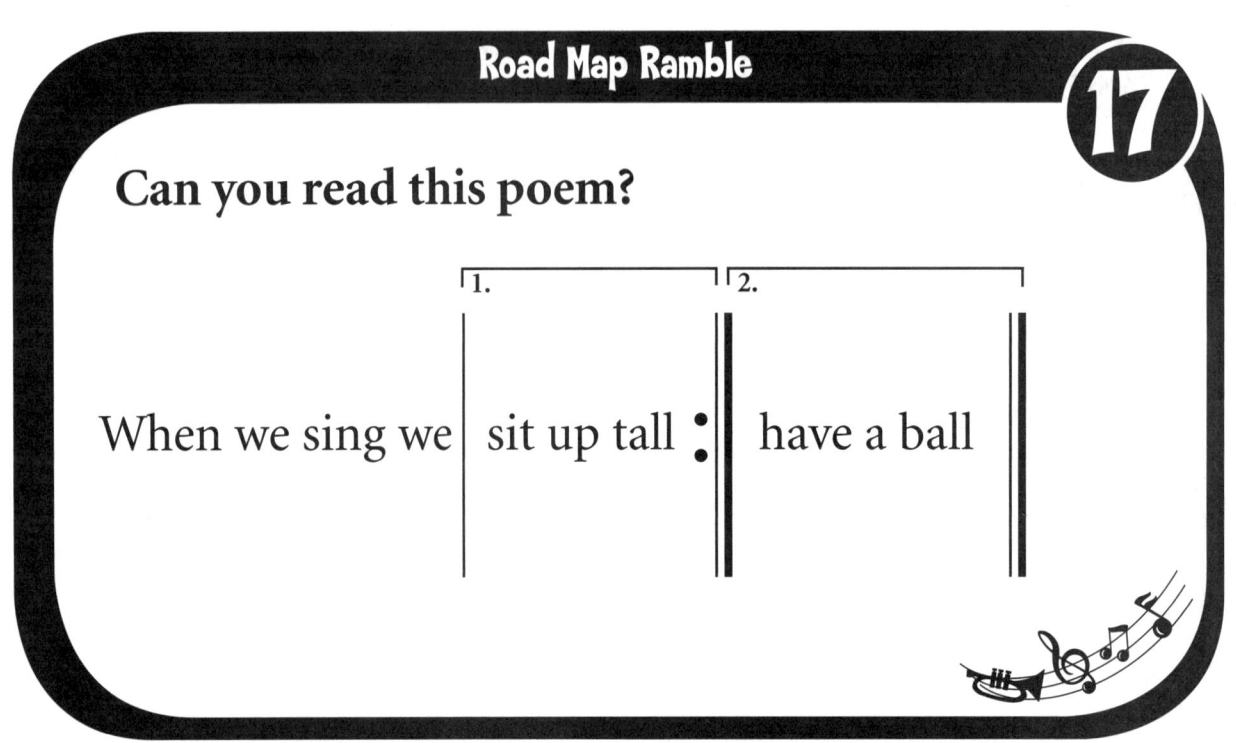

Road Map Ramble

Instructions: Copy one set of cards for each team. Cut out each card along the dotted line. Give each team a set of cards to play Fan-N-Pick.

Road Map Ramble

19

Can you read this poem?

	1.	2.
Find a penny	in a ditch :	and you're rich

Road Map Ramble

20

Can you read this poem?

	1.	2.
I like candy	it's so sweet :	what a treat!

Road Map Ramble

Instructions: Copy one set of cards for each team. Cut out each card along the dotted line. Give each team a set of cards to play Fan-N-Pick.

Road Map Ramble

21

Can you read this poem?

Tie that box up ‖ 1. with a string :‖ 2. for the King ‖

Road Map Ramble

22

Can you read this poem?

That girl thinks ‖ 1. she's a queen :‖ 2. I like beans! ‖

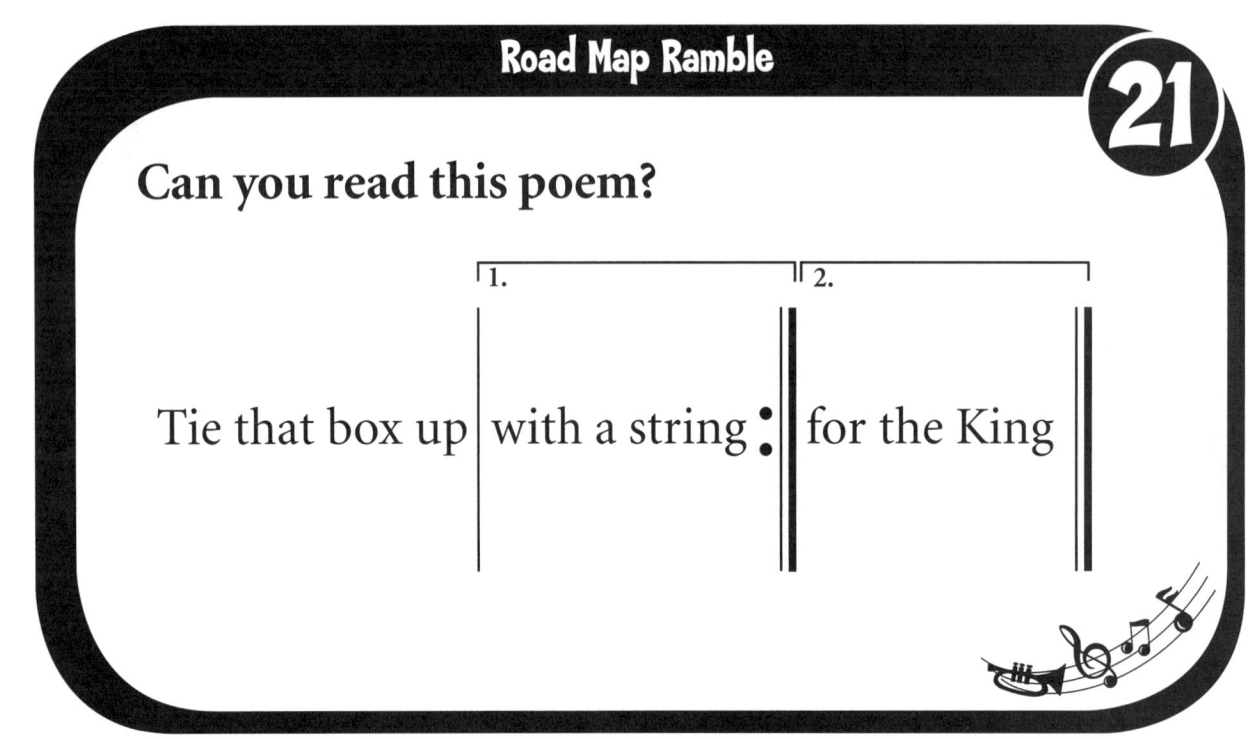

Road Map Ramble

Instructions: Copy one set of cards for each team. Cut out each card along the dotted line. Give each team a set of cards to play Fan-N-Pick.

Road Map Ramble

23

Can you read this poem?

	1.	2.
See the sun	watch it shine :‖	it's so fine ‖

Road Map Ramble

24

Can you read this poem?

	1.	2.
Ladybug	in my hat :‖	small and fat! ‖

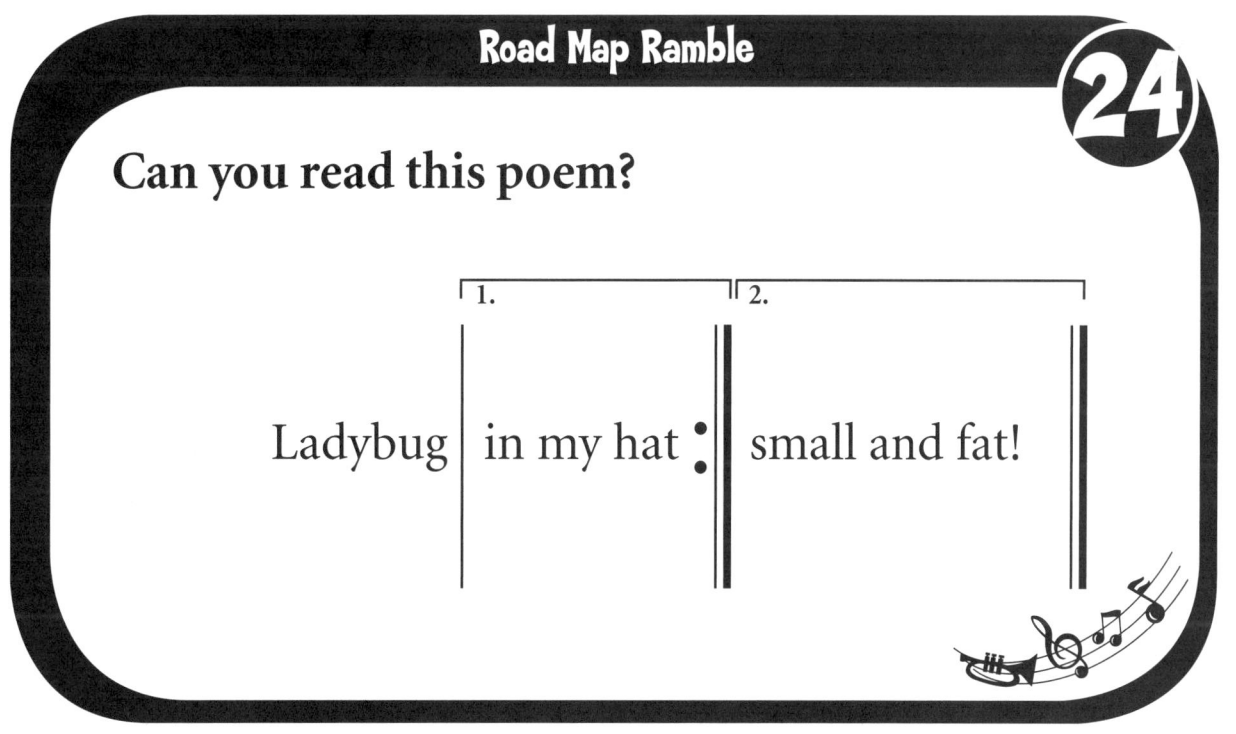

Road Map Ramble

Instructions: Copy one set of cards for each team. Cut out each card along the dotted line. Give each team a set of cards to play Fan-N-Pick.

Road Map Ramble

25

Can you read this pattern?

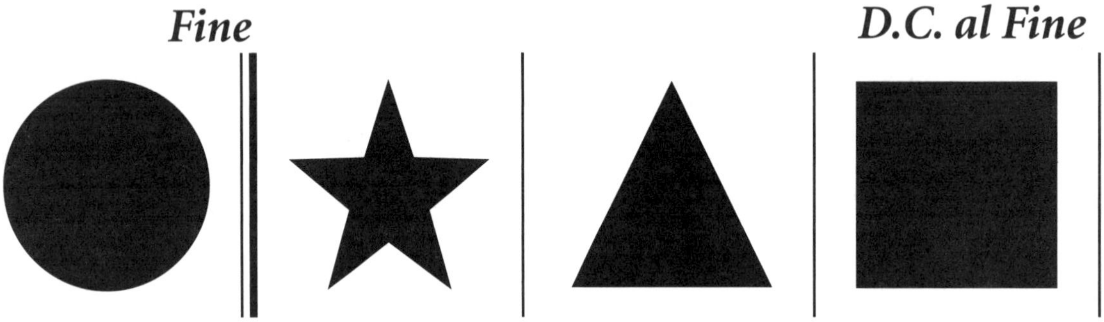

Road Map Ramble

26

Can you read this pattern?

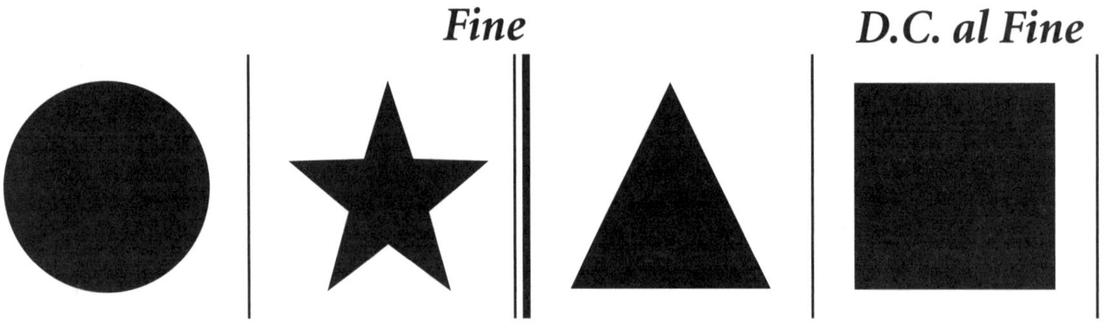

Road Map Ramble

Instructions: Copy one set of cards for each team. Cut out each card along the dotted line. Give each team a set of cards to play Fan-N-Pick.

Road Map Ramble

27

Can you read this pattern?

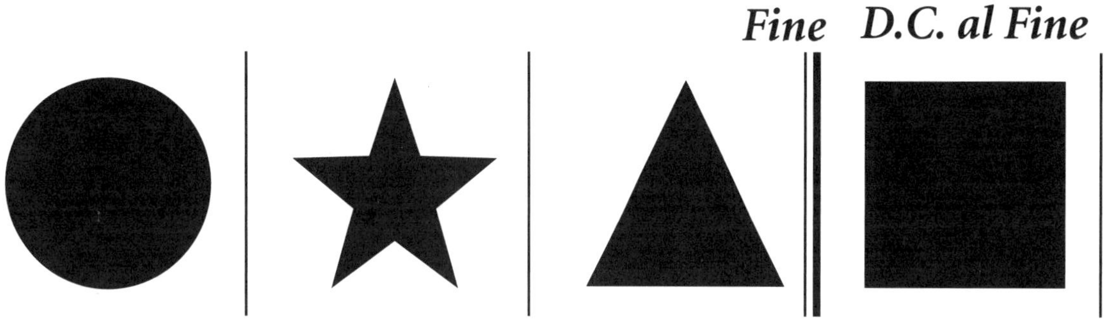

Road Map Ramble

28

Can you read this pattern?

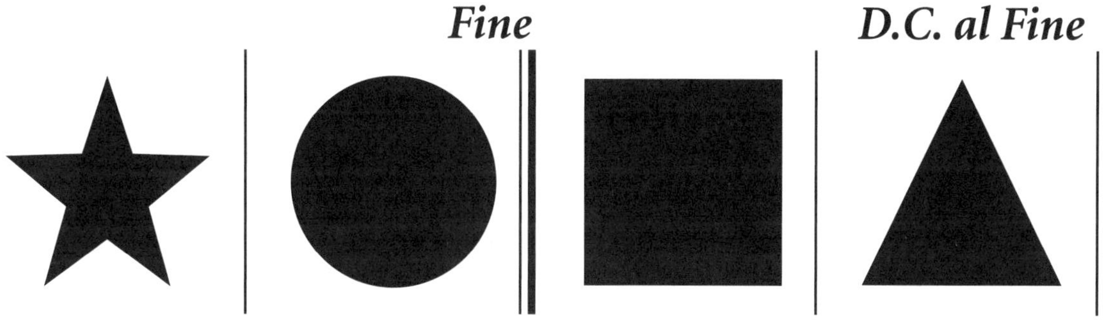

Road Map Ramble

Instructions: Copy one set of cards for each team. Cut out each card along the dotted line. Give each team a set of cards to play Fan-N-Pick.

Road Map Ramble

29

Can you read this pattern?

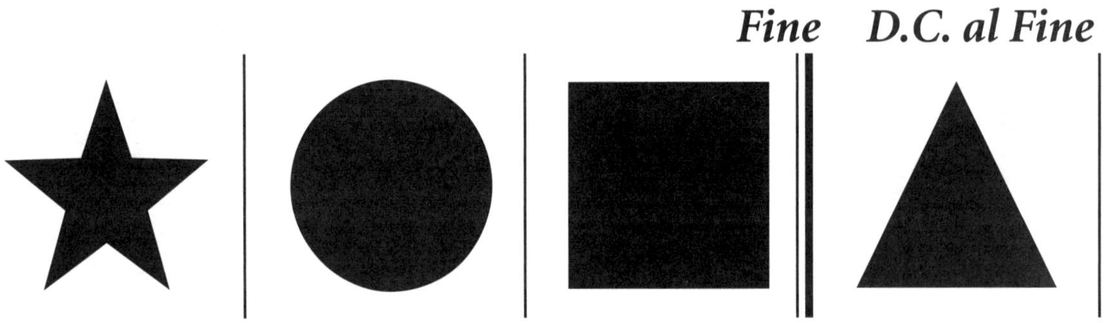

Road Map Ramble

30

Can you read this pattern?

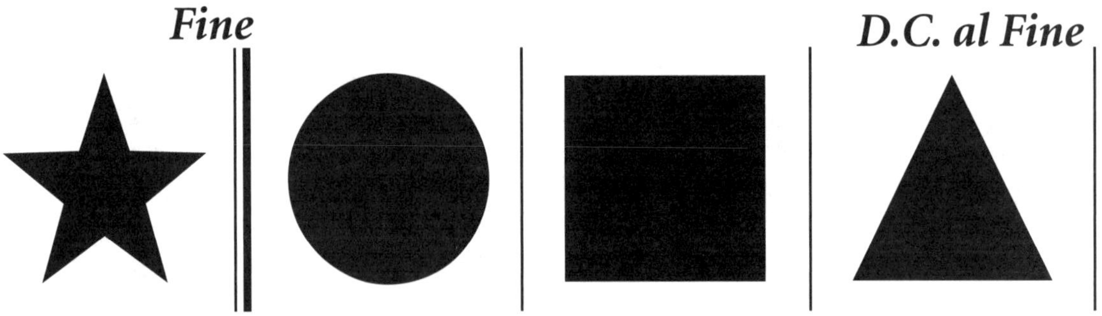

Road Map Ramble

Instructions: Copy one set of cards for each team. Cut out each card along the dotted line. Give each team a set of cards to play Fan-N-Pick.

Road Map Ramble

31

Can you read this pattern?

Road Map Ramble

32

Can you read this pattern?

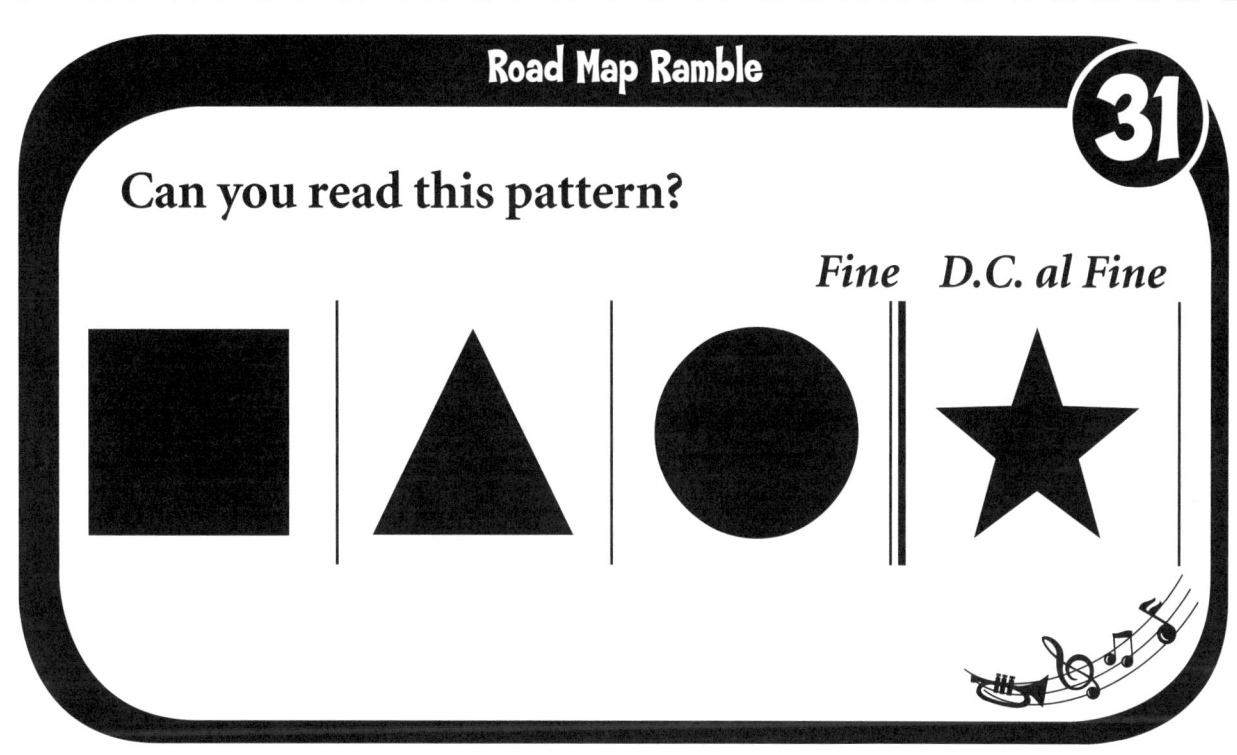

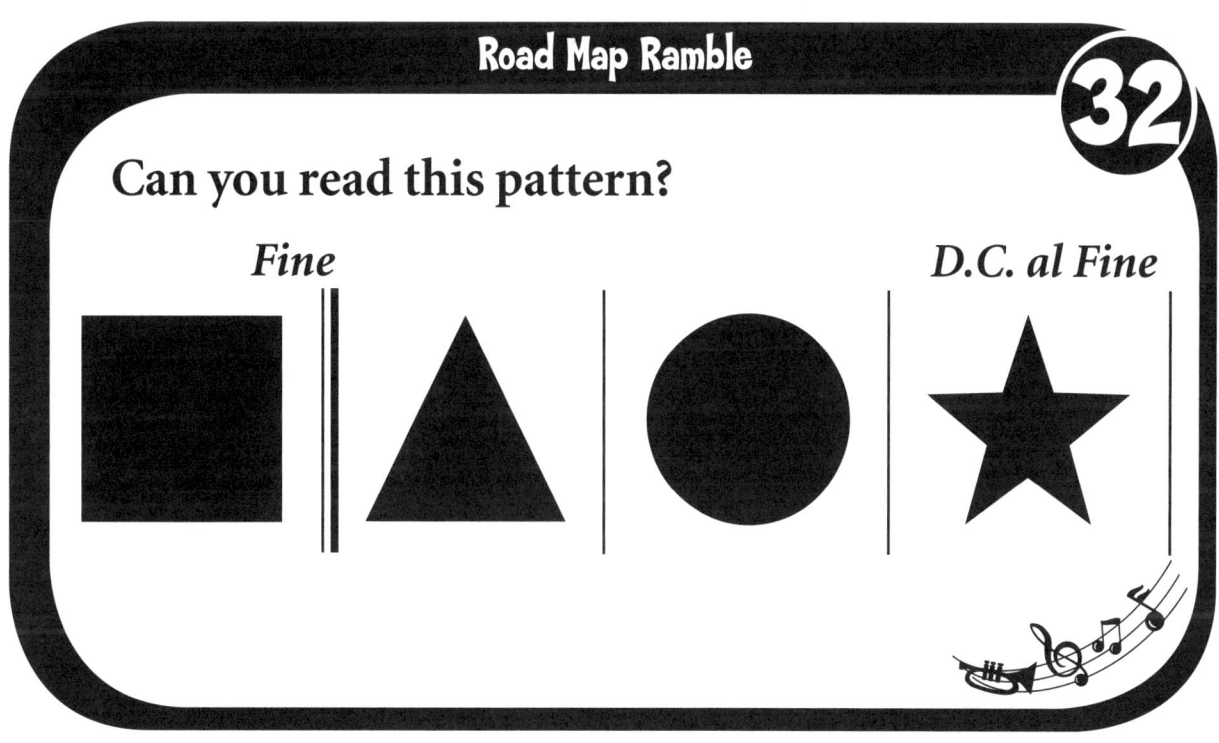

Road Map Ramble

Instructions: Copy one set of cards for each team. Cut out each card along the dotted line. Give each team a set of cards to play Fan-N-Pick.

Road Map Ramble

33

Can you read this pattern?

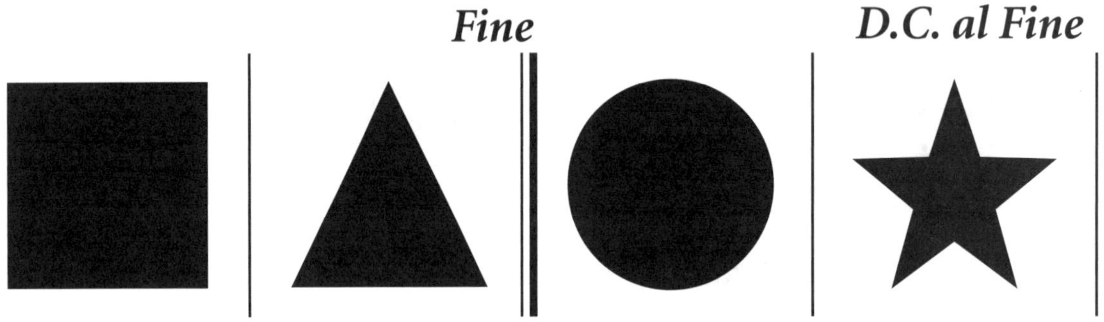

Road Map Ramble

34

Can you read this pattern?

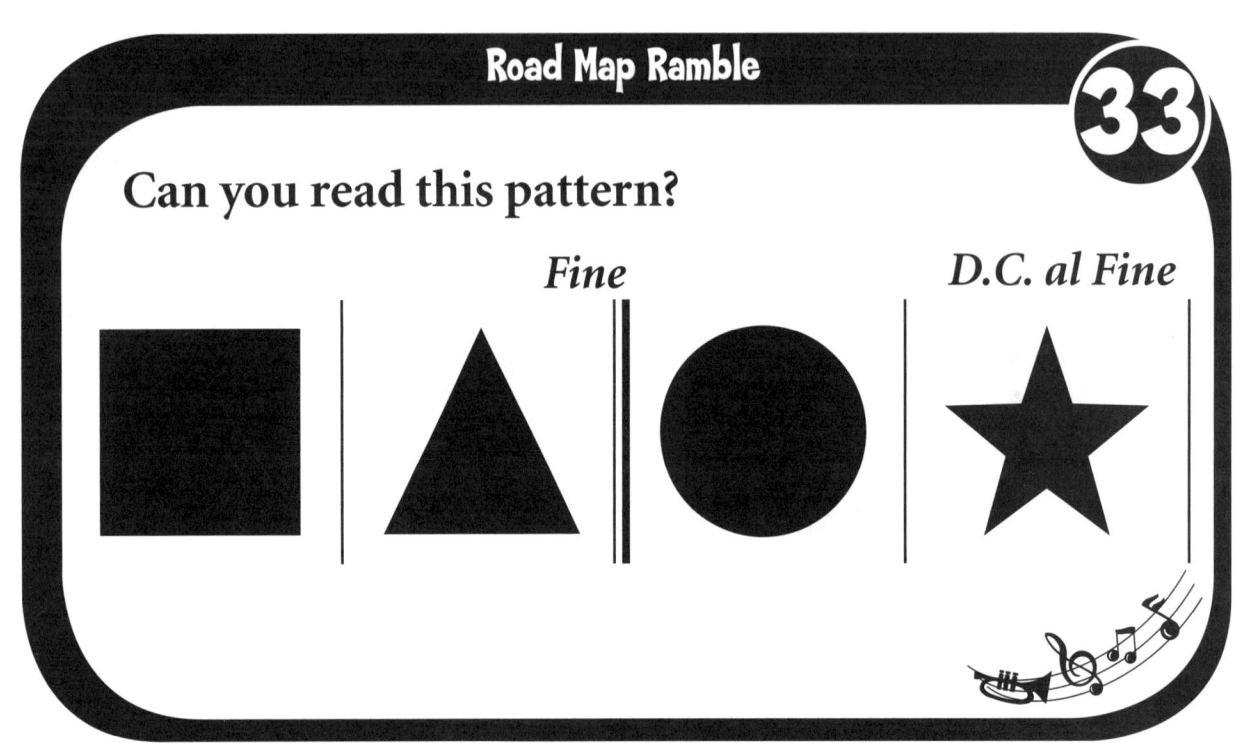

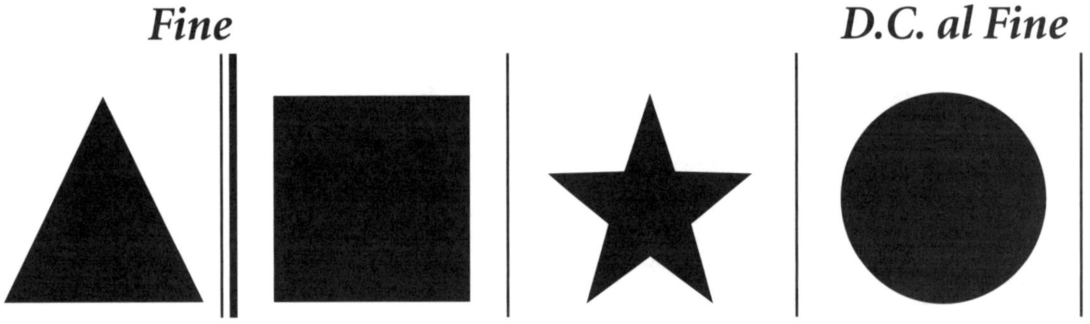

Road Map Ramble

Instructions: Copy one set of cards for each team. Cut out each card along the dotted line. Give each team a set of cards to play Fan-N-Pick.

Road Map Ramble

35

Can you read this pattern?

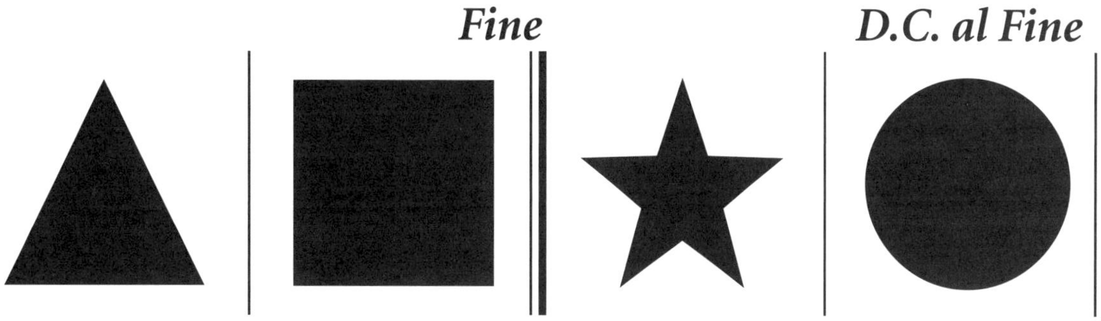

Road Map Ramble

36

Can you read this pattern?

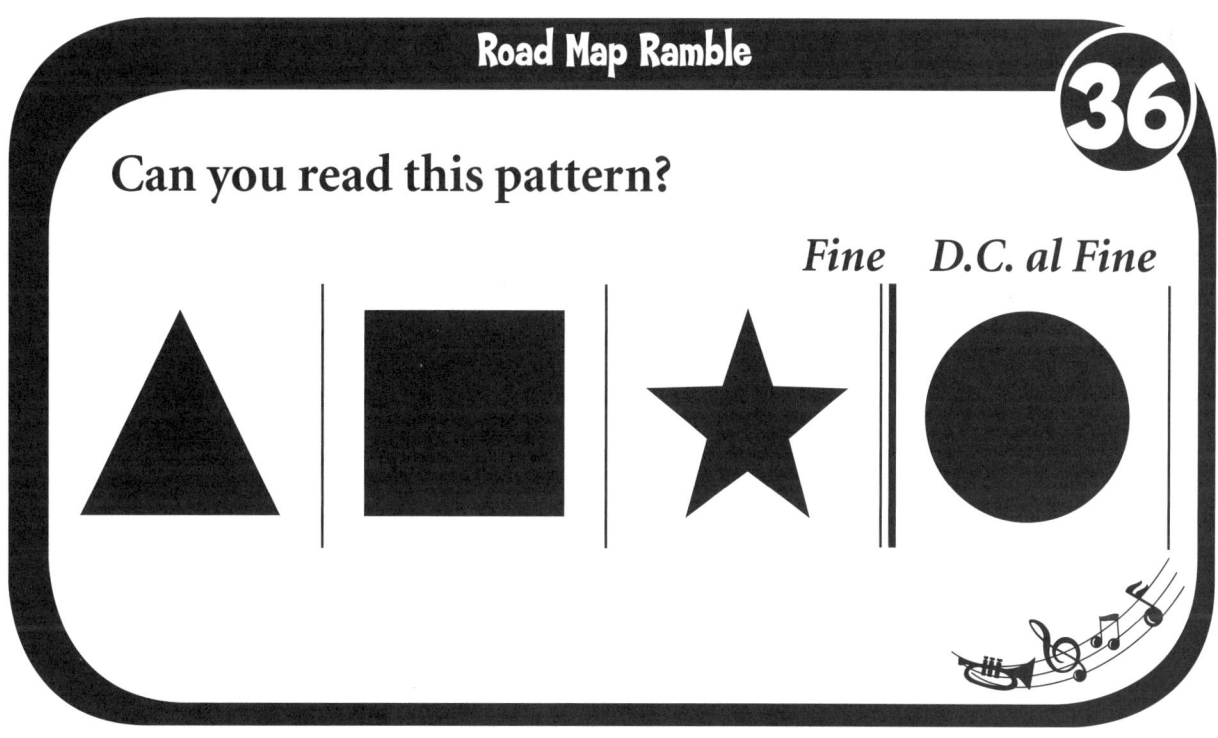

Road Map Ramble

Answer Key

Variations of verbal counting might include using numbers or vocabulary. For example, the answer to #1 might also sound like: "1, 2, 3-and, 4" or "quarter, quarter, eighth-eighth, quarter."

1. Ta Ta Ti-Ti Ta, Ta Ta Ti-Ti Ta
2. Ti-Ti Ti-Ti Ta Ta, Ti-Ti Ti-Ti Ta Ta
3. Ti-Ti Ta Ta (rest), Ti-Ti Ta Ta (rest)
4. Ta Ti-Ti Ta-ah, Ta Ti-Ti Ta-ah
5. Ti-Ti Ta (rest) Ta, Ti-Ti Ta (rest) Ta
6. Ta Ta-ah Ta, Ta Ta-ah Ta Ta
7. Ta-ah Ta Ta, Ta-ah Ta Ta
8. (rest) (rest) Ti-Ti Ta, (rest) (rest) Ti-Ti Ta
9. Ta Tri-ple-ti Ta Ta, Ta Tri-ple-ti Ta Ta
10. Tri-ple-ti Ta (rest) (rest), Tri-ple-ti Ta (rest) (rest)
11. Ta (rest) Tri-ple-ti Ta, Ta (rest) Tri-ple-ti Ta
12. Tri-ple-ti Tri-ple-ti Ta (rest), Tri-ple-ti Tri-ple-ti Ta (rest)
13. "Dog and cat in a house. Dog and cat chased a mouse."
14. "Pretty flower in a vase. Pretty flower full of grace."
15. "Kangaroo hop hop hops. Kangaroo never stops."
16. "See the rain pouring down. See the rain all over town."
17. "When we sing we sit up tall. When we sing we have a ball."
18. "Eat some soup from a bowl. Eat some soup with a troll."
19. "Find a penny in a ditch. Find a penny and you're rich."
20. "I like candy—it's so sweet. I like candy—what a treat!"
21. "Tie that box up with a string. Tie that box up for the King."
22. "That girl thinks she's a queen. That girl thinks I like beans!"
23. "See the sun, watch it shine. See the sun, it's so fine."
24. "Ladybug in my hat. Ladybug small and fat!"
25. Circle, star, triangle, square, circle
26. Circle, star, triangle, square, circle, star
27. Circle, star, triangle, square, circle, star, triangle
28. Star, circle, square, triangle, star, circle
29. Star, circle, square, triangle, star, circle, square
30. Star, circle, square, triangle, star
31. Square, triangle, circle, star, square, triangle, circle
32. Square, triangle, circle, star, square
33. Square, triangle, circle, star, square, triangle
34. Triangle, square, star, circle, triangle
35. Triangle, square, star, circle, triangle, square
36. Triangle square, star, circle, triangle, square, star

Interval Insanity: Harmonic Intervals

Instructions: Copy one set of cards for each team. Cut out each card along the dotted line. Give each team a set of cards to play Fan-N-Pick.

Interval Insanity: Harmonic Intervals

1

What kind of interval is this?

Interval Insanity: Harmonic Intervals

2

What kind of interval is this?

Interval Insanity: Harmonic Intervals

3

What kind of interval is this?

Interval Insanity: Harmonic Intervals

4

What kind of interval is this?

Interval Insanity: Harmonic Intervals

Instructions: Copy one set of cards for each team. Cut out each card along the dotted line. Give each team a set of cards to play Fan-N-Pick.

Interval Insanity: Harmonic Intervals

5

What kind of interval is this?

Interval Insanity: Harmonic Intervals

6

What kind of interval is this?

Interval Insanity: Harmonic Intervals

7

What kind of interval is this?

Interval Insanity: Harmonic Intervals

8

What kind of interval is this?

Interval Insanity: Harmonic Intervals

Instructions: Copy one set of cards for each team. Cut out each card along the dotted line. Give each team a set of cards to play Fan-N-Pick.

Interval Insanity: Harmonic Intervals

9

What kind of interval is this?

Interval Insanity: Harmonic Intervals

10

What kind of interval is this?

Interval Insanity: Harmonic Intervals

11

What kind of interval is this?

Interval Insanity: Harmonic Intervals

12

What kind of interval is this?

Interval Insanity: Harmonic Intervals

Instructions: Copy one set of cards for each team. Cut out each card along the dotted line. Give each team a set of cards to play Fan-N-Pick.

Interval Insanity: Harmonic Intervals

13

What kind of interval is this?

Interval Insanity: Harmonic Intervals

14

What kind of interval is this?

Interval Insanity: Harmonic Intervals

15

What kind of interval is this?

Interval Insanity: Harmonic Intervals

16

What kind of interval is this?

Interval Insanity: Harmonic Intervals

Instructions: Copy one set of cards for each team. Cut out each card along the dotted line. Give each team a set of cards to play Fan-N-Pick.

Interval Insanity: Harmonic Intervals

17

What kind of interval is this?

Interval Insanity: Harmonic Intervals

18

What kind of interval is this?

Interval Insanity: Harmonic Intervals

19

What kind of interval is this?

Interval Insanity: Harmonic Intervals

20

What kind of interval is this?

Interval Insanity: Harmonic Intervals

Instructions: Copy one set of cards for each team. Cut out each card along the dotted line. Give each team a set of cards to play Fan-N-Pick.

Interval Insanity: Harmonic Intervals — **21**

What kind of interval is this?

Interval Insanity: Harmonic Intervals — **22**

What kind of interval is this?

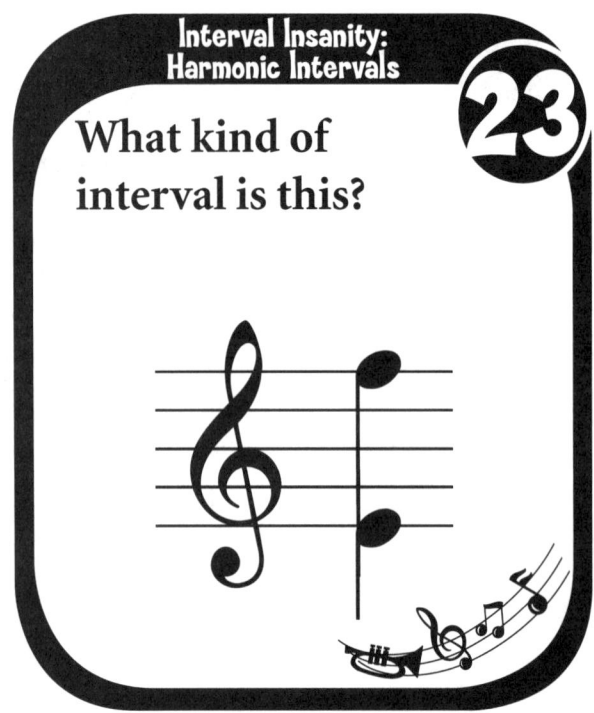

Interval Insanity: Harmonic Intervals — **23**

What kind of interval is this?

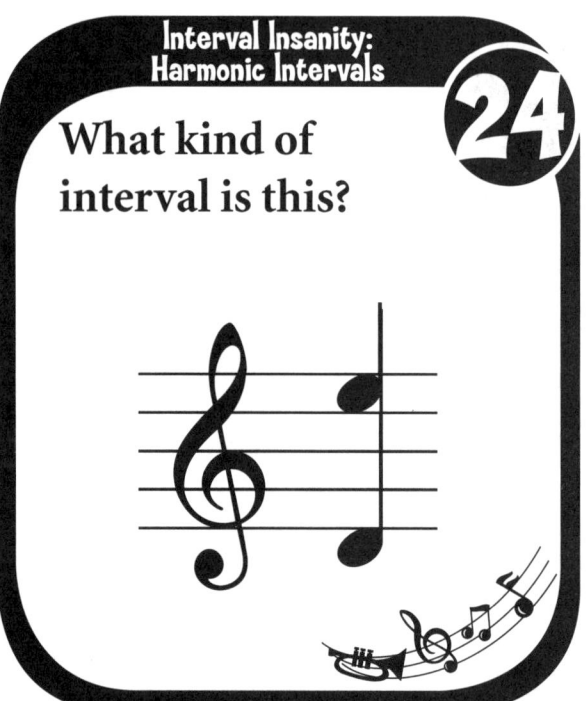

Interval Insanity: Harmonic Intervals — **24**

What kind of interval is this?

Interval Insanity: Harmonic Intervals

Answer Key

The "minor"/"major" designation is best suited for secondary level students; upper elementary students may simply give the ordinal number if teachers choose to utilize this structure at that level.

1. minor second
2. major second
3. major third
4. major second
5. augmented fourth
6. minor third
7. perfect fourth
8. minor third
9. perfect fifth
10. perfect fourth
11. perfect fifth
12. perfect fifth
13. major sixth
14. minor sixth
15. minor seventh
16. major sixth
17. octave
18. minor seventh
19. octave
20. major seventh
21. major ninth
22. octave
23. minor ninth
24. major ninth

Detailed Durations

Instructions: Copy one set of cards for each team. Cut out each card along the dotted line. Give each team a set of cards to play Fan-N-Pick. Matching cards may also be used for Mix-N-Match.

Detailed Durations 1

What does a whole note look like?

Detailed Durations 2

What kind of note is this?

Detailed Durations 3

What does a half note look like?

Detailed Durations 4

What kind of notes are these?

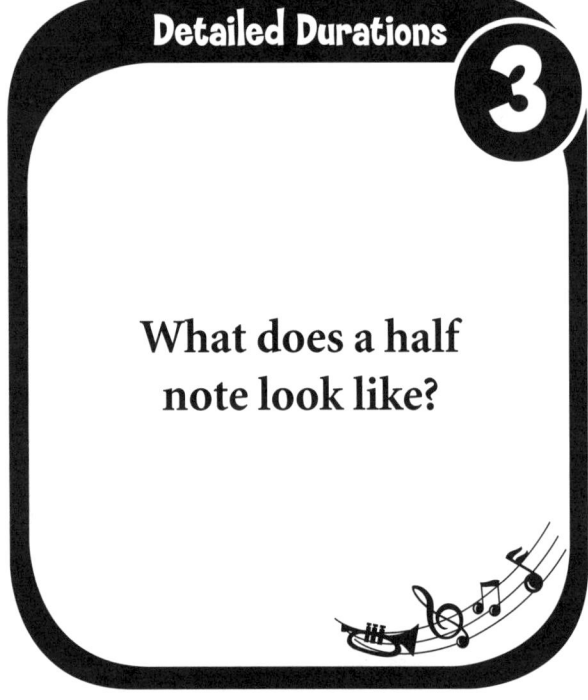

Detailed Durations

Instructions: Copy one set of cards for each team. Cut out each card along the dotted line. Give each team a set of cards to play Fan-N-Pick. Matching cards may also be used for Mix-N-Match.

Detailed Durations

5

What does a quarter note look like?

Detailed Durations

6

What kinds of notes are these?

Detailed Durations

7

What does an eighth note look like?

Detailed Durations

8

What kinds of notes are these?

Detailed Durations

Instructions: Copy one set of cards for each team. Cut out each card along the dotted line. Give each team a set of cards to play Fan-N-Pick. Matching cards may also be used for Mix-N-Match.

Detailed Durations **9**

What does a sixteenth note look like?

Detailed Durations **10**

What kind of note is this?

Detailed Durations **11**

What does a triplet look like?

Detailed Durations **12**

What kind of notes are these?

Detailed Durations

Instructions: Copy one set of cards for each team. Cut out each card along the dotted line. Give each team a set of cards to play Fan-N-Pick. Matching cards may also be used for Mix-N-Match.

Detailed Durations 13

What does a dotted half note look like?

Detailed Durations 14

What kinds of notes are these?

Detailed Durations 15

What does a dotted quarter note look like?

Detailed Durations 16

What kinds of notes are these?

Detailed Durations

Instructions: Copy one set of cards for each team. Cut out each card along the dotted line. Give each team a set of cards to play Fan-N-Pick. Matching cards may also be used for Mix-N-Match.

Detailed Durations 17

What does a whole rest look like?

Detailed Durations 18

What kind of rest is this?

Detailed Durations 19

What does a half rest look like?

Detailed Durations 20

What kind of rest is this?

Detailed Durations

Instructions: Copy one set of cards for each team. Cut out each card along the dotted line. Give each team a set of cards to play Fan-N-Pick. Matching cards may also be used for Mix-N-Match.

Detailed Durations — 21

What does a quarter rest look like?

Detailed Durations — 22

What kind of rest is this?

Detailed Durations — 23

What does an eighth rest look like?

Detailed Durations — 24

What kind of rest is this?

Detailed Durations

Instructions: Copy one set of cards for each team. Cut out each card along the dotted line. Give each team a set of cards to play Fan-N-Pick. Matching cards may also be used for Mix-N-Match.

Detailed Durations **25**

What does a dotted quarter rest look like?

Detailed Durations **26**

What kind of rest is this?

Detailed Durations **27**

What does a dotted half rest look like?

Detailed Durations **28**

What kind of rest is this?

Detailed Durations

Answer Key

1. oval with an open center
2. whole note
3. empty note head with a stem
4. half notes
5. filled note head with a stem
6. quarter notes
7. filled note head with a stem and one flag
8. eighth notes
9. filled note head with a stem and two flags
10. sixteenth note
11. three eighth notes connected with a number 3
12. triplet
13. empty note head with a stem and a dot
14. dotted half notes
15. filled note head with a stem and a dot
16. dotted quarter notes
17. solid rectangle hanging down from a line
18. whole rest
19. solid rectangle sitting on a line
20. half rest
21. slanted z with a curly tail
22. quarter rest
23. resembles a seven
24. eighth rest
25. slanted z with a curly tail and a dot
26. dotted quarter rest
27. solid rectangle sitting on a line with a dot
28. dotted half rest

What's My Rhythm?

Instructions: Copy one set of cards for each team. Cut out each card along the dotted line. Give each team a set of cards to play Fan-N-Pick.

What's My Rhythm?

Instructions: Copy one set of cards for each team. Cut out each card along the dotted line. Give each team a set of cards to play Fan-N-Pick.

What's My Rhythm?

Instructions: Copy one set of cards for each team. Cut out each card along the dotted line. Give each team a set of cards to play Fan-N-Pick.

What's My Rhythm?

Instructions: Copy one set of cards for each team. Cut out each card along the dotted line. Give each team a set of cards to play Fan-N-Pick.

What's My Rhythm?

Instructions: Copy one set of cards for each team. Cut out each card along the dotted line. Give each team a set of cards to play Fan-N-Pick.

What's My Rhythm?

Instructions: Copy one set of cards for each team. Cut out each card along the dotted line. Give each team a set of cards to play Fan-N-Pick.

What's My Rhythm?

Instructions: Copy one set of cards for each team. Cut out each card along the dotted line. Give each team a set of cards to play Fan-N-Pick.

What's My Rhythm?

Instructions: Copy one set of cards for each team. Cut out each card along the dotted line. Give each team a set of cards to play Fan-N-Pick.

What's My Rhythm?

Answer Key

Variations of verbal counting might include using the number system. For example, the answer for #1 might sound like, "1, 2-and, 3, 4."

1. Tree ap-ple Tree Tree
2. Tree Tree ap-ple Tree
3. ap-ple ap-ple ap-ple Tree
4. Tree ap-ple ap-ple Tree
5. Ta Ti-Ti Ta Ta
6. Ta Ta Ti-Ti Ta
7. Ti-Ti Ti-Ti Ti-Ti Ta
8. Ta Ti-Ti Ti-Ti Ta
9. ap-ple Tree ap-ple Tree
10. ap-ple ap-ple Tree Tree
11. ap-ple ap-ple Tree (rest)
12. (rest) Tree ap-ple Tree
13. Ti-Ti Ta Ti-Ti Ta
14. Ti-Ti Ti-Ti Ta Ta
15. Ti-Ti Ti-Ti Ta (rest)
16. (rest) Ta Ti-Ti Ta
17. Tree Tree Tree Tree
18. Tree Tree Tree (rest)
19. Tree (rest) Tree (rest)
20. Tree (rest) ap-ple Tree
21. Ta Ta Ta Ta
22. Ta Ta Ta (rest)
23. Ta (rest) Ta (rest)
24. Ta (rest) Ti-Ti Ta
25. Tree Tree (rest) (rest)
26. ap-ple Tree Tree (rest)
27. Tree (rest) Tree Tree
28. (rest) (rest) ap-ple Tree
29. Ta Ta (rest) (rest)
30. Ti-Ti Ta Ta (rest)
31. Ta (rest) Ta Ta
32. (rest) (rest) Ti-Ti Ta

Key Connections

Instructions: Copy one set of cards for each team. Cut out each card along the dotted line. Give each team a set of cards to play Fan-N-Pick. Matching cards may also be used for Mix-N-Match.

Key Connections 1

What key signatures does this represent?

Key Connections 2

What does the key signature for C Major (A minor) look like?

Key Connections 3

What key signatures does this represent?

Key Connections 4

What does the key signature for G Major (E minor) look like?

Key Connections

Instructions: Copy one set of cards for each team. Cut out each card along the dotted line. Give each team a set of cards to play Fan-N-Pick. Matching cards may also be used for Mix-N-Match.

Key Connections

5

What key signatures does this represent?

Key Connections

6

What does the key signature for D Major (B minor) look like?

Key Connections

7

What key signatures does this represent?

Key Connections

8

What does the key signature for A Major (F-sharp minor) look like?

Key Connections

Instructions: Copy one set of cards for each team. Cut out each card along the dotted line. Give each team a set of cards to play Fan-N-Pick. Matching cards may also be used for Mix-N-Match.

Key Connections 9

What key signatures does this represent?

Key Connections 10

What does the key signature for E Major (C-sharp minor) look like?

Key Connections 11

What key signatures does this represent?

Key Connections 12

What does the key signature for B Major (G-sharp minor) look like?

Key Connections

Instructions: Copy one set of cards for each team. Cut out each card along the dotted line. Give each team a set of cards to play Fan-N-Pick. Matching cards may also be used for Mix-N-Match.

Key Connections 13

What key signatures does this represent?

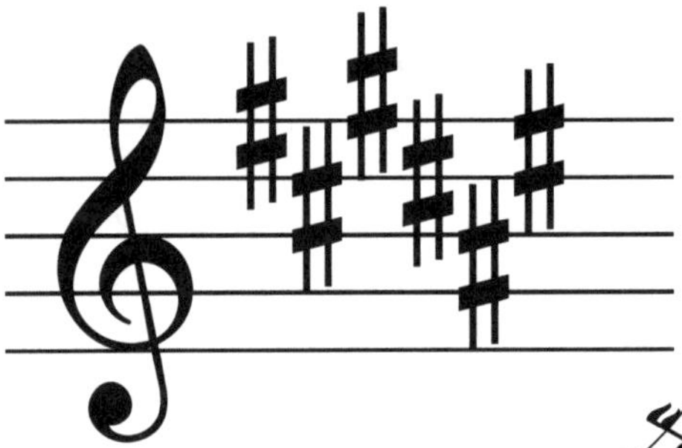

Key Connections 14

What does the key signature for F-sharp Major (D-sharp minor) look like?

Key Connections 15

What key signatures does this represent?

Key Connections 16

What does the key signature for C-sharp Major (A-sharp minor) look like?

Key Connections

Instructions: Copy one set of cards for each team. Cut out each card along the dotted line. Give each team a set of cards to play Fan-N-Pick. Matching cards may also be used for Mix-N-Match.

Key Connections 17

What key signatures does this represent?

Key Connections 18

What does the key signature for F Major (D minor) look like?

Key Connections 19

What key signatures does this represent?

Key Connections 20

What does the key signature for B-flat Major (G minor) look like?

Key Connections

Instructions: Copy one set of cards for each team. Cut out each card along the dotted line. Give each team a set of cards to play Fan-N-Pick. Matching cards may also be used for Mix-N-Match.

Key Connections

21

What key signatures does this represent?

Key Connections

22

What does the key signature for E-flat Major (C minor) look like?

Key Connections

23

What key signatures does this represent?

Key Connections

24

What does the key signature for A-flat Major (F minor) look like?

Key Connections

Instructions: Copy one set of cards for each team. Cut out each card along the dotted line. Give each team a set of cards to play Fan-N-Pick. Matching cards may also be used for Mix-N-Match.

Key Connections

25

What key signatures does this represent?

Key Connections

26

What does the key signature for D-flat Major (B flat-minor) look like?

Key Connections

27

What key signatures does this represent?

Key Connections

28

What does the key signature for G-flat Major (E-flat minor) look like?

Key Connections

Instructions: Copy one set of cards for each team. Cut out each card along the dotted line. Give each team a set of cards to play Fan-N-Pick. Matching cards may also be used for Mix-N-Match.

Key Connections 29

What key signatures does this represent?

Key Connections 30

What does the key signature for C-flat Major (A-flat minor) look like?

Key Connections 31

What key signatures does this represent?

Key Connections 32

How are D-flat Major and C-sharp Major related?

Key Connections

Answer Key

1 C Major (A minor)

2 

3 G Major (E minor)

4 

5 D Major (B minor)

6 

7 A Major (F♯ minor)

8 

9 E Major (C♯ minor)

10 

11 B Major (G♯ minor)

12 

13 F# Major (D♯ minor)

14 

15 C# Major (A♯ minor)

16 

17 F Major (D minor)

18 

19 B♭Major (G minor)

20 

21 E♭ Major (C minor)

22 

23 A♭ Major (F minor)

24 

25 D♭ Major (B♭ minor)

26 

27 G♭ Major (E♭ minor)

28 

29 C♭ Major (A♭ minor)

30 

31 D♭ Major and C♯ Major are enharmonic keys, and will sound alike.

32 D♭ Major and C♯ Major are enharmonic keys, and will sound alike.

Recorder Roundup

Instructions: Copy one set of cards for each team. Cut out each card along the dotted line. Give each team a set of cards to play Fan-N-Pick.

Recorder Roundup 1

Can you play this pattern?

Recorder Roundup 2

Can you play this pattern?

B B B (rest)

Recorder Roundup 3

Can you play this pattern?

Recorder Roundup 4

Can you play this pattern?

A A A (rest)

Recorder Roundup

Instructions: Copy one set of cards for each team. Cut out each card along the dotted line. Give each team a set of cards to play Fan-N-Pick.

Recorder Roundup **5**

Can you play this pattern?

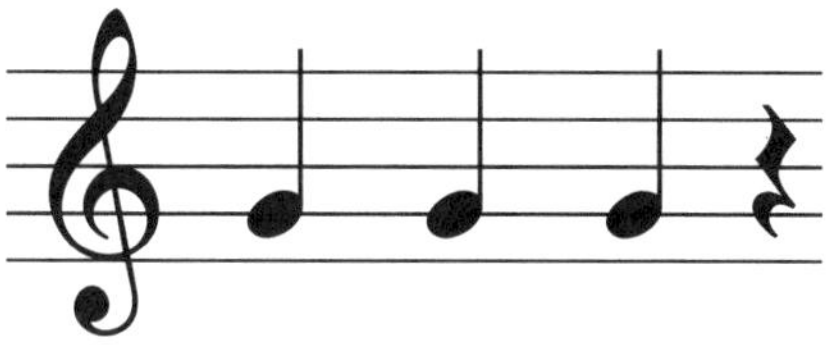

Recorder Roundup **6**

Can you play this pattern?

G G G (rest)

Recorder Roundup **7**

Can you play this pattern?

Recorder Roundup **8**

Can you play this pattern?

B B B B B

Recorder Roundup

Instructions: Copy one set of cards for each team. Cut out each card along the dotted line. Give each team a set of cards to play Fan-N-Pick.

Recorder Roundup **9**

Can you play this pattern?

Recorder Roundup **10**

Can you play this pattern?

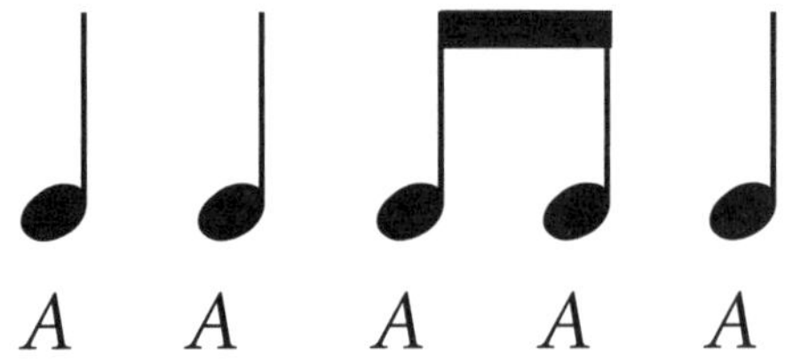

Recorder Roundup **11**

Can you play this pattern?

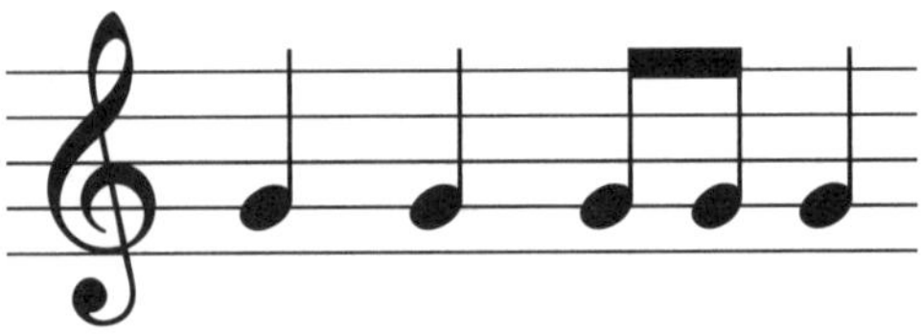

Recorder Roundup **12**

Can you play this pattern?

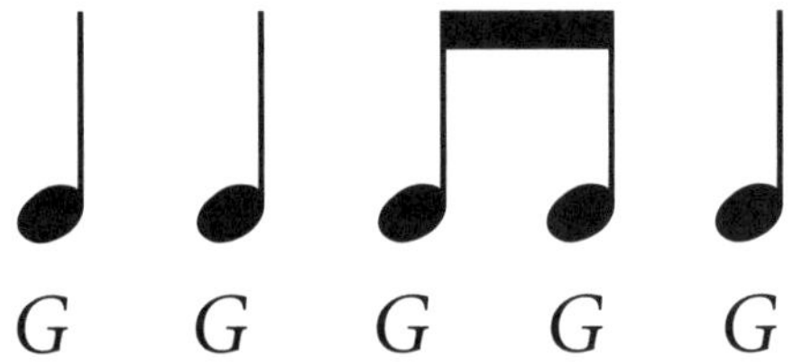

Recorder Roundup

Instructions: Copy one set of cards for each team. Cut out each card along the dotted line. Give each team a set of cards to play Fan-N-Pick.

Recorder Roundup 13

Can you play this pattern?

Recorder Roundup 14

Can you play this pattern?

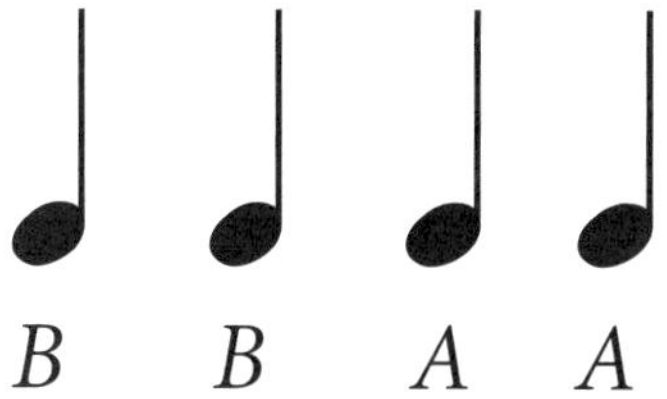

Recorder Roundup 15

Can you play this pattern?

Recorder Roundup 16

Can you play this pattern?

Kagan Publishing • 1 (800) 933-2667 • www.KaganOnline.com

Recorder Roundup

Instructions: Copy one set of cards for each team. Cut out each card along the dotted line. Give each team a set of cards to play Fan-N-Pick.

Recorder Roundup 17

Can you play this pattern?

Recorder Roundup 18

Can you play this pattern?

B B G (rest)

Recorder Roundup 19

Can you play this pattern?

Recorder Roundup 20

Can you play this pattern?

G G A A

Recorder Roundup

Instructions: Copy one set of cards for each team. Cut out each card along the dotted line. Give each team a set of cards to play Fan-N-Pick.

Recorder Roundup 21

Can you play this pattern?

Recorder Roundup 22

Can you play this pattern?

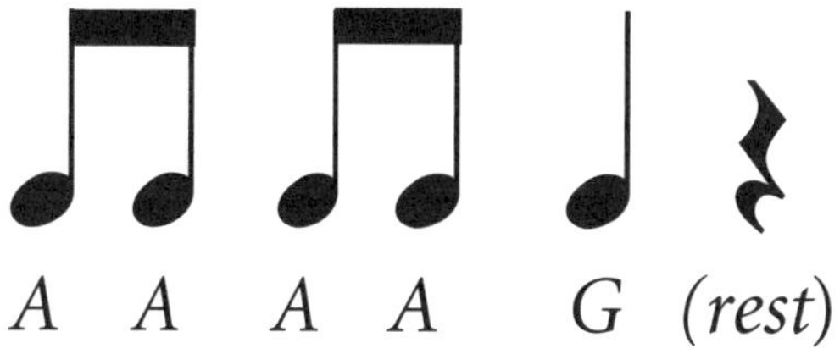

Recorder Roundup 23

Can you play this pattern?

Recorder Roundup 24

Can you play this pattern?

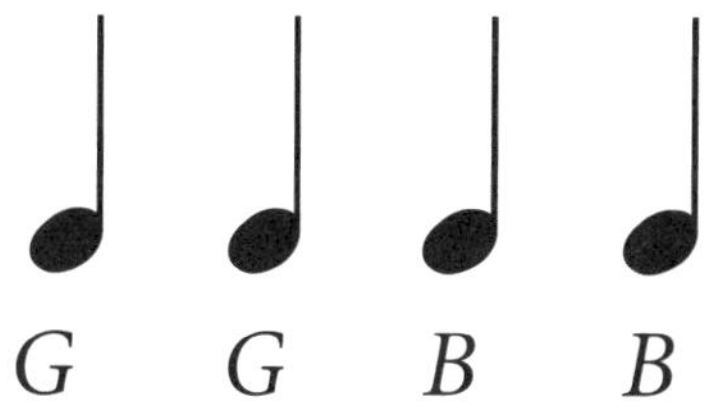

Recorder Roundup

Instructions: Copy one set of cards for each team. Cut out each card along the dotted line. Give each team a set of cards to play Fan-N-Pick.

Recorder Roundup

25

Can you play this pattern?

Recorder Roundup

26

Can you play this pattern?

B A G (rest)

Recorder Roundup

27

Can you play this pattern?

Recorder Roundup

28

Can you play this pattern?

G A B (rest)

Recorder Roundup

Instructions: Copy one set of cards for each team. Cut out each card along the dotted line. Give each team a set of cards to play Fan-N-Pick.

Recorder Roundup 29

Can you play this pattern?

Recorder Roundup 30

Can you play this pattern?

A B G (rest)

Recorder Roundup 31

Can you play this pattern?

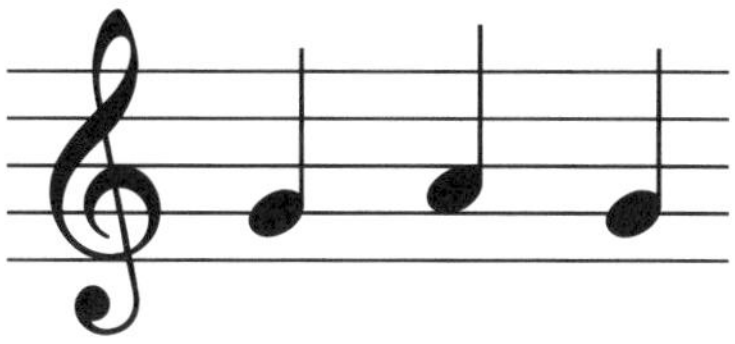

Recorder Roundup 32

Can you play this pattern?

G A G

Recorder Roundup

Instructions: Copy one set of cards for each team. Cut out each card along the dotted line. Give each team a set of cards to play Fan-N-Pick.

Recorder Roundup 33

Can you play this pattern?

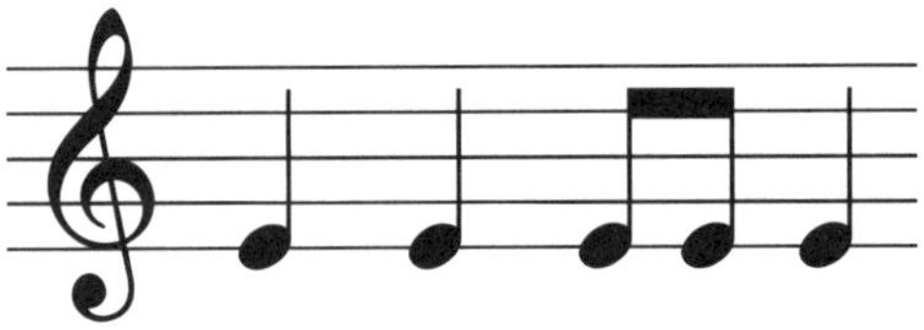

Recorder Roundup 34

Can you play this pattern?

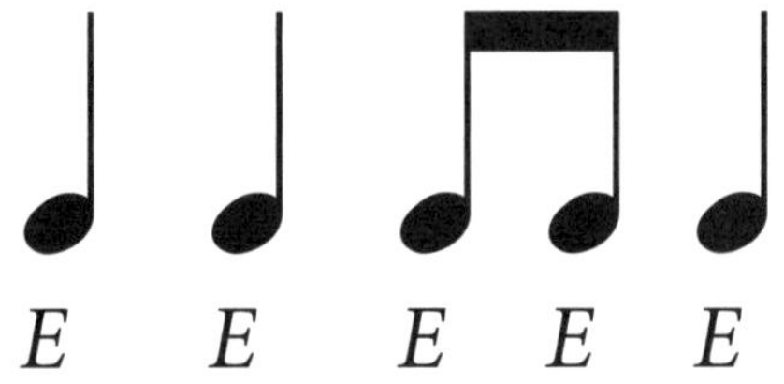

Recorder Roundup 35

Can you play this pattern?

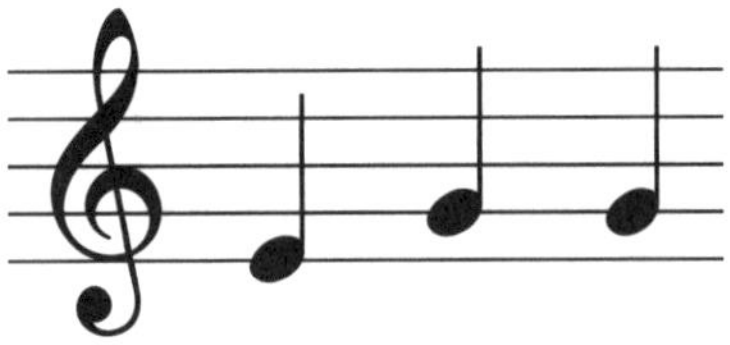

Recorder Roundup 36

Can you play this pattern?

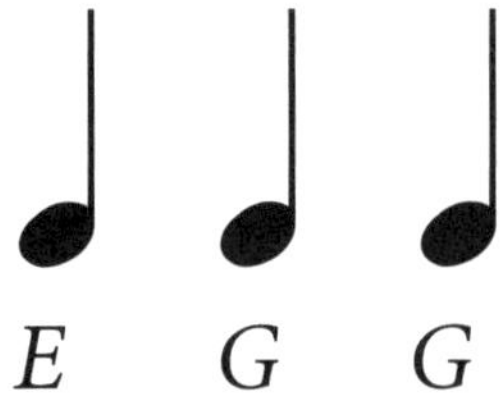

Recorder Roundup

Instructions: Copy one set of cards for each team. Cut out each card along the dotted line. Give each team a set of cards to play Fan-N-Pick.

Recorder Roundup 37

Can you play this pattern?

Recorder Roundup 38

Can you play this pattern?

A G E

Recorder Roundup 39

Can you play this pattern?

Recorder Roundup 40

Can you play this pattern?

E E E (rest)

Recorder Roundup

Instructions: Copy one set of cards for each team. Cut out each card along the dotted line. Give each team a set of cards to play Fan-N-Pick.

Recorder Roundup 41

Can you play this pattern?

Recorder Roundup 42

Can you play this pattern?

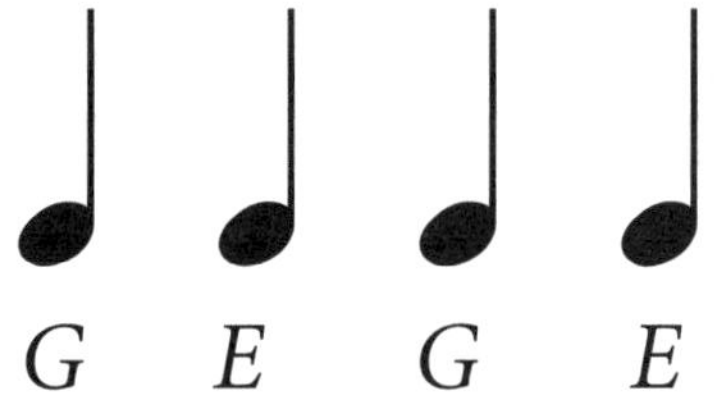

Recorder Roundup 43

Can you play this pattern?

Recorder Roundup 44

Can you play this pattern?

Recorder Roundup

Instructions: Copy one set of cards for each team. Cut out each card along the dotted line. Give each team a set of cards to play Fan-N-Pick.

Recorder Roundup 45

Can you play this pattern?

Recorder Roundup 46

Can you play this pattern?

G A G E

Recorder Roundup 47

Can you play this pattern?

Recorder Roundup 48

Can you play this pattern?

E E G G A (rest)

Recorder Roundup

Instructions: Copy one set of cards for each team. Cut out each card along the dotted line. Give each team a set of cards to play Fan-N-Pick.

Recorder Roundup 49

Can you play this pattern?

Recorder Roundup 50

Can you play this pattern?

G E E

Recorder Roundup 51

Can you play this pattern?

Recorder Roundup 52

Can you play this pattern?

A G E

Recorder Roundup

Instructions: Copy one set of cards for each team. Cut out each card along the dotted line. Give each team a set of cards to play Fan-N-Pick.

Recorder Roundup 53

Can you play this pattern?

Recorder Roundup 54

Can you play this pattern?

Recorder Roundup 55

Can you play this pattern?

Recorder Roundup 56

Can you play this pattern?

Recorder Roundup

Instructions: Copy one set of cards for each team. Cut out each card along the dotted line. Give each team a set of cards to play Fan-N-Pick.

Recorder Roundup
57

Can you play this pattern?

Recorder Roundup
58

Can you play this pattern?

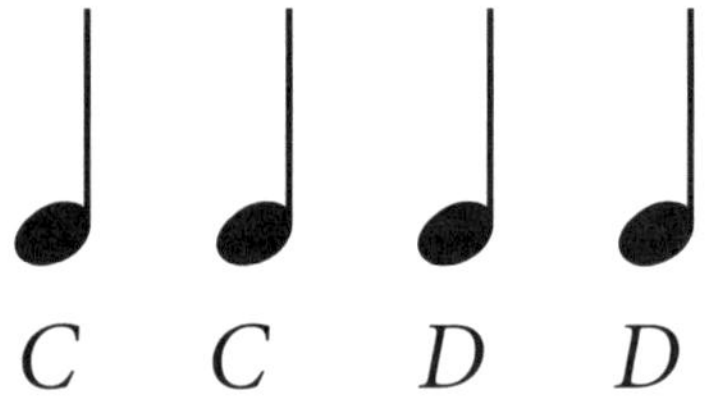

Recorder Roundup
59

Can you play this pattern?

Recorder Roundup
60

Can you play this pattern?

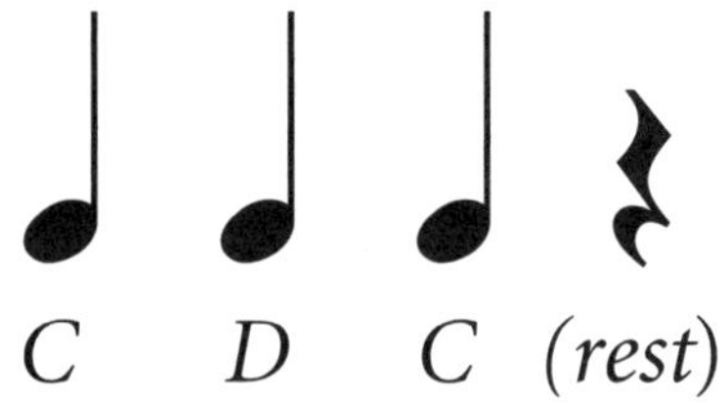

Recorder Roundup

Instructions: Copy one set of cards for each team. Cut out each card along the dotted line. Give each team a set of cards to play Fan-N-Pick.

Recorder Roundup 61

Can you play this pattern?

Recorder Roundup 62

Can you play this pattern?

Recorder Roundup 63

Can you play this pattern?

Recorder Roundup 64

Can you play this pattern?

Recorder Roundup

Instructions: Copy one set of cards for each team. Cut out each card along the dotted line. Give each team a set of cards to play Fan-N-Pick.

Recorder Roundup 65

Can you play this pattern?

Recorder Roundup 66

Can you play this pattern?

C D D E (rest)

Recorder Roundup 67

Can you play this pattern?

Recorder Roundup 68

Can you play this pattern?

D E C (rest)

Recorder Roundup

Instructions: Copy one set of cards for each team. Cut out each card along the dotted line. Give each team a set of cards to play Fan-N-Pick.

Recorder Roundup

69

Can you play this pattern?

Recorder Roundup

70

Can you play this pattern?

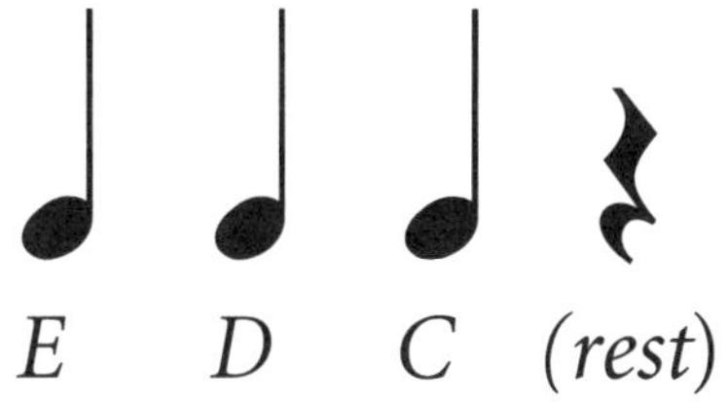

Recorder Roundup

71

Can you play this pattern?

Recorder Roundup

72

Can you play this pattern?

Recorder Roundup

Instructions: Copy one set of cards for each team. Cut out each card along the dotted line. Give each team a set of cards to play Fan-N-Pick.

Recorder Roundup

73

Can you play this pattern?

Recorder Roundup

74

Can you play this pattern?

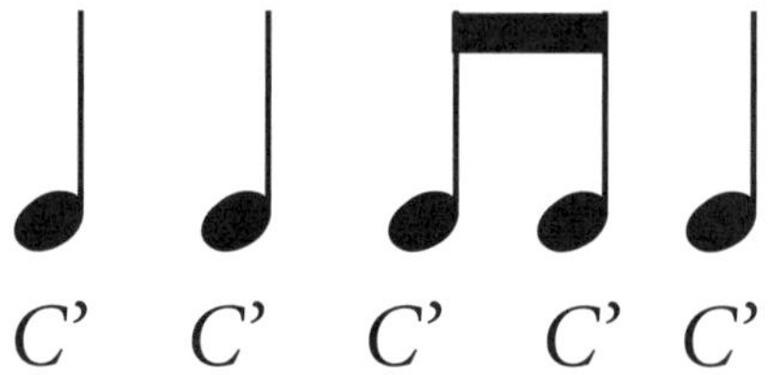

Recorder Roundup

75

Can you play this pattern?

Recorder Roundup

76

Can you play this pattern?

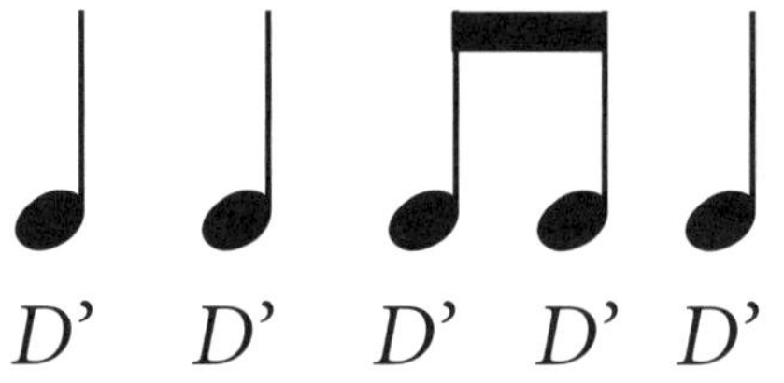

Recorder Roundup

Instructions: Copy one set of cards for each team. Cut out each card along the dotted line. Give each team a set of cards to play Fan-N-Pick.

Recorder Roundup 77

Can you play this pattern?

Recorder Roundup 78

Can you play this pattern?

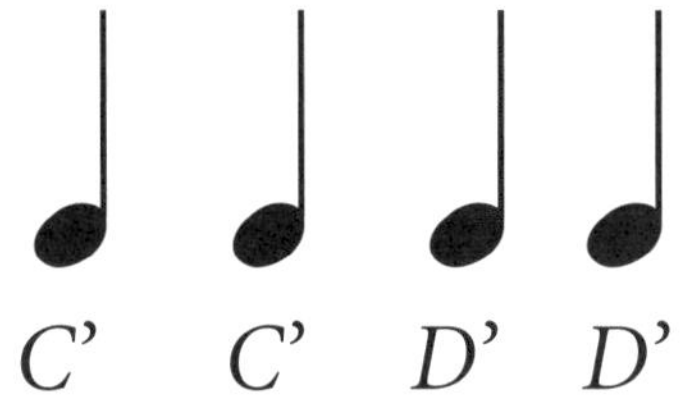

Recorder Roundup 79

Can you play this pattern?

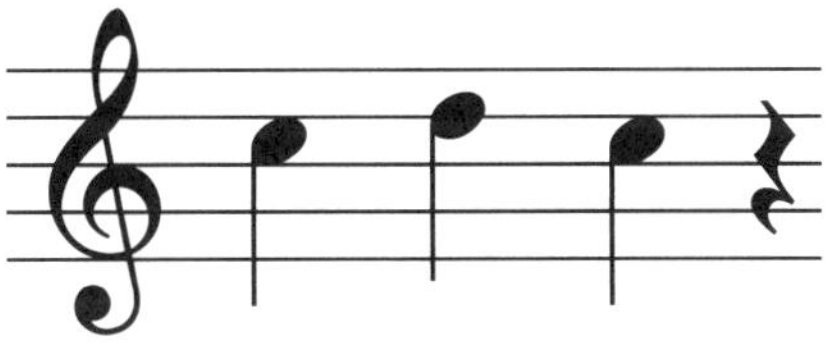

Recorder Roundup 80

Can you play this pattern?

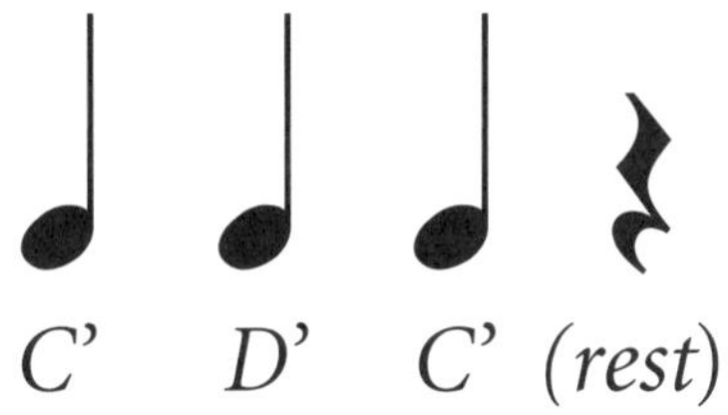

Recorder Roundup

Instructions: Copy one set of cards for each team. Cut out each card along the dotted line. Give each team a set of cards to play Fan-N-Pick.

Recorder Roundup **81**

Can you play this pattern?

Recorder Roundup **82**

Can you play this pattern?

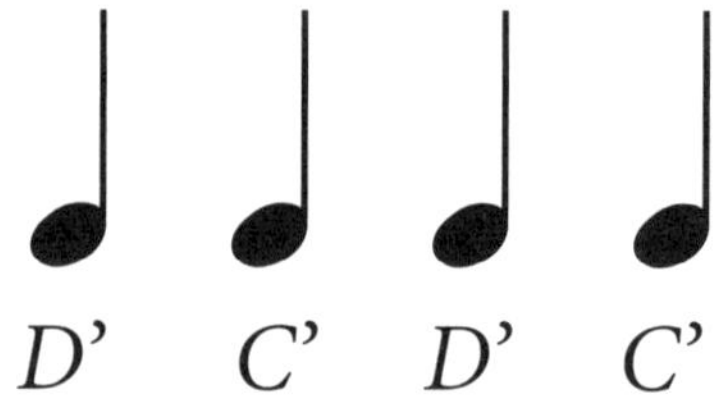

Recorder Roundup **83**

Can you play this pattern?

Recorder Roundup **84**

Can you read this pattern?

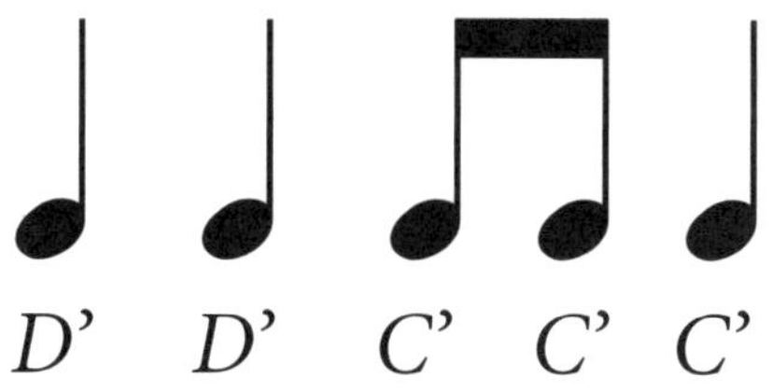

Recorder Roundup

Answer Key

1. B B B (rest)
2. B B B (rest)
3. A A A (rest)
4. A A A (rest)
5. G G G (rest)
6. G G G (rest)
7. B B B B B
8. B B B B B
9. A A A A A
10. A A A A A
11. G G G G G
12. G G G G G
13. B B A A
14. B B A A
15. A A A B B
16. A A A B B
17. B B G (rest)
18. B B G (rest)
19. G G A A
20. G G A A
21. A A A A G (rest)
22. A A A A G (rest)
23. G G B B
24. G G B B
25. B A G (rest)
26. B A G (rest)
27. G A B (rest)
28. G A B (rest)
29. A B G (rest)
30. A B G (rest)
31. G A G
32. G A G
33. E E E E E
34. E E E E E
35. E G G
36. E G G
37. A G E
38. A G E
39. E E E (rest)
40. E E E (rest)
41. G E G E
42. G E G E
43. G E E E
44. G E E E
45. G A G E
46. G A G E
47. E E G G A (rest)
48. E E G G A (rest)
49. G E E
50. G E E
51. A G E
52. A G E
53. C C C C C
54. C C C C C
55. D D D D D
56. D D D D D
57. C C D D
58. C C D D
59. C D C (rest)
60. C D C (rest)
61. D D C C C
62. D D C C C
63. E C D C
64. E C D C
65. C D D E (rest)
66. C D D E (rest)
67. D E C (rest)
68. D E C (rest)
69. E D C (rest)
70. E D C (rest)
71. E E D D C C
72. E E D D C C
73. C' C' C' C' C'
74. C' C' C' C' C'
75. D' D' D' D' D'
76. D' D' D' D' D'
77. C' C' D' D'
78. C' C' D' D'
79. C' D' C' (rest)
80. C' D' C' (rest)
81. D' C' D' C'
82. D' C' D' C'
83. D' D' C' C' C'
84. D' D' C' C' C'

Fan-N-Pick Job Tents

Instructions: Copy one set of Job Tents for each team. Cut out each Job Tent along the dotted line and fold along the solid line. Each team member has one Job Tent standing in front of him or her. Pass the tents clockwise as each question card has been answered so everyone has the opportunity to do each of the jobs.

"Pick a card, any card!"

My job is to fan out the cards for the teammate on my left.

1

Fan the Cards

Fan-N-Pick Job Tent

"Can you tell me....?"

My job is to pick a card and read the question to the teammate on my left and provide think time.

2

Pick a Card

Fan-N-Pick Job Tent

Fan-N-Pick Job Tents

Instructions: Copy one set of Job Tents for each team. Cut out each Job Tent along the dotted line and fold along the solid line. Each team member has one Job Tent standing in front of him or her. Pass the tents clockwise as each question card has been answered so everyone has the opportunity to do each of the jobs.

My job is to answer the question on the card.

"The answer is..."

3

Answer

Fan-N-Pick Job Tent

My job is to check for a correct answer.

"You got it!" "Great job!"

Or, I might need to coach.

"Listen/Look again." "Think about..."

4

Praise or Coach

Fan-N-Pick Job Tent

Fan-N-Pick Job Mat

Instructions: Copy one mat for each team. Cut out along the dotted line. Place this mat in the center of each team. Rotate as each question has been answered so everyone has the opportunity to do each of the jobs.

Fan-N-Pick Job Mat

1 Fan the Cards

2 Pick a Card, Read the Question, Provide Think Time

3 Answer

4 Praise, Coach, Paraphrase

Large Blank Card Template

Instructions: Use this blank card template to create your own Fan-N-Pick question cards.

Small Blank Card Template

Instructions: Use this blank card template to create your own Fan-N-Pick question cards.

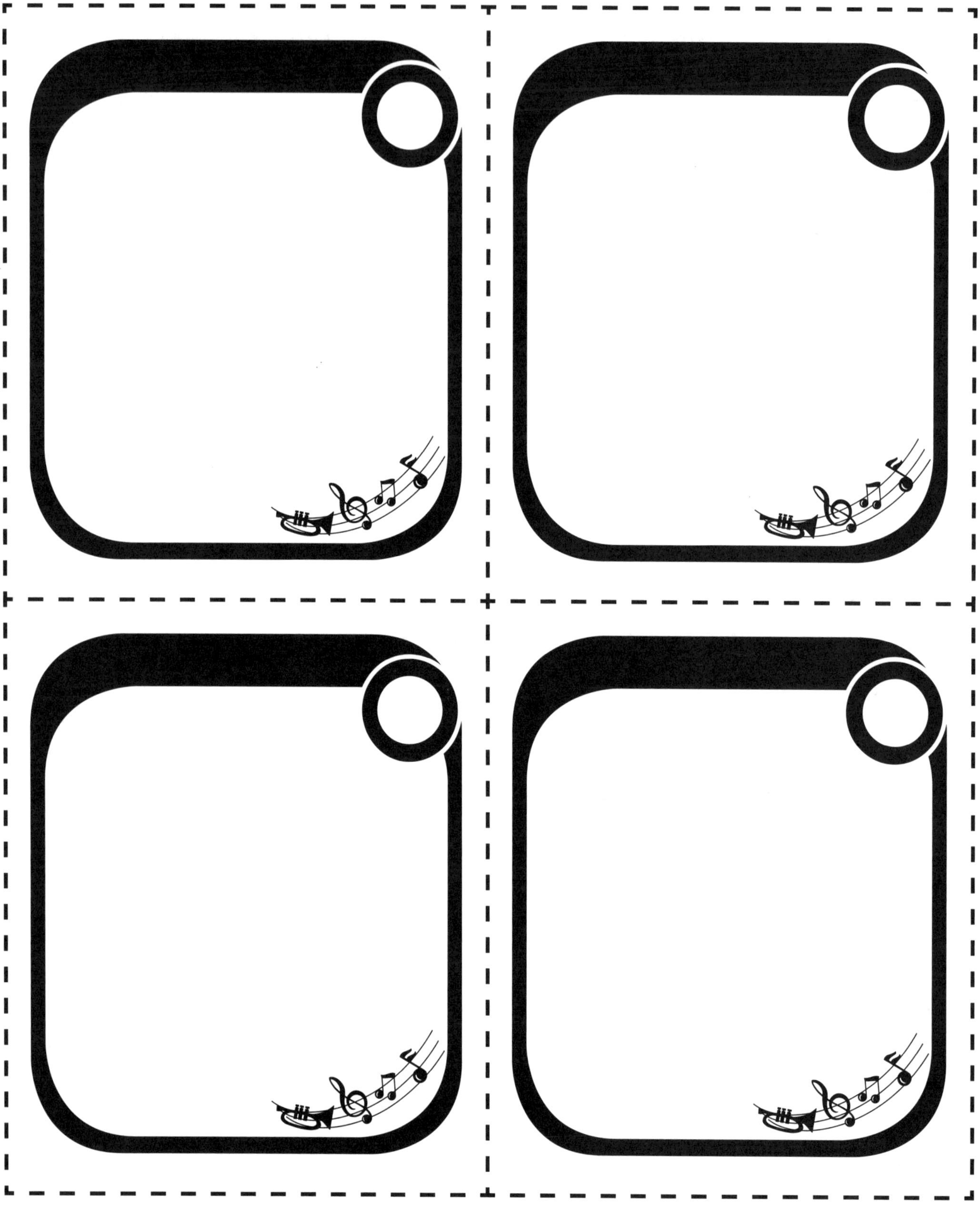

Structure 3

Showdown

Structure 3

Showdown

When the Showdown Maestro calls, "Showdown!" teammates all display their own answers. Teammates either celebrate, or tutor then celebrate.

Steps

Setup: Students sit in teams of four. Each student has something on which to write answers (write-on/wipe-off board, paper, etc.). Each team receives one set of question cards.

1 Teacher selects the Showdown Maestro.
The teacher assigns one student on each team to be the Showdown Maestro for the first round.

2 Maestro picks a card and reads the question.
The Showdown Maestro draws the top card from the stack, reads the question aloud, and provides think time. In our Symbol Scene example, the Maestro picks a symbol card and asks, "*What is the name of this symbol?*" and displays the card to teammates.

3 Students respond individually.
Each student working independently, including the Showdown Maestro, writes his or her answer. For example, students would write the word *accent* or draw the symbol for an accent mark, depending on the card drawn.

4 Students signal when ready.
After everyone has finished writing, teammates signal they are ready by turning their boards/papers over and putting their writing utensils down, or by giving a "thumbs-up" signal as agreed upon by the team prior to starting the structure.

5 Showdown!
The Showdown Maestro calls "*Showdown!*" and everyone reveals their answer. The Maestro leads the checking as teammates compare and discuss their answers. If all are correct, the team celebrates. If someone has answered incorrectly, teammates tutor, then celebrate.

6 Rotate role of Maestro and continue structure.
The team member to the left of the first Showdown Maestro becomes the Maestro for the next round, and the structure is repeated from Step 2.

Sample Activity

Symbol Scene: **Cards printed with music notation symbols or questions about those symbols are stacked facedown in the center of the team's work area.**

Benefits

- All students are actively involved.
- Students interact with their teammates.
- Students learn and practice social skills: patience, leadership, responsibility, tutoring, praising, and disagreeing appropriately.
- Students rely on each other, rather than on the teacher, to check for accuracy in responses to the questions.
- By using different sets of cards, many music concepts can be reinforced.
- Showdown can be used as a pretest, as a review of concepts, or as an informal assessment through teacher observation while monitoring the teams.

Hints

- **Model.** Teacher models the role of Maestro while leading a team through each step of the structure. Remind everyone to use "team voices" so that all can participate in the structure simultaneously without interfering with other teams.
- **Creating Cards.** Upper elementary and secondary level students can create their own cards, based on review sheet information. Questions should be limited to those with only one correct answer, or high-consensus answers. True-False, Fill-in-the-Blank, Fact-or-Opinion, and Multiple-Choice formats are examples of knowledge building (content mastery) questions.
- **Visual for Maestro.** An object, such as a conductor's baton, is given to the Maestro. The baton is passed to the next teammate as he or she assumes the role of the Maestro.
- **Question/Symbol Card Sets.** The teacher has the option to choose only the cards with symbols or only the cards with questions about the notation.
- **Answer Keys.** Answer keys for this structure are provided to assist substitute teachers or Showdown Maestros.

Showdown

Structure 3

Showdown (continued)

Variations

- **Teacher as Maestro.** Students (in teams) listen to a question from the teacher, and all write and compare/check/celebrate within teams.
- **No-Card Modifications.** Questions may be written on a handout given to each team, or displayed by a projector. As each question is asked, the Showdown Maestro for the next round takes the next question in turn.

Principles

P **Positive Interdependence:** Students are on the same side and celebrate their successes as a team.

I **Individual Accountability:** Students are accountable when showing their answers to teammates, tutoring their teammates when needed, and praising or celebrating when the correct response is given.

E **Equal Participation:** Students have equal participation during the rotation of the role of Showdown Maestro, and in responding individually to every question.

S **Simultaneous Interaction:** 100% are writing and showing answers; 25% are asking the question and leading the team.

Showdown Activities

Additional Activities for Showdown Cards

Card sets can also be used for Structure 1: Quiz-Quiz-Trade and Structure 2: Fan-N-Pick.

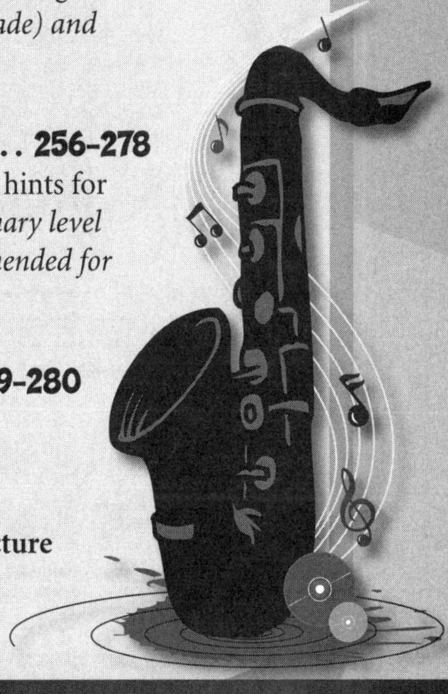

Symbol Scene

Instructions: Copy one set of cards for each team. Give each team a set of cards to play Showdown. Matching cards may also be used for Mix-N-Match.

Symbol Scene

1

What is the name of this symbol?

$>$

Symbol Scene

2

What does the symbol for an "accent" look like?

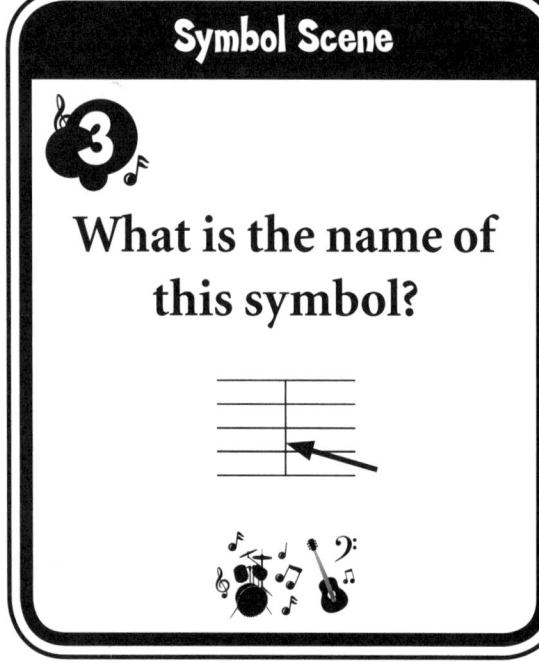

Symbol Scene

3

What is the name of this symbol?

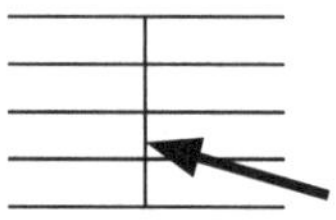

Symbol Scene

4

What does a "bar line" look like?

Symbol Scene

Instructions: Copy one set of cards for each team. Give each team a set of cards to play Showdown. Matching cards may also be used for Mix-N-Match.

Symbol Scene

5

What is the name of this symbol?

Symbol Scene

6

What does the symbol for a "bass clef" look like?

Symbol Scene

7

What is the name of this symbol?

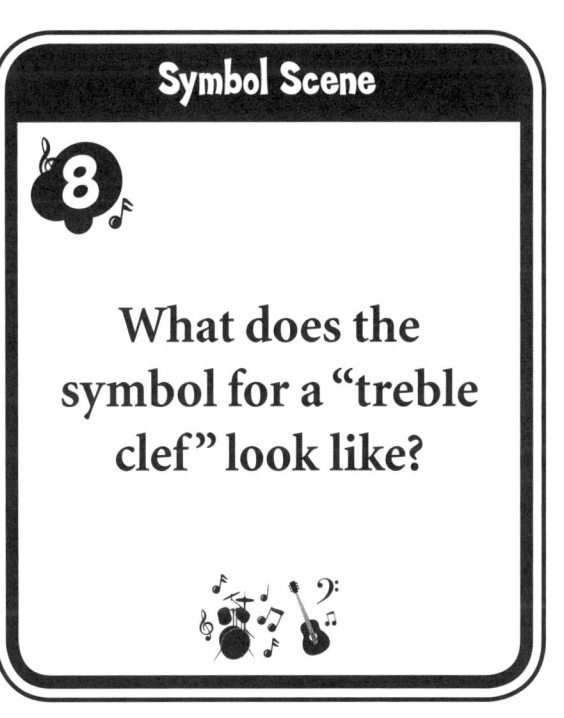

Symbol Scene

8

What does the symbol for a "treble clef" look like?

Symbol Scene

Instructions: Copy one set of cards for each team. Give each team a set of cards to play Showdown. Matching cards may also be used for Mix-N-Match.

Symbol Scene

9

What is the name of this symbol?

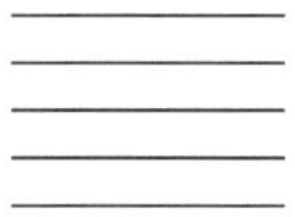

Symbol Scene

10

What does a "staff" look like in music notation?

Symbol Scene

11

What is the name of this symbol?

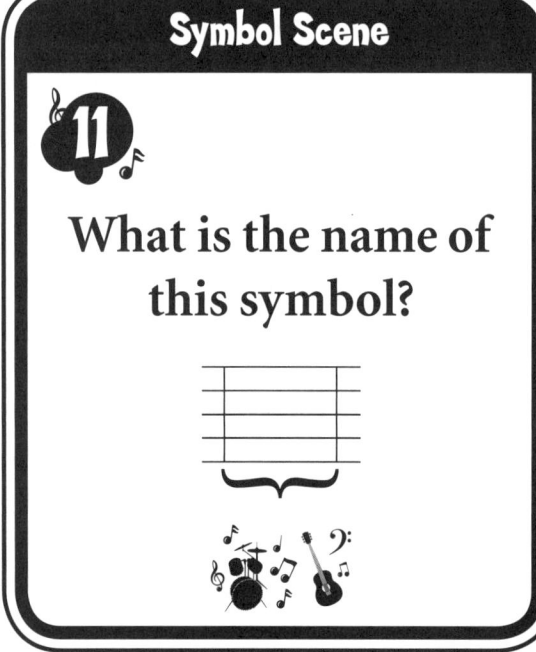

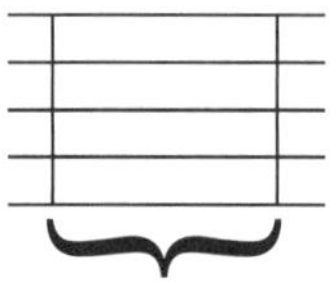

Symbol Scene

12

What does a "measure" look like?

Symbol Scene

Instructions: Copy one set of cards for each team. Give each team a set of cards to play Showdown. Matching cards may also be used for Mix-N-Match.

Symbol Scene

13

What is the name of this symbol?

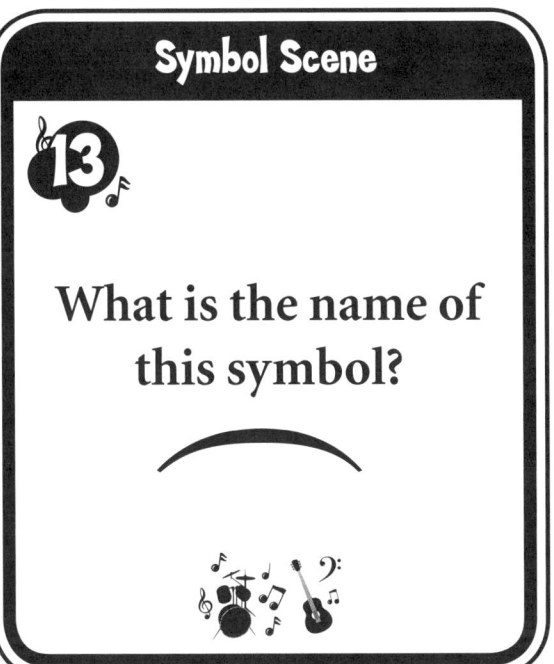

Symbol Scene

14

What does the symbol for a "slur" look like?

Symbol Scene

15

What is the name of this symbol?

,

Symbol Scene

16

What does the symbol for a "breath mark" look like in music notation?

Symbol Scene

Instructions: Copy one set of cards for each team. Give each team a set of cards to play Showdown. Matching cards may also be used for Mix-N-Match.

Symbol Scene

17

What is the name of this symbol?

Symbol Scene

18

What does a "double bar line" mean in music notation?

Symbol Scene

19

What is the name of this symbol?

Symbol Scene

20

What does the symbol for a "fermata" look like?

Symbol Scene

Instructions: Copy one set of cards for each team. Give each team a set of cards to play Showdown. Matching cards may also be used for Mix-N-Match.

Symbol Scene

21

What does this word tell you?

Fine

Symbol Scene

22

What is the word that means the music has finished, but isn't usually found at the end of the music notation?

Symbol Scene

23

What is the name of this symbol?

𝄌

Symbol Scene

24

What does the symbol for a "coda" look like?

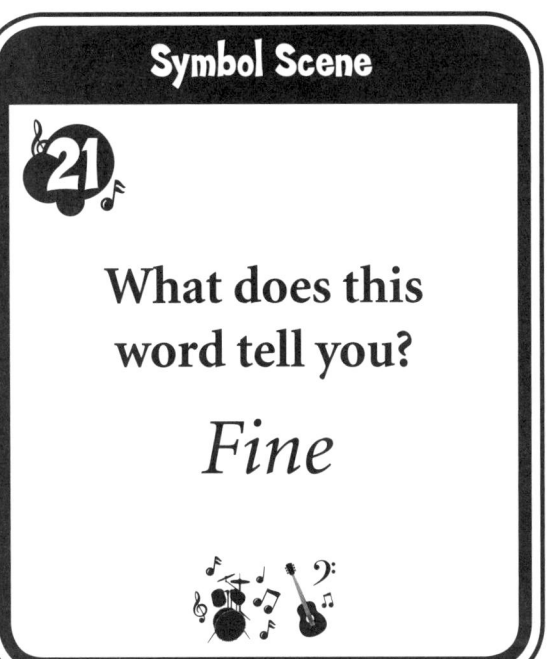

Symbol Scene

Instructions: Copy one set of cards for each team. Give each team a set of cards to play Showdown. Matching cards may also be used for Mix-N-Match.

Symbol Scene

25

What is the name of this symbol?

♭

Symbol Scene

26

What does the symbol for a "flat sign" look like?

Symbol Scene

27

What is the name of this symbol?

♯

Symbol Scene

28

What does the symbol for a "sharp sign" look like?

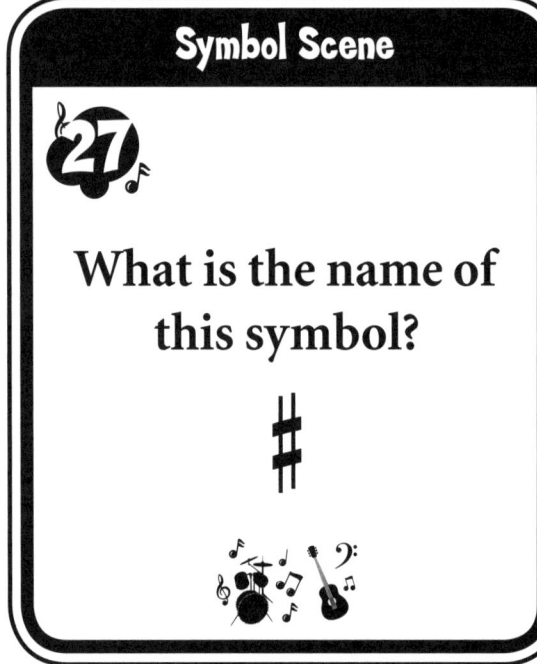

Symbol Scene

Instructions: Copy one set of cards for each team. Give each team a set of cards to play Showdown. Matching cards may also be used for Mix-N-Match.

Symbol Scene

29

What is the name of this symbol?

$\begin{matrix}2\\4\end{matrix}$

Symbol Scene

30

What does a "meter signature" tell you about the music?

Symbol Scene

31

What is the name of this symbol?

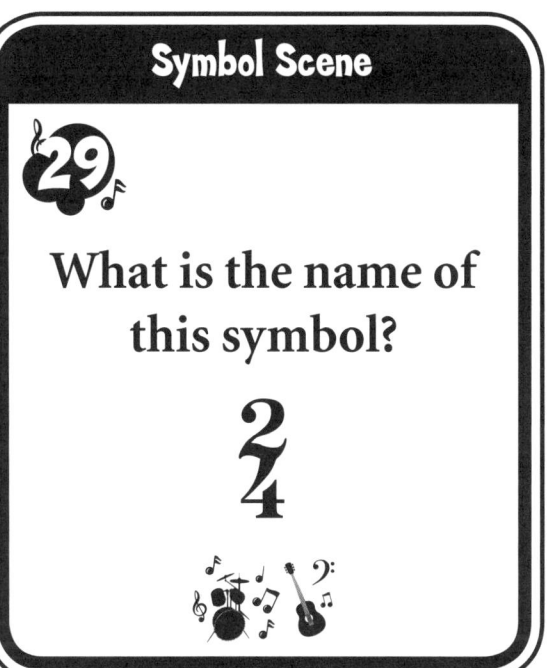

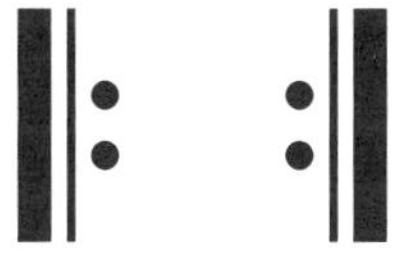

Symbol Scene

32

What does the symbol for a "repeat sign" look like?

Symbol Scene

Instructions: Copy one set of cards for each team. Give each team a set of cards to play Showdown. Matching cards may also be used for Mix-N-Match.

Symbol Scene

33

What is the name of this symbol?

𝄋

Symbol Scene

34

What does the symbol for a "segno" look like?

Symbol Scene

35

What is the name of this symbol?

8va

Symbol Scene

36

What does an "octave mark" symbol mean about how the music will sound?

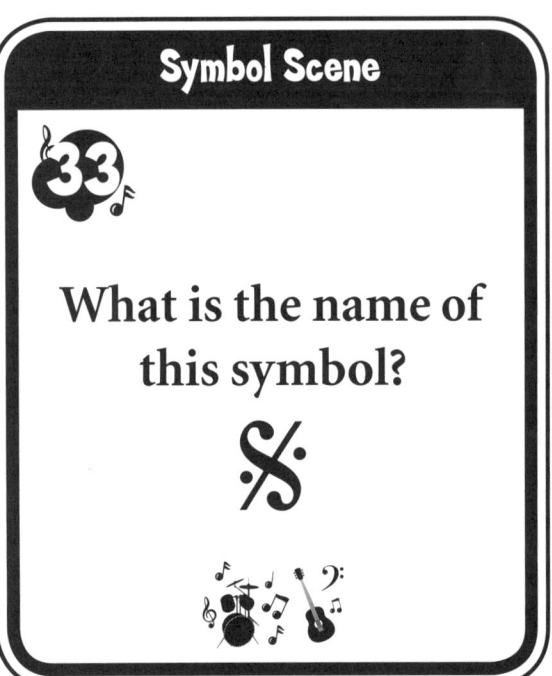

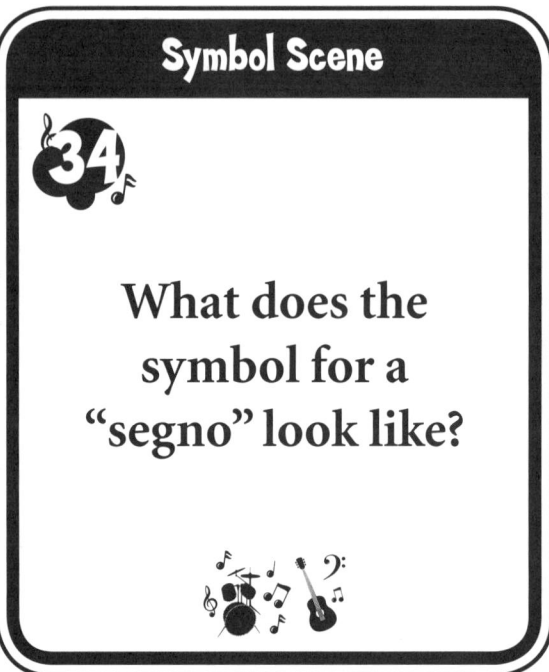

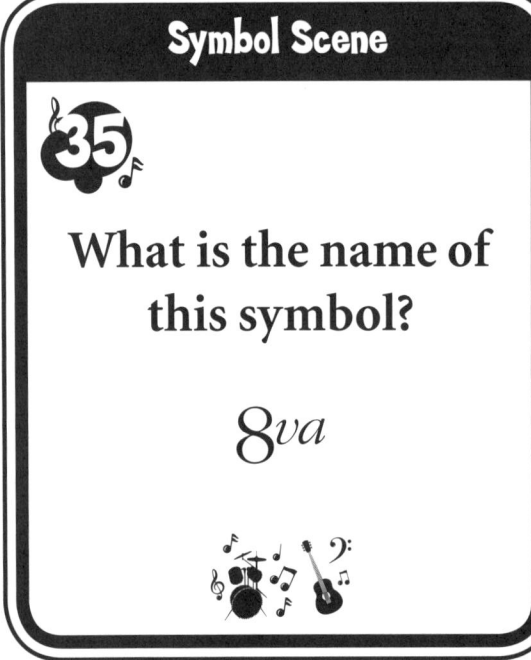

Symbol Scene

Instructions: Copy one set of cards for each team. Give each team a set of cards to play Showdown. Matching cards may also be used for Mix-N-Match.

Symbol Scene

37

What is the name of this symbol?

Symbol Scene

38

What does the symbol for a "trill" look like?

Symbol Scene

39

What is the name of this symbol?

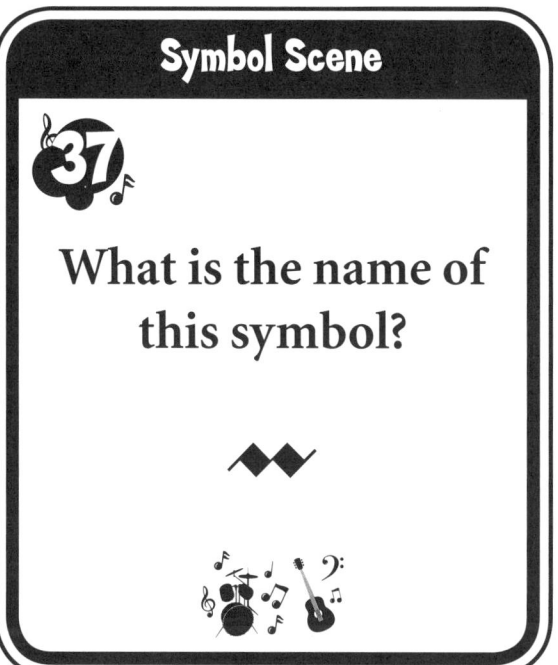

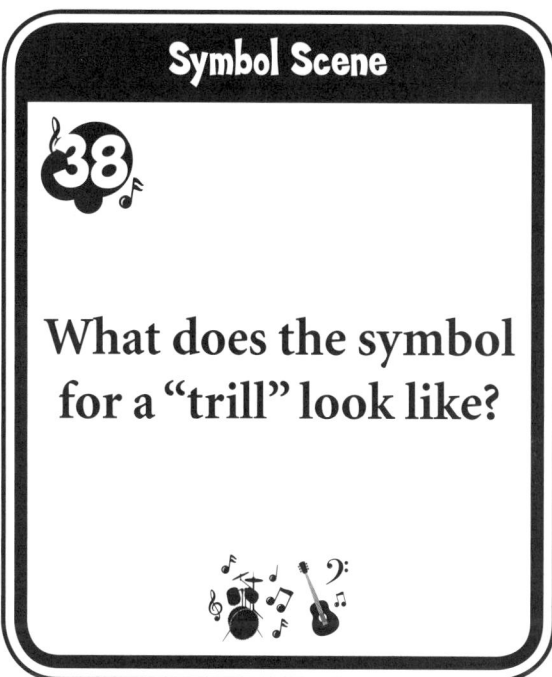

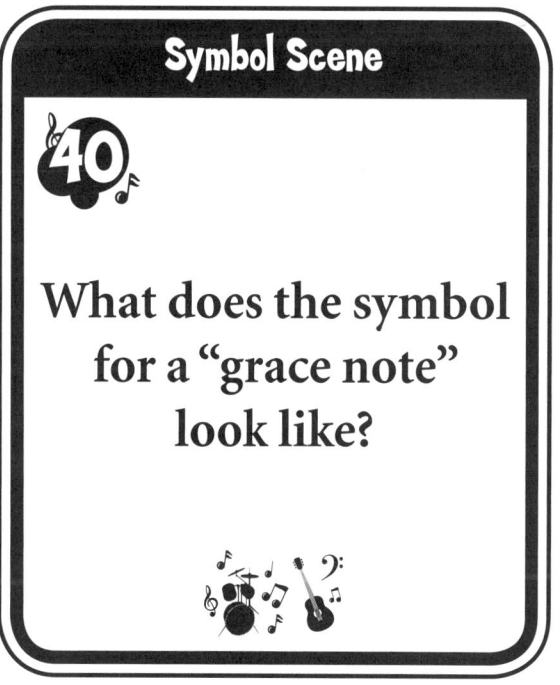

Symbol Scene

40

What does the symbol for a "grace note" look like?

Symbol Scene

Instructions: Copy one set of cards for each team. Give each team a set of cards to play Showdown. Matching cards may also be used for Mix-N-Match.

Symbol Scene

41

What does this music notation symbol mean?

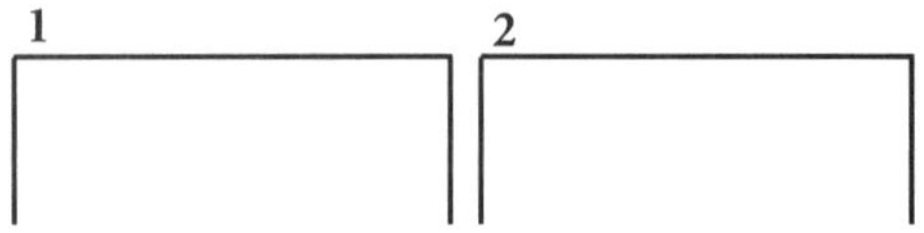

Symbol Scene

42

What music notation symbol tells you that the second time you perform a phrase or section, it will end differently than the first time?

Symbol Scene

43

What is the meaning of this musical term?

D.C. al Fine

Symbol Scene

44

What musical term tells you to go back to the beginning and finish when you arrive at a certain Italian word?

Symbol Scene

Answer Key

1. accent
2. >
3. bar line
4. used to separate measures
5. bass clef
6. 𝄢
7. treble clef
8. 𝄞
9. staff
10. 
11. measure
12. 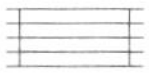
13. slur
14. ⌒
15. breath mark
16. ’
17. double bar line
18. end of song or music
19. fermata
20. 𝄐
21. the music has finished
22. *Fine*
23. coda
24. 𝄌
25. flat sign
26. ♭
27. sharp sign
28. ♯
29. meter signature
30. the number of beats per measure and the kind of note that counts as one beat
31. repeat sign
32. 𝄆 𝄇
33. segno
34. 𝄋
35. octave mark
36. notes are sounded one octave higher or lower than written
37. trill
38. 
39. grace note
40. 
41. the second time you perform a phrase or section, it will end differently than the first time
42. 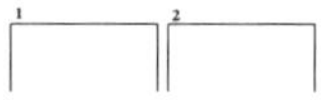

43. go back to the beginning and finish when you arrive at *D.C. al Fine*
44. *D.C. al Fine*

Word Wizard: Bass Clef

Instructions: Copy one set of cards for each team. Give each team a set of cards to play Showdown.

Word Wizard: Bass Clef

1

What word does this pattern spell?

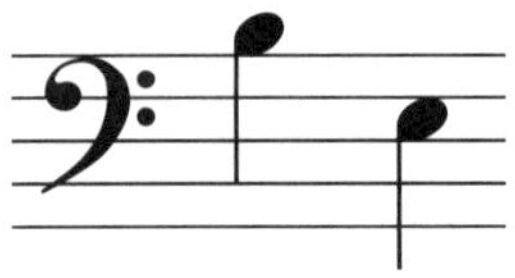

Word Wizard: Bass Clef

2

What word does this pattern spell?

Word Wizard: Bass Clef

3

What word does this pattern spell?

Word Wizard: Bass Clef

4

What word does this pattern spell?

Word Wizard: Bass Clef

Instructions: Copy one set of cards for each team. Give each team a set of cards to play Showdown.

Word Wizard: Bass Clef

5

What word does this pattern spell?

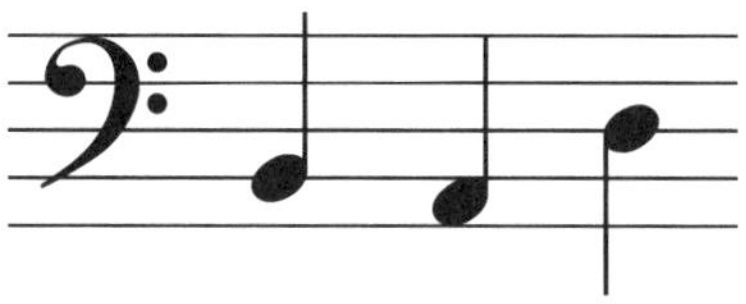

Word Wizard: Bass Clef

6

What word does this pattern spell?

Word Wizard: Bass Clef

7

What word does this pattern spell?

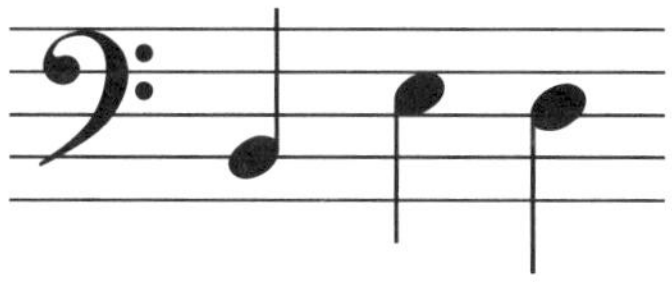

Word Wizard: Bass Clef

8

What word does this pattern spell?

Word Wizard: Bass Clef

Instructions: Copy one set of cards for each team. Give each team a set of cards to play Showdown.

Word Wizard: Bass Clef

9

What word does this pattern spell?

Word Wizard: Bass Clef

10

What word does this pattern spell?

Word Wizard: Bass Clef

11

What word does this pattern spell?

Word Wizard: Bass Clef

12

What word does this pattern spell?

Word Wizard: Bass Clef

Instructions: Copy one set of cards for each team. Give each team a set of cards to play Showdown.

Word Wizard: Bass Clef

13

What word does this pattern spell?

Word Wizard: Bass Clef

14

What word does this pattern spell?

Word Wizard: Bass Clef

15

What word does this pattern spell?

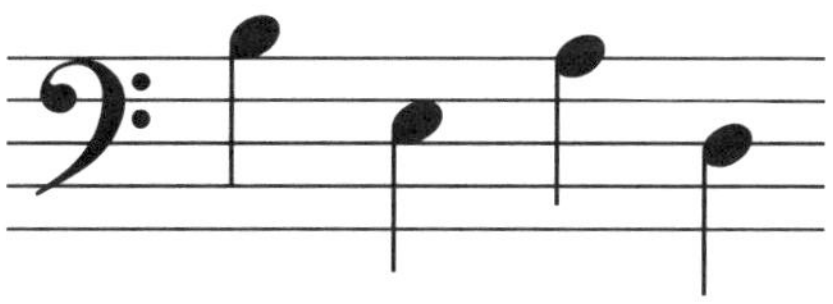

Word Wizard: Bass Clef

16

What word does this pattern spell?

Word Wizard: Bass Clef

Instructions: Copy one set of cards for each team. Give each team a set of cards to play Showdown.

Word Wizard: Bass Clef

17

What word does this pattern spell?

Word Wizard: Bass Clef

18

What word does this pattern spell?

Word Wizard: Bass Clef

19

What word does this pattern spell?

Word Wizard: Bass Clef

20

What word does this pattern spell?

Word Wizard: Bass Clef

Instructions: Copy one set of cards for each team. Give each team a set of cards to play Showdown.

Word Wizard: Bass Clef

21

What word does this pattern spell?

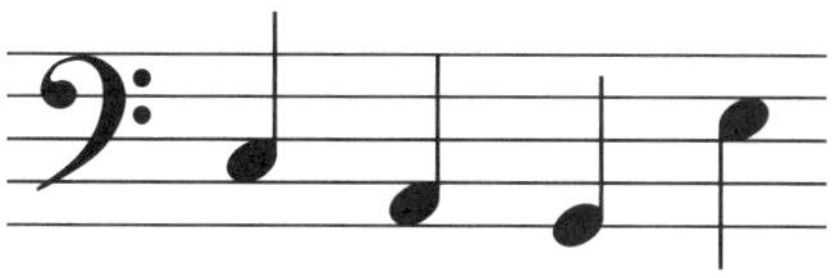

Word Wizard: Bass Clef

22

What word does this pattern spell?

Word Wizard: Bass Clef

23

What word does this pattern spell?

Word Wizard: Bass Clef

24

What word does this pattern spell?

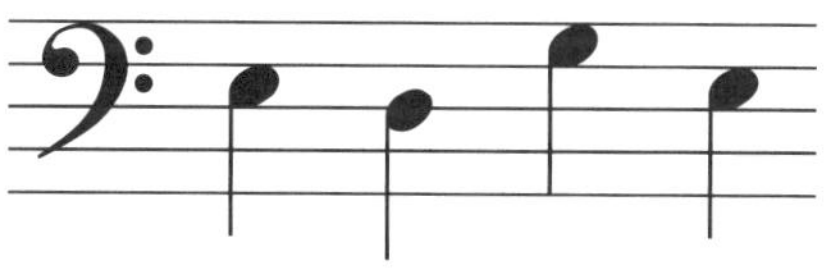

Word Wizard: Bass Clef

Instructions: Copy one set of cards for each team. Give each team a set of cards to play Showdown.

Word Wizard: Bass Clef

25

What word does this pattern spell?

Word Wizard: Bass Clef

26

What word does this pattern spell?

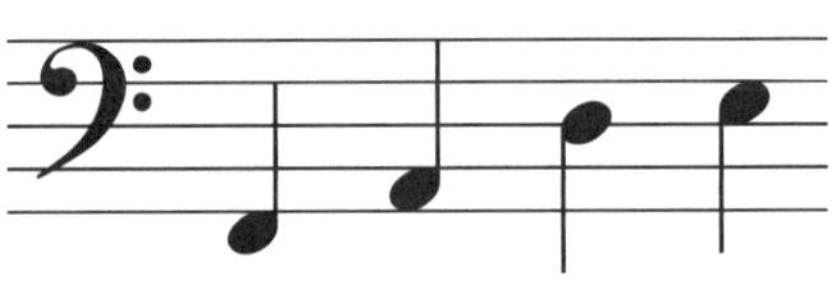

Word Wizard: Bass Clef

27

What word does this pattern spell?

Word Wizard: Bass Clef

28

What word does this pattern spell?

Word Wizard: Bass Clef

Instructions: Copy one set of cards for each team. Give each team a set of cards to play Showdown.

Word Wizard: Bass Clef

29

What word does this pattern spell?

Word Wizard: Bass Clef

30

What word does this pattern spell?

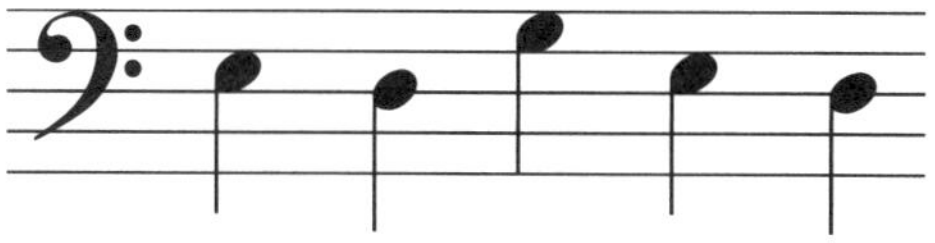

Word Wizard: Bass Clef

31

What word does this pattern spell?

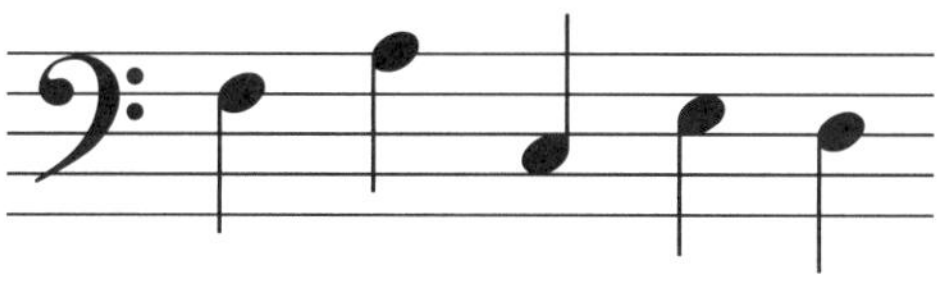

Word Wizard: Bass Clef

32

What word does this pattern spell?

Word Wizard: Bass Clef

Instructions: Copy one set of cards for each team. Give each team a set of cards to play Showdown.

Word Wizard: Bass Clef

33

What word does this pattern spell?

Word Wizard: Bass Clef

34

What word does this pattern spell?

Word Wizard: Bass Clef

35

What word does this pattern spell?

Word Wizard: Bass Clef

36

What word does this pattern spell?

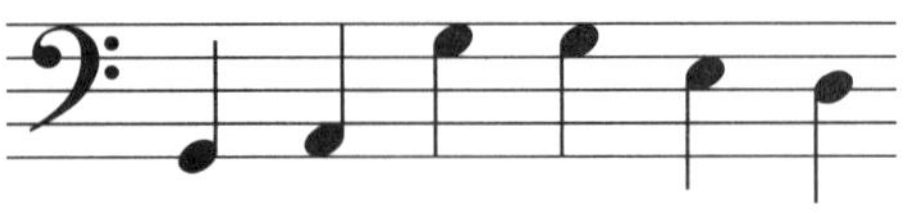

Word Wizard: Bass Clef

Answer Key

1. BE
2. ACE
3. ADE
4. AGE
5. BAD
6. BAG
7. BED
8. BEE
9. BEG
10. EGG
11. FED
12. GAB
13. GAG
14. GEE
15. BEAD
16. BEEF
17. AGED
18. ACED
19. DEAD
20. CAFE
21. CAGE
22. DEAF
23. DEED
24. EDGE
25. FACE
26. FADE
27. FEED
28. CAGED
29. DECAF
30. EDGED
31. FACED
32. FADED
33. BAGGED
34. BEADED
35. BEGGED
36. GAGGED

Interval Insanity: Melodic Intervals

Instructions: Copy one set of cards for each team. Give each team a set of cards to play Showdown.

Interval Insanity: Melodic Intervals

1

What kind of interval is this? Is it ascending or descending?

Interval Insanity: Melodic Intervals

2

What kind of interval is this? Is it ascending or descending?

Interval Insanity: Melodic Intervals

3

What kind of interval is this? Is it ascending or descending?

Interval Insanity: Melodic Intervals

4

What kind of interval is this? Is it ascending or descending?

Interval Insanity: Melodic Intervals

Instructions: Copy one set of cards for each team. Give each team a set of cards to play Showdown.

Interval Insanity: Melodic Intervals

5

What kind of interval is this? Is it ascending or descending?

Interval Insanity: Melodic Intervals

6

What kind of interval is this? Is it ascending or descending?

Interval Insanity: Melodic Intervals

7

What kind of interval is this? Is it ascending or descending?

Interval Insanity: Melodic Intervals

8

What kind of interval is this? Is it ascending or descending?

Interval Insanity: Melodic Intervals

Instructions: Copy one set of cards for each team. Give each team a set of cards to play Showdown.

Interval Insanity: Melodic Intervals

9

What kind of interval is this? Is it ascending or descending?

Interval Insanity: Melodic Intervals

10

What kind of interval is this? Is it ascending or descending?

Interval Insanity: Melodic Intervals

11

What kind of interval is this? Is it ascending or descending?

Interval Insanity: Melodic Intervals

12

What kind of interval is this? Is it ascending or descending?

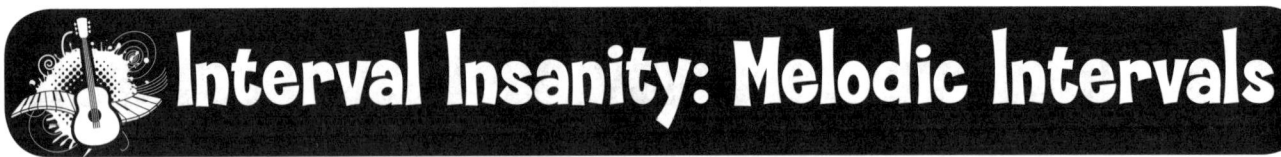

Interval Insanity: Melodic Intervals

Instructions: Copy one set of cards for each team. Give each team a set of cards to play Showdown.

Interval Insanity: Melodic Intervals

13

What kind of interval is this? Is it ascending or descending?

Interval Insanity: Melodic Intervals

14

What kind of interval is this? Is it ascending or descending?

Interval Insanity: Melodic Intervals

15

What kind of interval is this? Is it ascending or descending?

Interval Insanity: Melodic Intervals

16

What kind of interval is this? Is it ascending or descending?

Interval Insanity: Melodic Intervals

Instructions: Copy one set of cards for each team. Give each team a set of cards to play Showdown.

Interval Insanity: Melodic Intervals

17

What kind of interval is this? Is it ascending or descending?

Interval Insanity: Melodic Intervals

18

What kind of interval is this? Is it ascending or descending?

Interval Insanity: Melodic Intervals

19

What kind of interval is this? Is it ascending or descending?

Interval Insanity: Melodic Intervals

20

What kind of interval is this? Is it ascending or descending?

Interval Insanity: Melodic Intervals

Instructions: Copy one set of cards for each team. Give each team a set of cards to play Showdown.

Interval Insanity: Melodic Intervals

21

What kind of interval is this? Is it ascending or descending?

Interval Insanity: Melodic Intervals

22

What kind of interval is this? Is it ascending or descending?

Interval Insanity: Melodic Intervals

23

What kind of interval is this? Is it ascending or descending?

Interval Insanity: Melodic Intervals

24

What kind of interval is this? Is it ascending or descending?

Interval Insanity: Melodic Intervals

Answer Key

The "minor"/"major," etc., designation in parentheses is best suited for secondary level students; upper elementary students may simply give the ordinal number if teachers choose to utilize this structure at that level.

1. descending (perfect) 5th
2. ascending (major) 2nd
3. ascending (perfect) 4th
4. descending (minor) 3rd
5. ascending (minor) 6th
6. descending (perfect) 5th
7. descending octave
8. ascending (major) 7th
9. descending (minor) 6th
10. ascending (perfect) 5th
11. ascending octave
12. descending (minor) 7th
13. ascending (major) 2nd
14. neither—repeated tones
15. descending (perfect) 4th
16. ascending (minor) 3rd
17. ascending (minor) 2nd
18. neither—repeated tones
19. ascending (major) 3rd
20. neither—repeated tones
21. ascending (major) 2nd
22. ascending (perfect) 4th
23. descending octave
24. descending (major) 6th

Family Focus

Instructions: Copy one set of cards for each team. Give each team a set of cards to play Showdown.

Family Focus

1

What are the names of the 4 families of instruments?

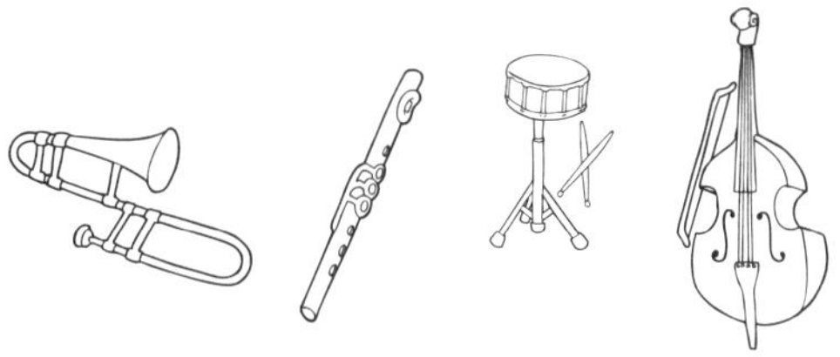

Family Focus

2

What family does the violin belong to?

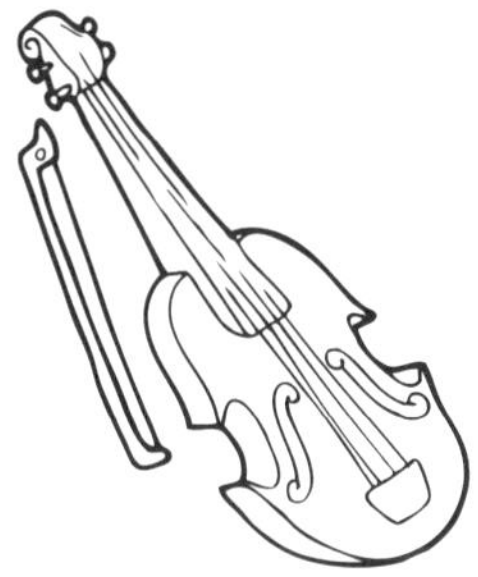

Family Focus

3

What family does the viola belong to?

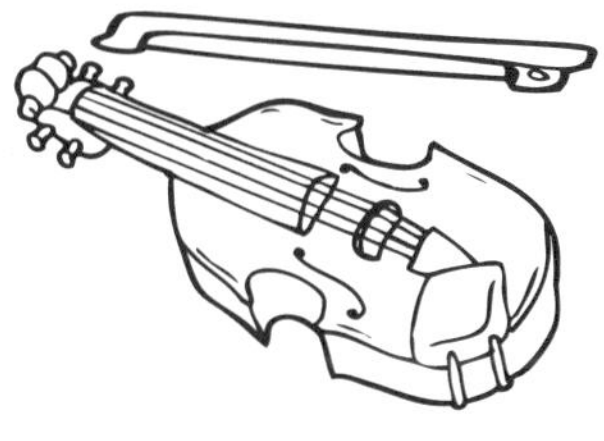

Family Focus

4

What family does the cello belong to?

Family Focus

Instructions: Copy one set of cards for each team. Give each team a set of cards to play Showdown.

Family Focus

5

What family does the double bass belong to?

Family Focus

6

What family does the guitar belong to?

Family Focus

7

What family does the banjo belong to?

Family Focus

8

What family does the autoharp belong to?

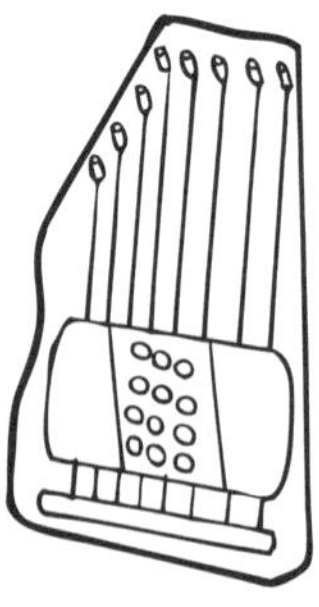

Family Focus

Instructions: Copy one set of cards for each team. Give each team a set of cards to play Showdown.

Family Focus

9

What family does the harp belong to?

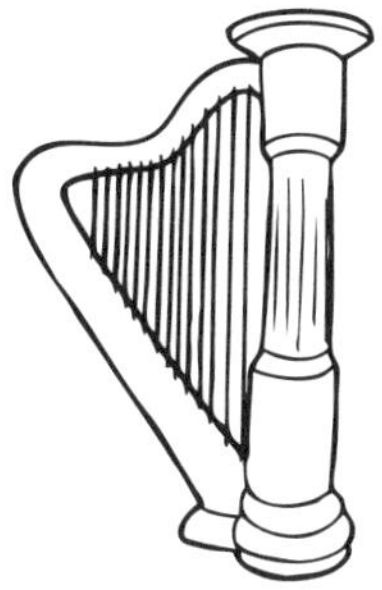

Family Focus

10

What family does the mandolin belong to?

Family Focus

11

What family does the mountain (Appalachian) dulcimer belong to?

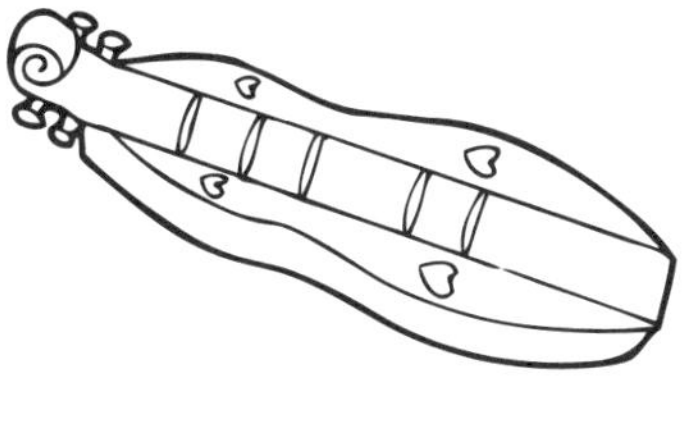

Family Focus

12

What family does the piccolo belong to?

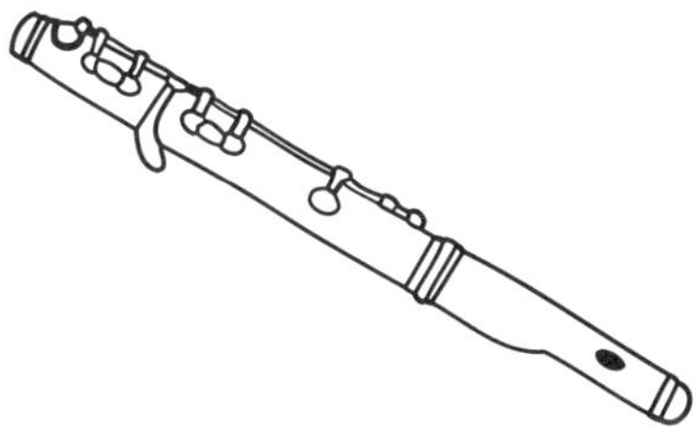

Family Focus

Instructions: Copy one set of cards for each team. Give each team a set of cards to play Showdown.

Family Focus

13

What family does the flute belong to?

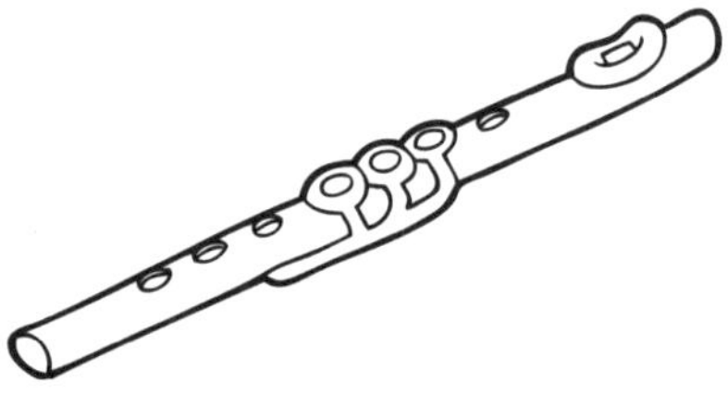

Family Focus

14

What family does the clarinet belong to?

Family Focus

15

What family does the oboe belong to?

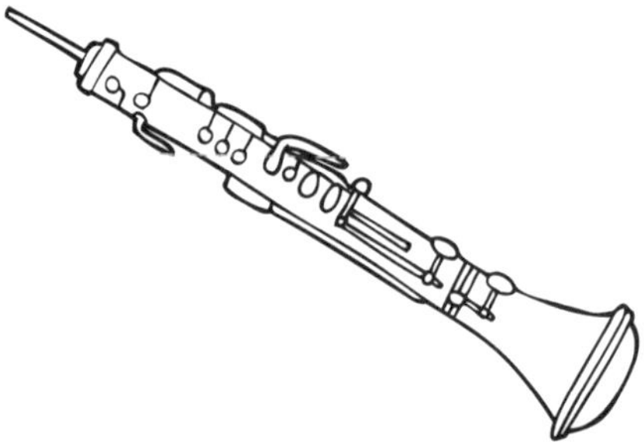

Family Focus

16

What family does the bassoon belong to?

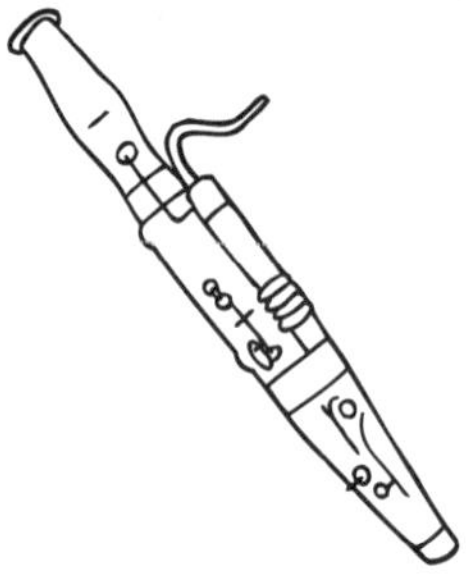

Family Focus

Instructions: Copy one set of cards for each team. Give each team a set of cards to play Showdown.

Family Focus

17

What family does the saxophone belong to?

Family Focus

18

What family does the trumpet belong to?

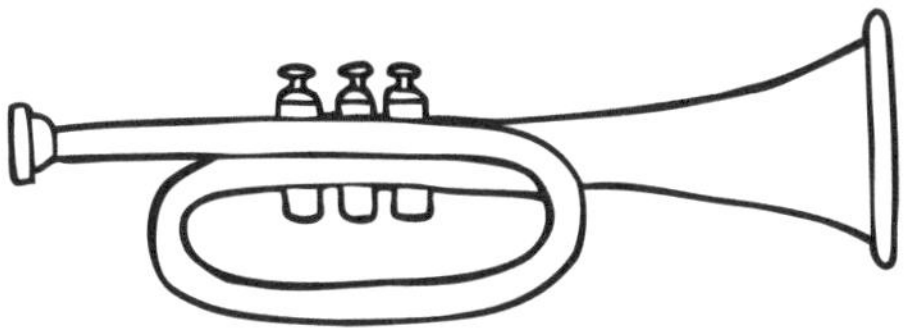

Family Focus

19

What family does the trombone belong to?

Family Focus

20

What family does the French horn belong to?

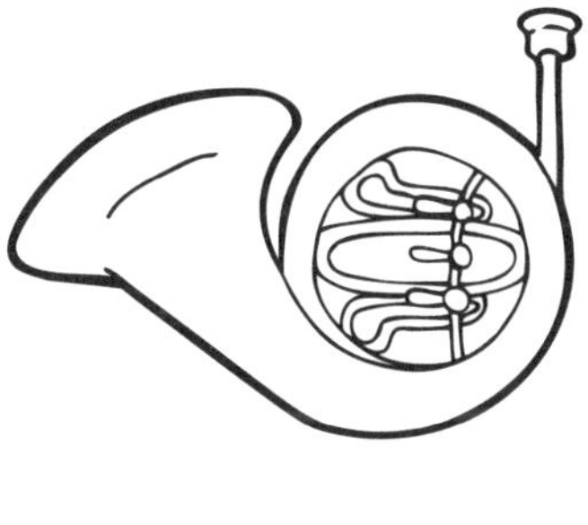

Family Focus

Instructions: Copy one set of cards for each team. Give each team a set of cards to play Showdown.

Family Focus

21

What family does the tuba belong to?

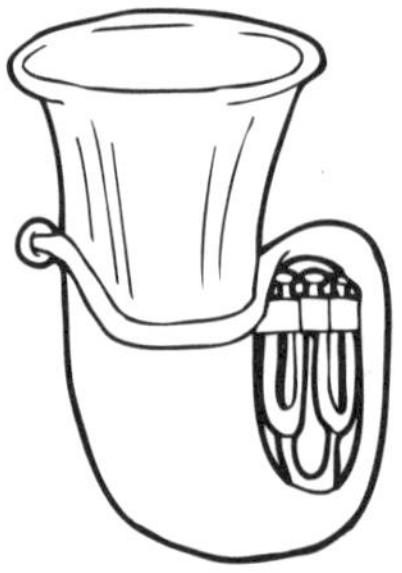

Family Focus

22

What family does the bass drum belong to?

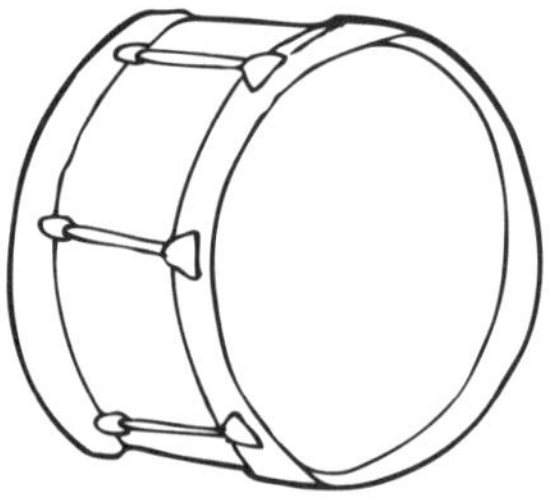

Family Focus

23

What family does the bongo drums belong to?

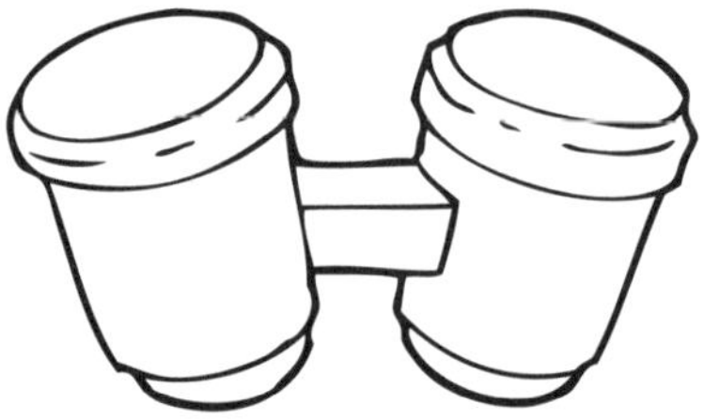

Family Focus

24

What family do the castanets belong to?

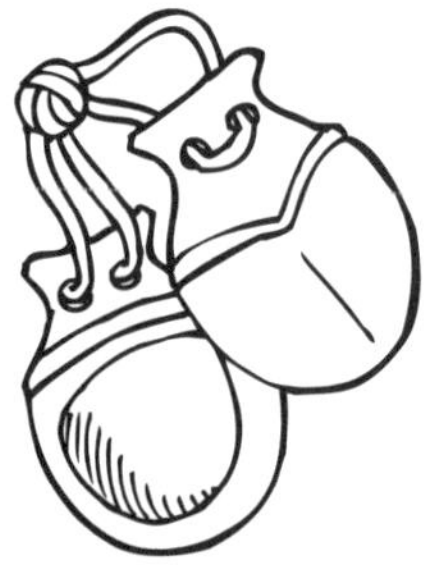

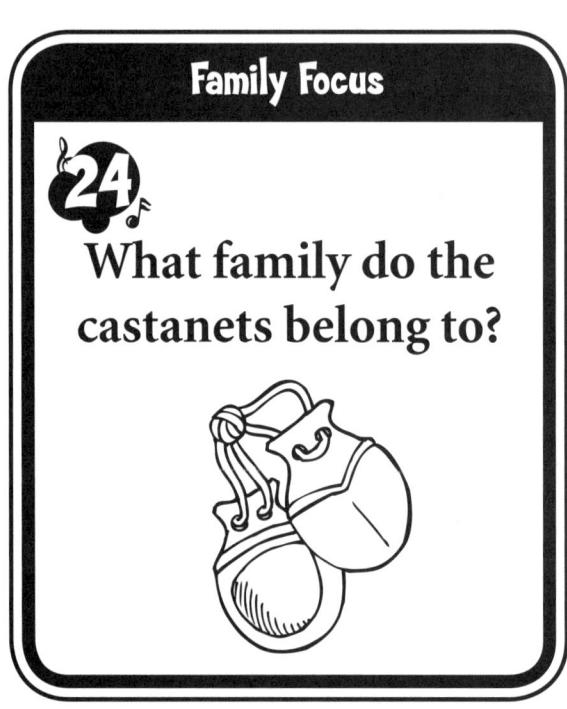

Family Focus

Instructions: Copy one set of cards for each team. Give each team a set of cards to play Showdown.

Family Focus

25

What family does the conga drum belong to?

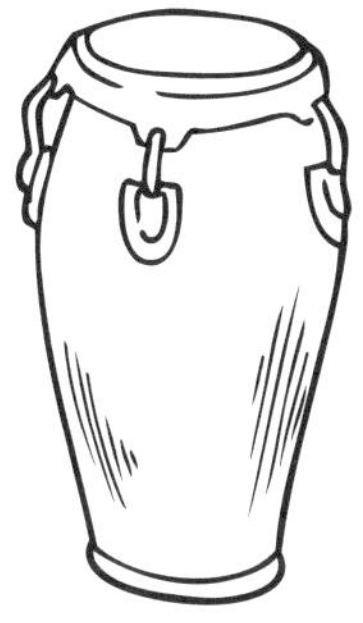

Family Focus

26

What family does the cowbell belong to?

Family Focus

27

What family does the guiro belong to?

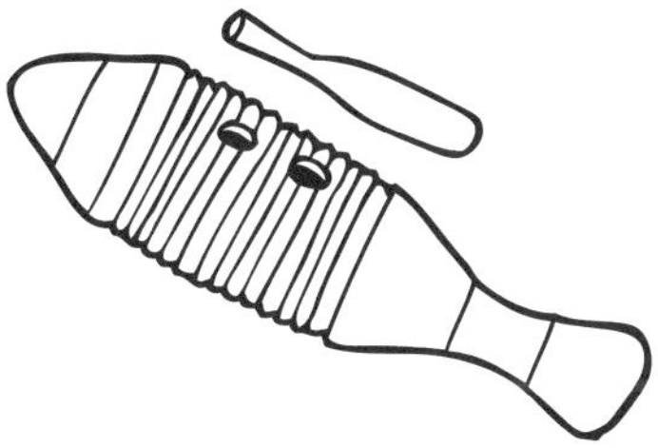

Family Focus

28

What family do the cymbals belong to?

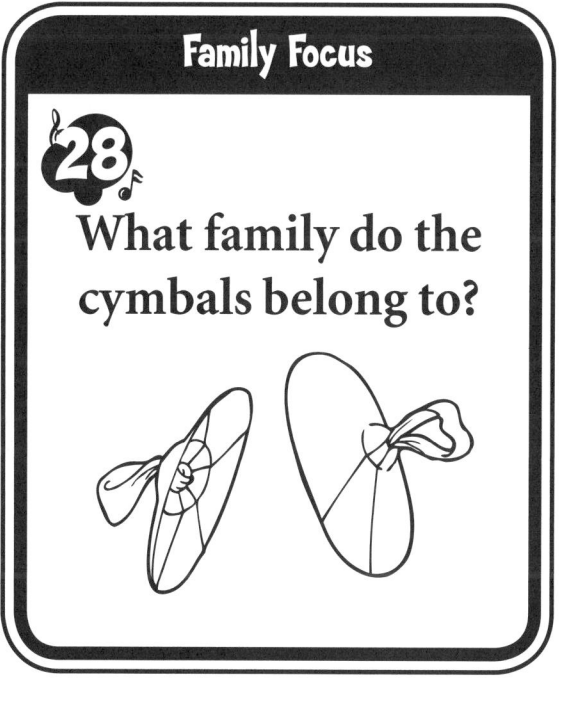

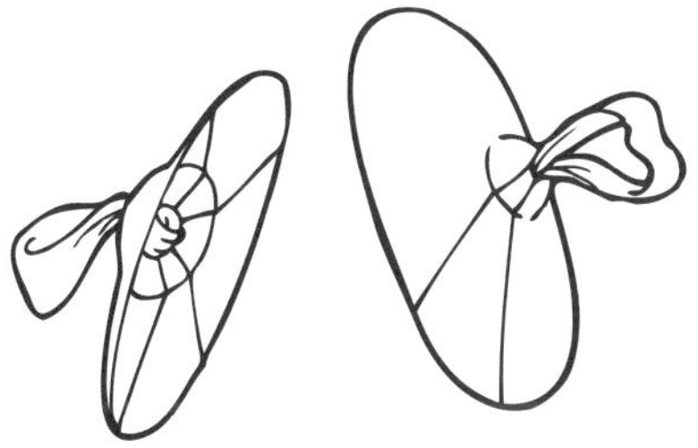

Family Focus

Instructions: Copy one set of cards for each team. Give each team a set of cards to play Showdown.

Family Focus

29

What family does the wood block belong to?

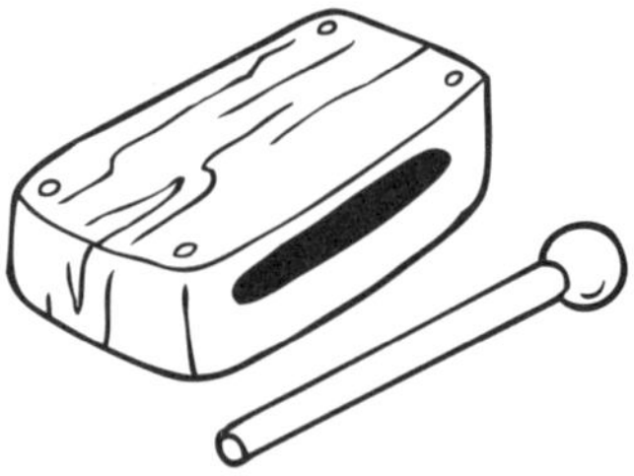

Family Focus

30

What family does the snare drum belong to?

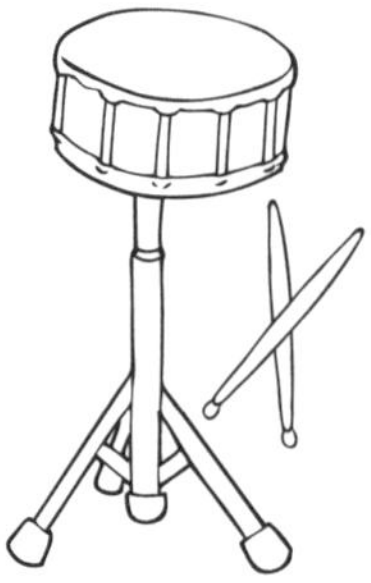

Family Focus

31

What family do the chimes belong to?

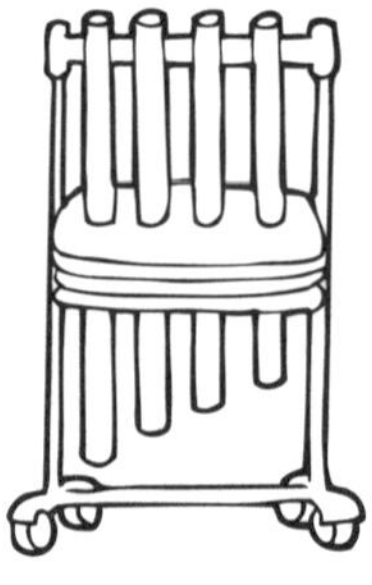

Family Focus

32

What family do the maracas belong to?

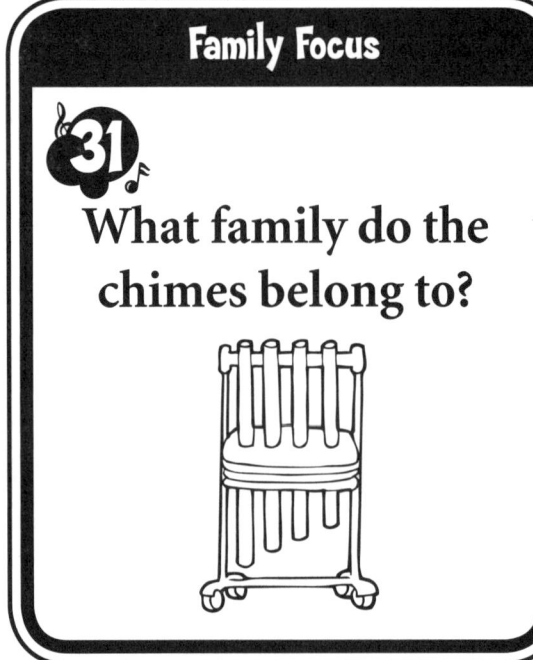

Family Focus

Instructions: Copy one set of cards for each team. Give each team a set of cards to play Showdown.

Family Focus

33

What family do the sandpaper blocks belong to?

Family Focus

34

What family does the tambourine belong to?

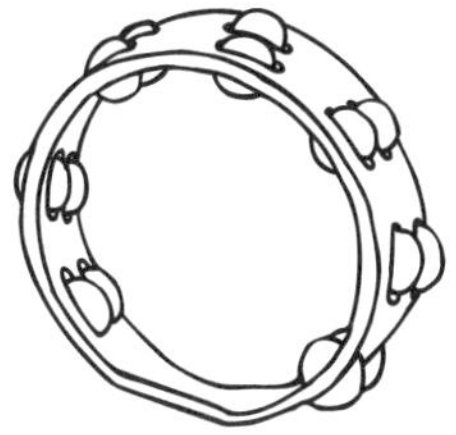

Family Focus

35

What family does the timpani drum belong to?

Family Focus

36

What family does the triangle belong to?

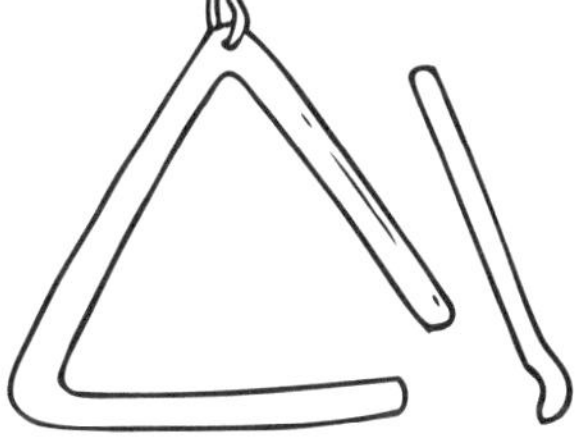

Family Focus

Instructions: Copy one set of cards for each team. Give each team a set of cards to play Showdown.

Family Focus

37

What family does the bagpipe belong to?

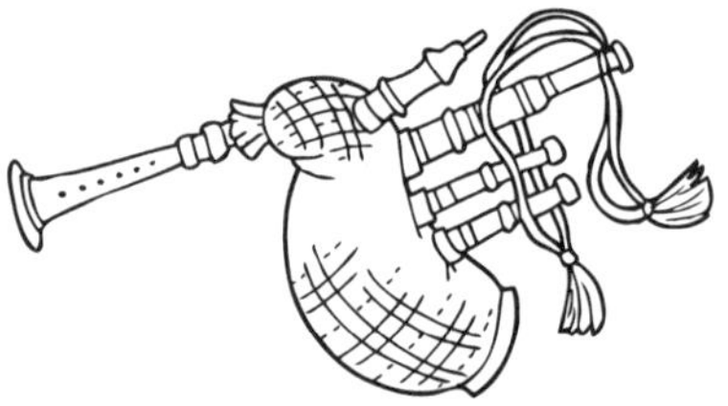

Family Focus

38

What family does the grand piano belong to?

Family Focus

39

What family does the xylophone belong to?

Family Focus

40

What family does the African tongue ("talking") drum belong to?

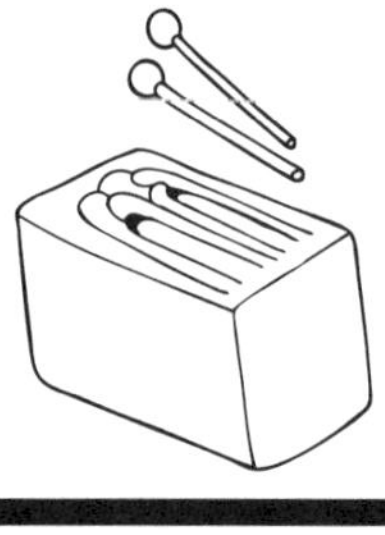

Family Focus

Instructions: Copy one set of cards for each team. Give each team a set of cards to play Showdown.

Family Focus

41

How many players are in a duet?

Family Focus

42

How many players are in a trio?

Family Focus

43

How many players are in a quartet?

Family Focus

44

How many players are in a quintet?

Family Focus

Instructions: Copy one set of cards for each team. Give each team a set of cards to play Showdown.

Family Focus

45

Who is the person that everyone in the orchestra watches for musical cues?

Family Focus

46

Which instrument is responsible for helping everyone tune up before a performance?

Family Focus

47

What type of ensemble is missing the entire string section of instruments?

Family Focus

48

Can you name 3 instruments found in a bluegrass band?

Family Focus

Instructions: Copy one set of cards for each team. Give each team a set of cards to play Showdown.

Family Focus

49

Can you name at least 2 instruments that are commonly used to accompany singing?

Family Focus

50

How many players are usually in a jazz combo?

Family Focus

51

What instruments are usually found in a rock band?

Family Focus

52

What instruments are usually found in a jazz combo?

Family Focus

Instructions: Copy one set of cards for each team. Give each team a set of cards to play Showdown.

Family Focus

53

What instrument does the orchestra's concertmaster play?

Family Focus

54

What family does the harmonica belong to?

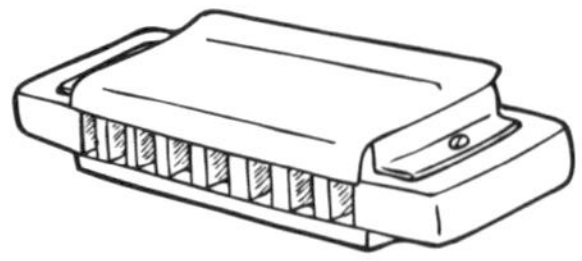

Family Focus

55

What instruments are usually found in a string quartet?

Family Focus

56

What brass instrument plays with a woodwind quintet?

Family Focus
Answer Key

1. Strings, Woodwinds, Percussion, Brass
2. Strings
3. Strings
4. Strings
5. Strings
6. Strings
7. Strings
8. Strings
9. Strings
10. Strings
11. Strings
12. Woodwinds
13. Woodwinds
14. Woodwinds
15. Woodwinds
16. Woodwinds
17. Woodwinds
18. Brass
19. Brass
20. Brass
21. Brass
22. Percussion
23. Percussion
24. Percussion
25. Percussion
26. Percussion
27. Percussion
28. Percussion
29. Percussion
30. Percussion
31. Percussion
32. Percussion
33. Percussion
34. Percussion
35. Percussion
36. Percussion
37. Woodwinds
38. Percussion
39. Percussion
40. Percussion
41. two
42. three
43. four
44. five
45. conductor
46. oboe
47. concert or marching band
48. banjo, mandolin, double bass, guitar, fiddle (violin)
49. piano, guitar, banjo, autoharp, dulcimer, organ, ukulele
50. four
51. electric guitar, electric bass, drum set ("trap set"), keyboard, synthesizer
52. piano, saxophone, double bass, drum set ("trap set")
53. violin
54. Woodwinds
55. 2 violins, viola, cello
56. French horn

Melody Madness

Instructions: Copy one set of cards for each team. Give each team a set of cards to play Showdown.

Melody Madness

1

How does this melody move?

Melody Madness

2

How does this melody move?

Melody Madness

3

How does this melody move?

Melody Madness

4

How does this melody move?

Melody Madness

Instructions: Copy one set of cards for each team. Give each team a set of cards to play Showdown.

Melody Madness

5

How does this melody move?

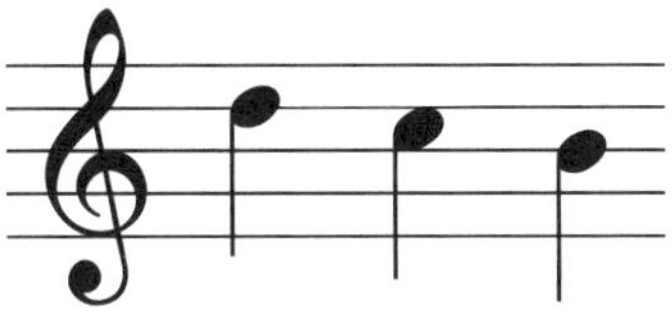

Melody Madness

6

How does this melody move?

Melody Madness

7

How does this melody move?

Melody Madness

8

How does this melody move?

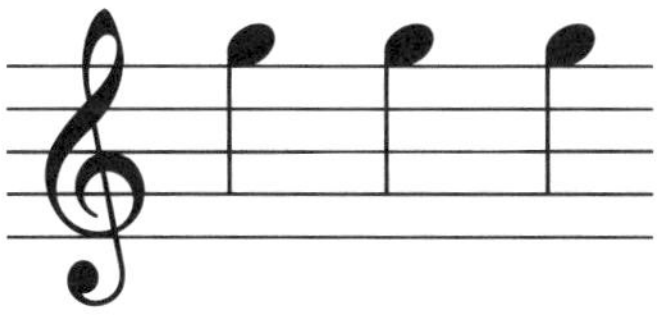

Melody Madness

Instructions: Copy one set of cards for each team. Give each team a set of cards to play Showdown.

Melody Madness

9

How does this melody move?

Melody Madness

10

How does this melody move?

Melody Madness

11

How does this melody move?

Melody Madness

12

How does this melody move?

Melody Madness

Instructions: Copy one set of cards for each team. Give each team a set of cards to play Showdown.

Melody Madness

13

How does this melody move?

Melody Madness

14

How does this melody move?

Melody Madness

15

How does this melody move?

Melody Madness

16

How does this melody move?

Melody Madness

Instructions: Copy one set of cards for each team. Give each team a set of cards to play Showdown.

Melody Madness

17

How does this melody move?

Melody Madness

18

How does this melody move?

Melody Madness

19

How does this melody move?

Melody Madness

20

How does this melody move?

Melody Madness

Instructions: Copy one set of cards for each team. Give each team a set of cards to play Showdown.

Melody Madness

21

How does this melody move?

Melody Madness

22

How does this melody move?

Melody Madness

23

How does this melody move?

Melody Madness

24

How does this melody move?

Melody Madness

Answer Key

1. leaps
2. leaps
3. leaps
4. repeated tones
5. steps
6. steps
7. repeated tones
8. repeated tones
9. steps
10. leaps
11. steps
12. leaps
13. steps
14. steps
15. repeated tones
16. steps
17. repeated tones
18. leaps
19. steps
20. leaps
21. steps
22. leaps
23. repeated tones
24. steps

Treble Clef Triumph

Instructions: Copy one set of cards for each team. Give each team a set of cards to play Showdown.

Treble Clef Triumph

1

What note is on the first ledger line below the treble clef staff?

Treble Clef Triumph

2

What is the letter name of this note?

Treble Clef Triumph

3

What note is on the first line of the treble clef staff?

Treble Clef Triumph

4

What is the letter name of this note?

Treble Clef Triumph

Instructions: Copy one set of cards for each team. Give each team a set of cards to play Showdown.

Treble Clef Triumph

5

What note is on the third line of the treble clef staff?

Treble Clef Triumph

6

What is the letter name of this note?

Treble Clef Triumph

7

What note is on the fourth line of the treble clef staff?

Treble Clef Triumph

8

What is the letter name of this note?

Treble Clef Triumph

Instructions: Copy one set of cards for each team. Give each team a set of cards to play Showdown.

Treble Clef Triumph

9

What note is on the second line of the treble clef staff?

Treble Clef Triumph

10

What is the letter name of this note?

Treble Clef Triumph

11

What note is in the second space of the treble clef staff?

Treble Clef Triumph

12

What is the letter name of this note?

Treble Clef Triumph

Instructions: Copy one set of cards for each team. Give each team a set of cards to play Showdown.

Treble Clef Triumph

13

What note is on the fifth line of the treble clef staff?

Treble Clef Triumph

14

What is the letter name of this note?

Treble Clef Triumph

15

What note is in the first space of the treble clef staff?

Treble Clef Triumph

16

What is the letter name of this note?

Treble Clef Triumph

Instructions: Copy one set of cards for each team. Give each team a set of cards to play Showdown.

Treble Clef Triumph

17

What note is in the third space of the treble clef staff?

Treble Clef Triumph

18

What is the letter name of this note?

Treble Clef Triumph

19

What note is in the fourth space of the treble clef staff?

Treble Clef Triumph

20

What is the letter name of this note?

Treble Clef Triumph

Instructions: Copy one set of cards for each team. Give each team a set of cards to play Showdown.

Treble Clef Triumph

21

What note is in the space just below the treble clef staff?

Treble Clef Triumph

22

What is the letter name of this note?

Treble Clef Triumph

23

What note is in the space just above the treble clef staff?

Treble Clef Triumph

24

What is the letter name of this note?

Treble Clef Triumph

Instructions: Copy one set of cards for each team. Give each team a set of cards to play Showdown.

Treble Clef Triumph

25

What note is on the first ledger line above the treble clef staff?

Treble Clef Triumph

26

What is the letter name of this note?

Treble Clef Triumph

27

What note is in the space just above the first ledger line above the treble clef staff?

Treble Clef Triumph

28

What is the letter name of this note?

Treble Clef Triumph

Instructions: Copy one set of cards for each team. Give each team a set of cards to play Showdown.

Treble Clef Triumph

29

What note is in the space just below the first ledger line below the treble clef staff?

Treble Clef Triumph

30

What is the letter name of this note?

Treble Clef Triumph

31

What note is on the second ledger line above the treble clef staff?

Treble Clef Triumph

32

What is the letter name of this note?

Treble Clef Triumph

Answer Key

1. Middle C
2. Middle C
3. E
4. E
5. B
6. B
7. D
8. D
9. G
10. G
11. A
12. A
13. F
14. F
15. F
16. F
17. C
18. C
19. E
20. E
21. D
22. D
23. G
24. G
25. A
26. A
27. B
28. B
29. B
30. B
31. C
32. C

What Am I?

Instructions: Copy one set of cards for each team. Give each team a set of cards to play Showdown.

What Am I?

1 What am I?

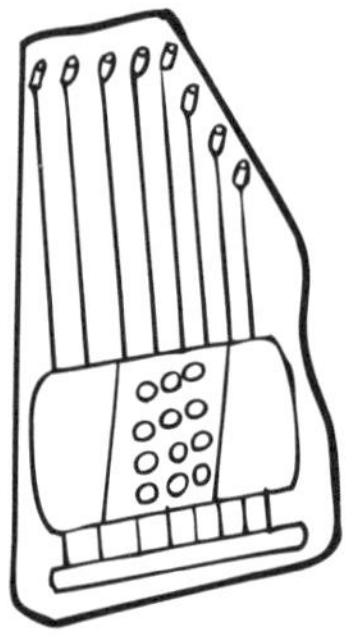

What Am I?

2 What am I?

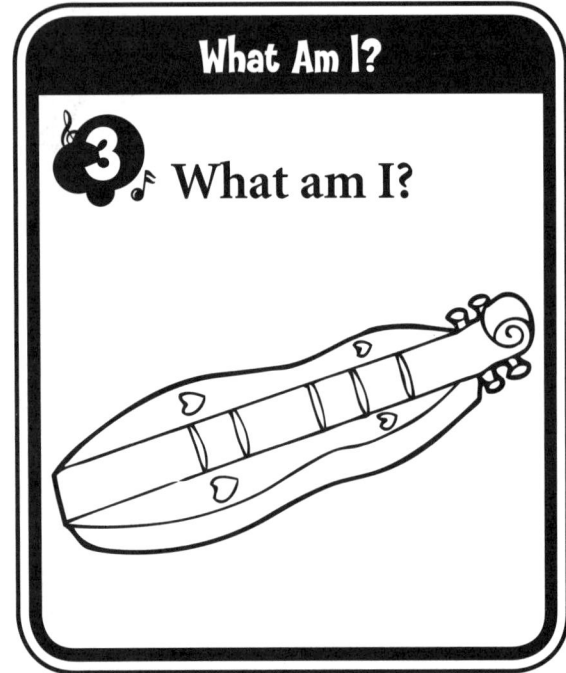

What Am I?

3 What am I?

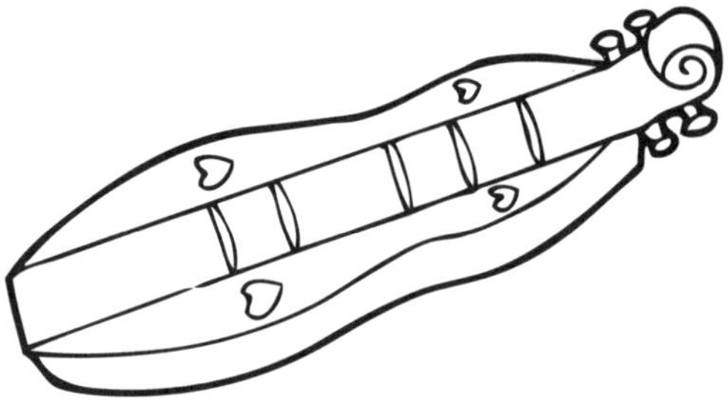

What Am I?

4 What am I?

What Am I?

Instructions: Copy one set of cards for each team. Give each team a set of cards to play Showdown.

What Am I?

1 **Hints:**

1. I am a stringed folk instrument.
2. I am played by pushing a button and strumming.
3. I play chords to accompany singing.

What Am I?

2 **Hints:**

1. I am a stringed folk instrument.
2. I am played by pressing on strings and strumming.
3. I play in bluegrass bands.
4. I can play melody or harmony.
5. My body looks like a drum.

What Am I?

3 **Hints:**

1. I am a stringed folk instrument.
2. I am played by pressing on strings and strumming.
3. I can play in both old time claw hammer and bluegrass finger-picking styles.
4. I can play melody or harmony.
5. My body has a teardrop or an hourglass shape.

What Am I?

4 **Hints:**

1. I am a stringed folk instrument.
2. I am played by pressing on strings and strumming.
3. I am the most popular folk instrument.
4. I can play melody or harmony.
5. I play chords to accompany singing.

What Am I?

Instructions: Copy one set of cards for each team. Give each team a set of cards to play Showdown.

What Am I?

5 What am I?

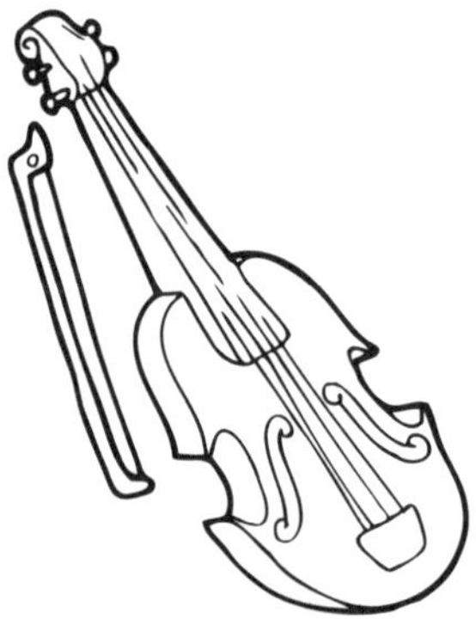

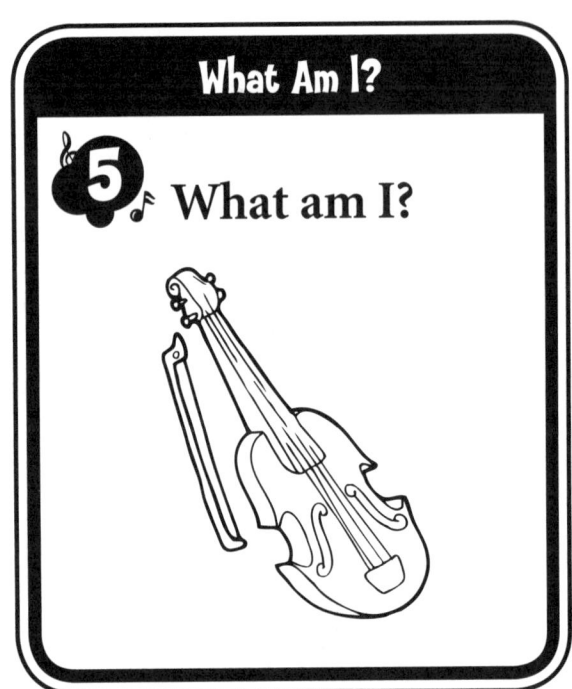

What Am I?

6 What am I?

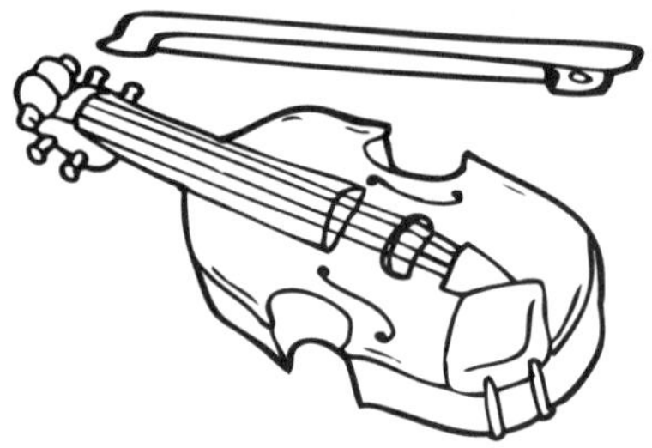

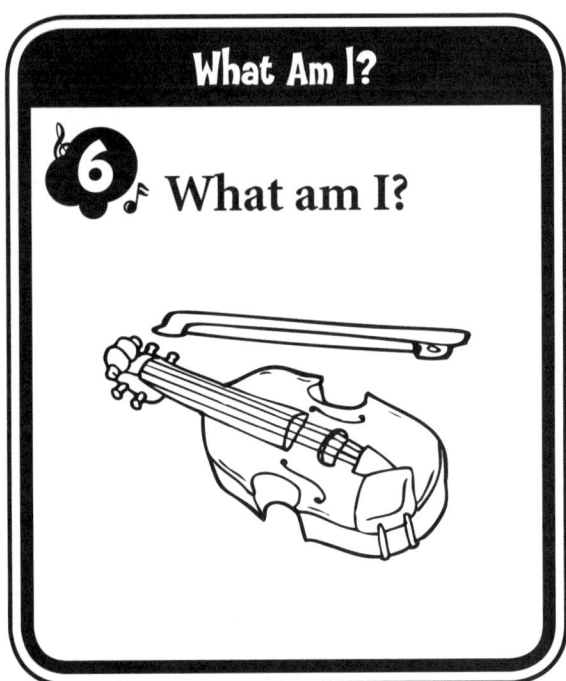

What Am I?

7 What am I?

What Am I?

8 What am I?

What Am I?

Instructions: Copy one set of cards for each team. Give each team a set of cards to play Showdown.

What Am I?

5 **Hints:**

1. I am a stringed orchestra instrument.
2. I am the highest voice in the string section.
3. I usually play the melody of the music.
4. I am usually played with a bow.
5. I can be played by plucking the strings.

What Am I?

6 **Hints:**

1. I am a stringed orchestra instrument.
2. I am the second highest voice in the string section.
3. I am usually played with a bow.
4. I can be played by plucking the strings.

What Am I?

7 **Hints:**

1. I am a stringed orchestra instrument.
2. I am the second lowest voice in the string section.
3. I have a deep, rich tone.
4. I am usually played with a bow.
5. I can be played by plucking the strings.

What Am I?

8 **Hints:**

1. I am a stringed orchestra instrument.
2. I am the lowest voice in the string section.
3. I rarely play the melody of the music.
4. I am often played with a bow.
5. I can be played by plucking the strings.

What Am I?

Instructions: Copy one set of cards for each team. Give each team a set of cards to play Showdown.

What Am I?

9 What am I?

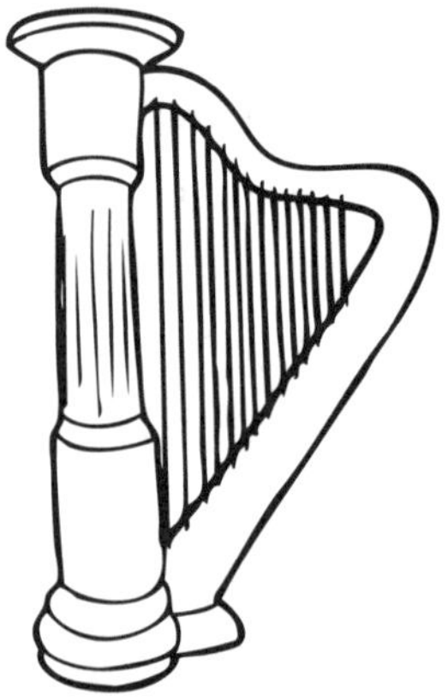

What Am I?

10 What am I?

What Am I?

11 What am I?

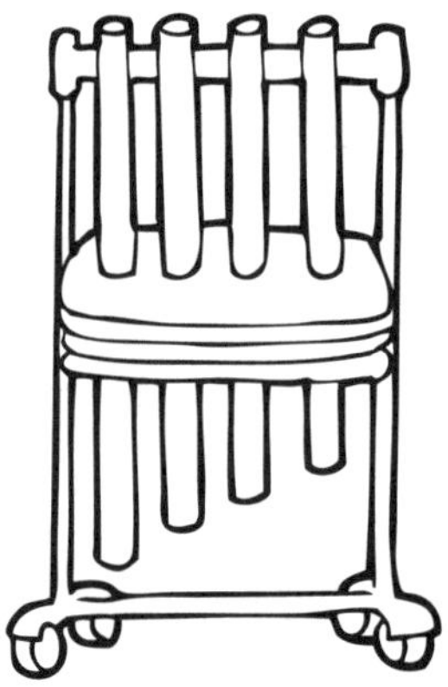

What Am I?

12 What am I?

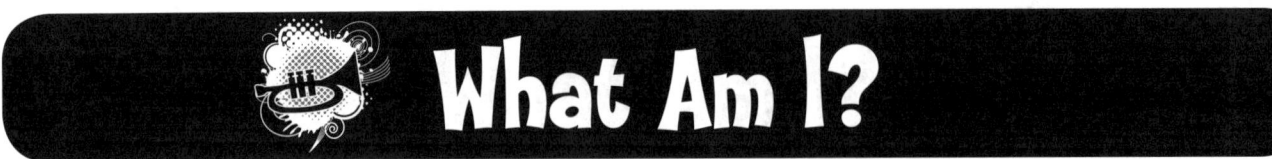

What Am I?

Instructions: Copy one set of cards for each team. Give each team a set of cards to play Showdown.

What Am I?

9 **Hints:**

1. I am a stringed orchestra instrument.
2. I am played by plucking or strumming the strings.
3. I am not a regular member of the orchestra.
4. My sound is sometimes called "heavenly."
5. I am very tall.

What Am I?

10 **Hints:**

1. I am a percussion instrument.
2. I have 88 keys.
3. I can play melodies and harmonies at the same time.
4. I can be found in many homes.
5. I play with many different ensembles.

What Am I?

11 **Hints:**

1. I am a percussion instrument.
2. I am a set of tuned metal rods.
3. I am usually found in an orchestra.
4. I am played with a small metal hammer.

What Am I?

12 **Hints:**

1. I am a percussion instrument.
2. I am made of metal, usually brass.
3. I have a round shape.
4. My sound can last a long time.

What Am I?

Instructions: Copy one set of cards for each team. Give each team a set of cards to play Showdown.

What Am I?

13 What am I?

What Am I?

14 What am I?

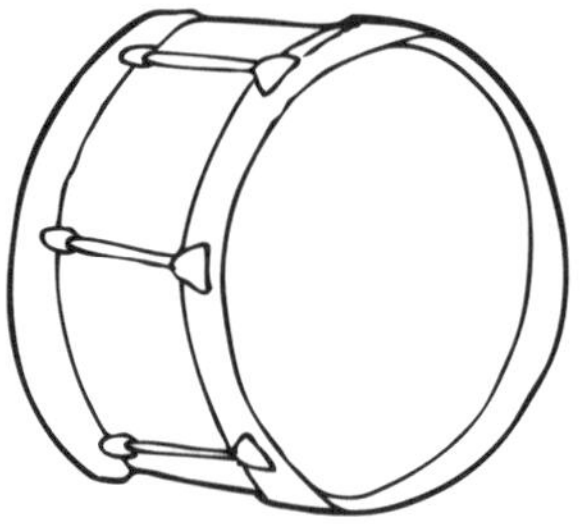

What Am I?

15 What am I?

What Am I?

16 What am I?

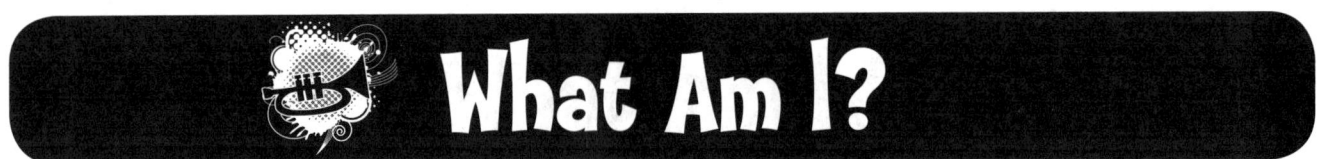

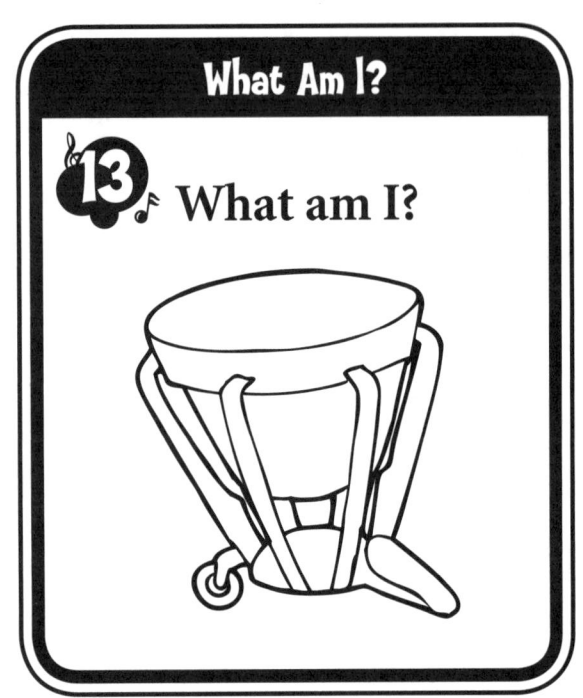

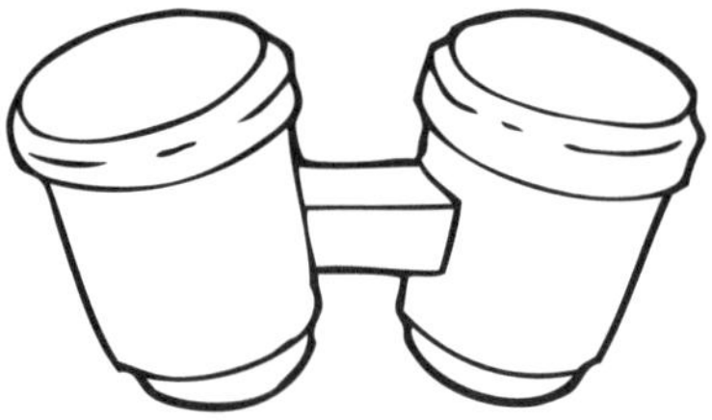

What Am I?

Instructions: Copy one set of cards for each team. Give each team a set of cards to play Showdown.

What Am I?

13 **Hints:**

1. I am a percussion instrument made of skin.
2. My body shape looks like a teakettle.
3. I am played with soft felt mallets.
4. I am usually found in an orchestra.
5. I can change my pitch.

What Am I?

14 **Hints:**

1. I am a percussion instrument made of skin.
2. I make a very deep sound.
3. I am played with large soft mallets.
4. I am found in marching bands and orchestras.

What Am I?

15 **Hints:**

1. I am a percussion instrument made of skin.
2. I am played with hands.
3. I am tall and narrow.
4. I am larger at the top than at the bottom.
5. I come from Latin America.

What Am I?

16 **Hints:**

1. I am a percussion instrument made of skin.
2. I am actually a pair—there are two of me hooked together.
3. I am played with hands and fingers.
4. I come from Latin America.

What Am I?

Instructions: Copy one set of cards for each team. Give each team a set of cards to play Showdown.

What Am I?

17 What am I?

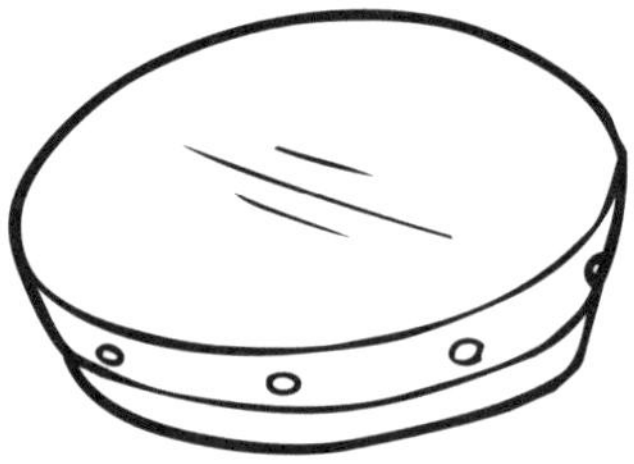

What Am I?

18 What am I?

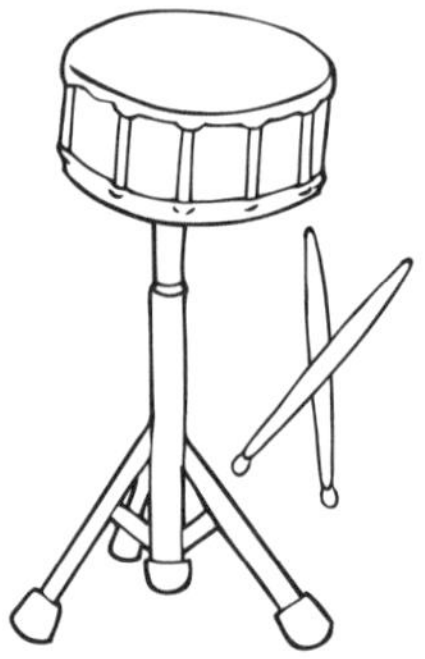

What Am I?

19 What am I?

What Am I?

20 What am I?

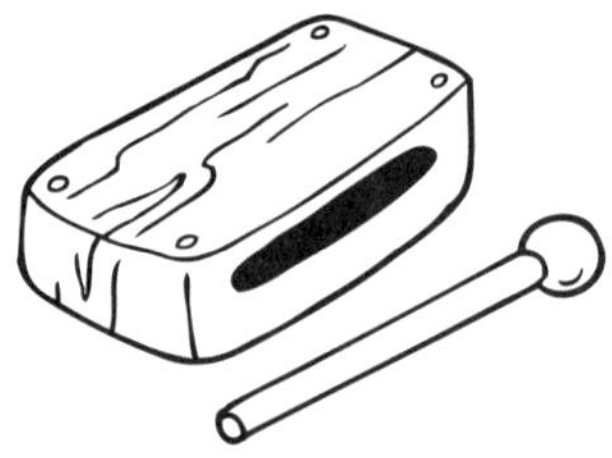

What Am I?

Instructions: Copy one set of cards for each team. Give each team a set of cards to play Showdown.

What Am I?

17 **Hints:**

1. I am a percussion instrument made of skin.
2. I am played with hands.
3. I am short and round.
4. If I am not played correctly, I sound like a cardboard box.

What Am I?

18 **Hints:**

1. I am a percussion instrument made of skin.
2. I am played with wooden sticks or a brush.
3. I have rattles attached under my head.
4. I can be found in a marching band or an orchestra.

What Am I?

19 **Hints:**

1. I am a percussion instrument made of wood.
2. I am played with mallets.
3. I have many wooden bars that are tuned to different pitches.

What Am I?

20 **Hints:**

1. I am a percussion instrument made of wood.
2. I am played by tapping a wooden mallet on my body.
3. I make a rather loud sound.

What Am I?

Instructions: Copy one set of cards for each team. Give each team a set of cards to play Showdown.

What Am I?

21 What am I?

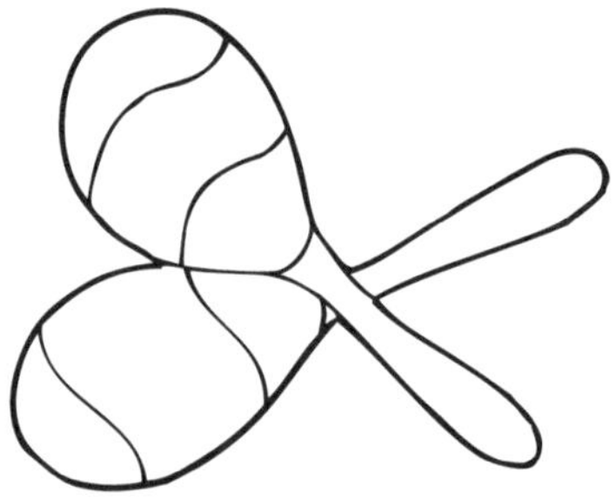

What Am I?

22 What am I?

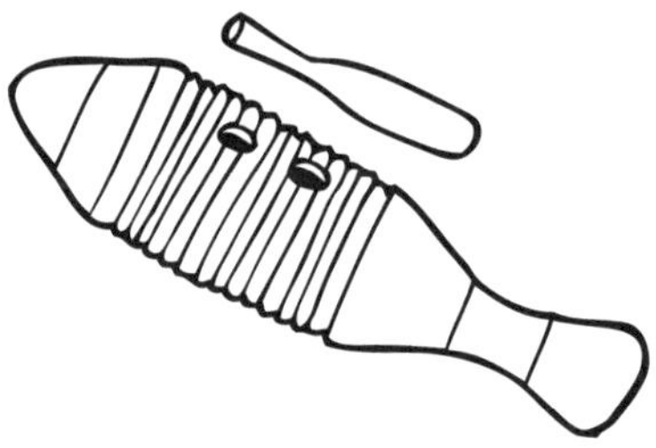

What Am I?

23 What am I?

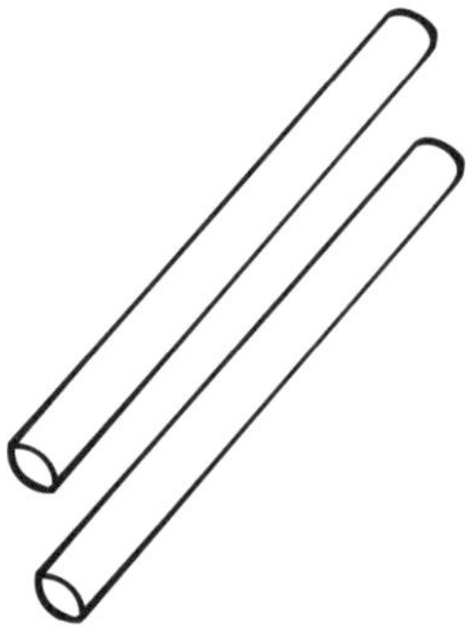

What Am I?

24 What am I?

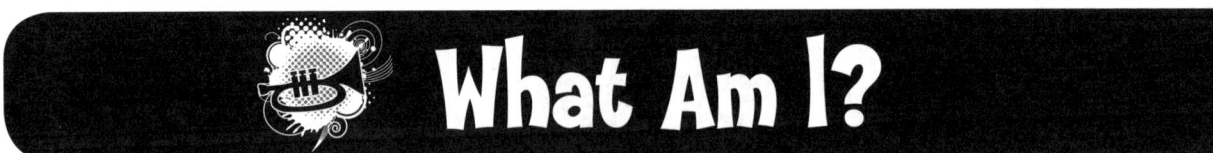

What Am I?

Instructions: Copy one set of cards for each team. Give each team a set of cards to play Showdown.

What Am I?

21 **Hints:**

1. I am a percussion instrument made of wood.
2. I am played by shaking.
3. I am often played in pairs.
4. I come from Latin America.

What Am I?

22 **Hints:**

1. I am a percussion instrument made of wood.
2. I am played by scraping.
3. I resemble a fish.
4. I come from Latin America.

What Am I?

23 **Hints:**

1. I am a percussion instrument made of wood.
2. I am played in pairs.
3. I am played by tapping one on top of the other.
4. I come from Native American tradition.

What Am I?

24 **Hints:**

1. I am a percussion instrument made of wood with metal beads.
2. I am played by rubbing the beads against a hand.
3. I come from Latin America.

What Am I?

Instructions: Copy one set of cards for each team. Give each team a set of cards to play Showdown.

What Am I?

25 What am I?

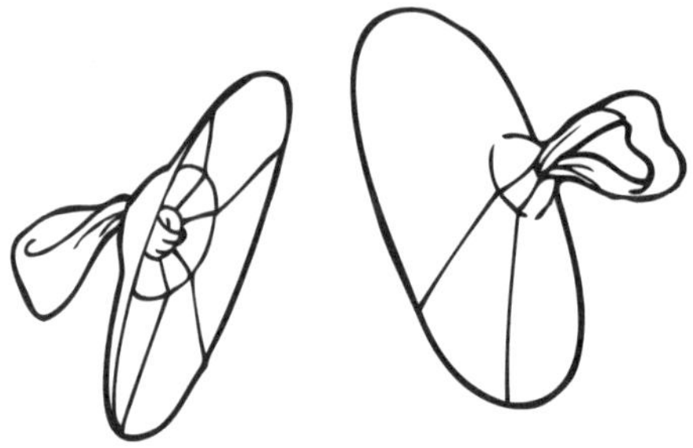

What Am I?

26 What am I?

What Am I?

27 What am I?

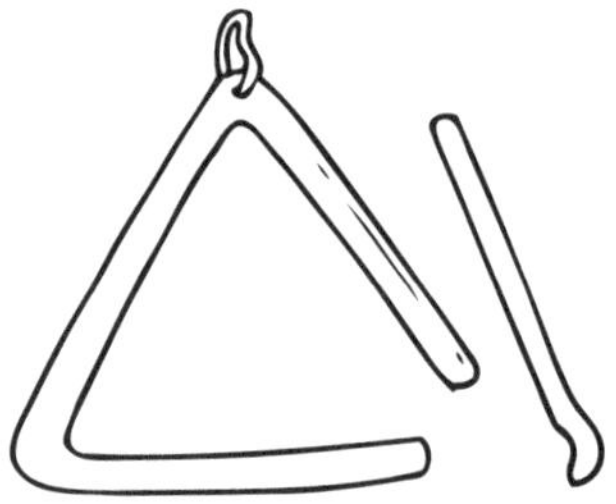

What Am I?

28 What am I?

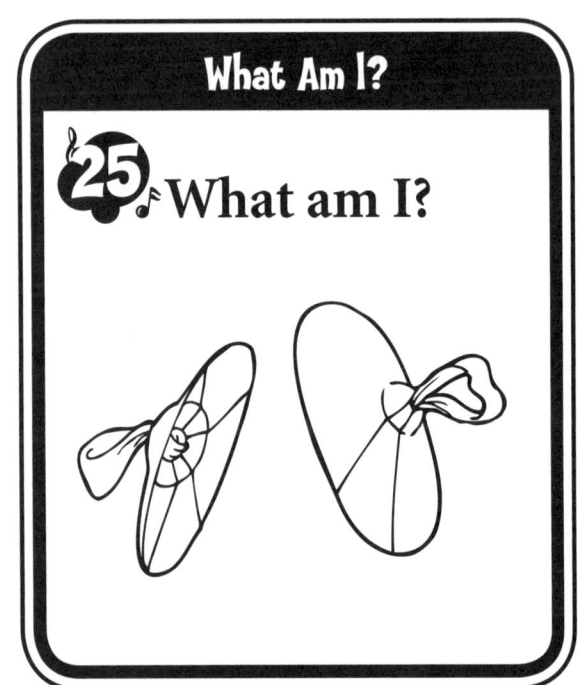

What Am I?

Instructions: Copy one set of cards for each team. Give each team a set of cards to play Showdown.

What Am I?

25

Hints:

1. I am a percussion instrument made of metal.
2. I am usually played in pairs.
3. I am played by crashing one against the other.
4. I can be found in a marching band or an orchestra.

What Am I?

26

Hints:

1. I am a percussion instrument made of metal.
2. I am played in pairs.
3. I am played by gently tapping one against the other.
4. I make a quiet sound.

What Am I?

27

Hints:

1. I am a percussion instrument made of metal.
2. My name sounds like a shape.
3. I am played by tapping a metal rod against one side of me.
4. I can be loud or quiet.

What Am I?

28

Hints:

1. I am a percussion instrument made of metal.
2. I am played by shaking.
3. I am often heard in Christmas music.

What Am I?

Instructions: Copy one set of cards for each team. Give each team a set of cards to play Showdown.

What Am I?

29 What am I?

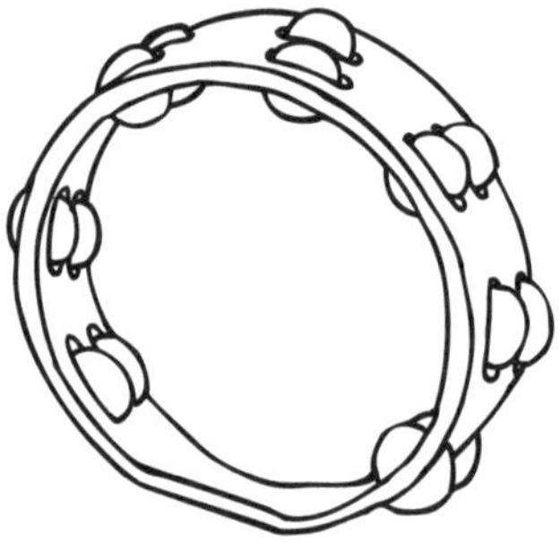

What Am I?

30 What am I?

What Am I?

31 What am I?

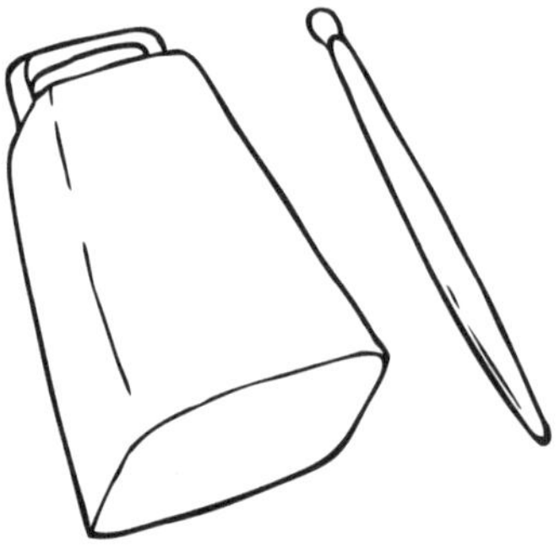

What Am I?

32 What am I?

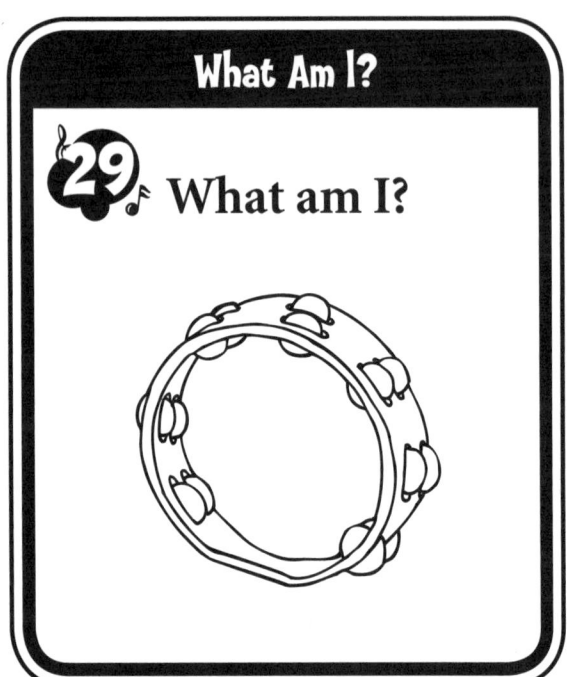

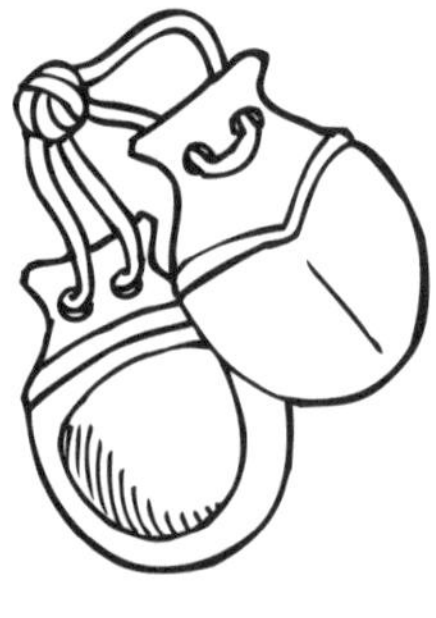

What Am I?

Instructions: Copy one set of cards for each team. Give each team a set of cards to play Showdown.

What Am I?

29 **Hints:**

1. I am a percussion instrument made of skin and metal.
2. I am played by shaking or by tapping.
3. I have one or two rows of jingles around my body.
4. I have a round shape.
5. I can also be headless, without the skin covering my body.

What Am I?

30 **Hints:**

1. I am a percussion instrument made of wood.
2. I am played in pairs.
3. I am played by gently rubbing one against the other.
4. I make a quiet sound.

What Am I?

31 **Hints:**

1. I am a percussion instrument made of metal.
2. I am played by tapping a stick against my side.
3. Sometimes there is a metal clapper inside me so I am played by shaking.
4. I make a loud sound.

What Am I?

32 **Hints:**

1. I am a percussion instrument made of wood.
2. I am played in pairs.
3. I am played by clicking one against the other.
4. I am often played by Flamenco dancers in Spain.

What Am I?

Instructions: Copy one set of cards for each team. Give each team a set of cards to play Showdown.

What Am I?

33 **What am I?**

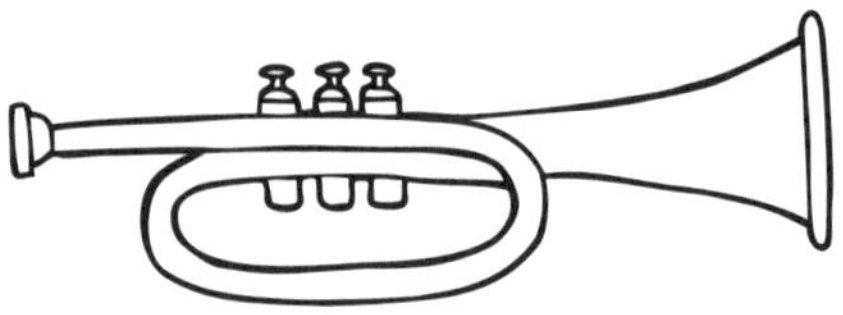

What Am I?

34 **What am I?**

What Am I?

35 **What am I?**

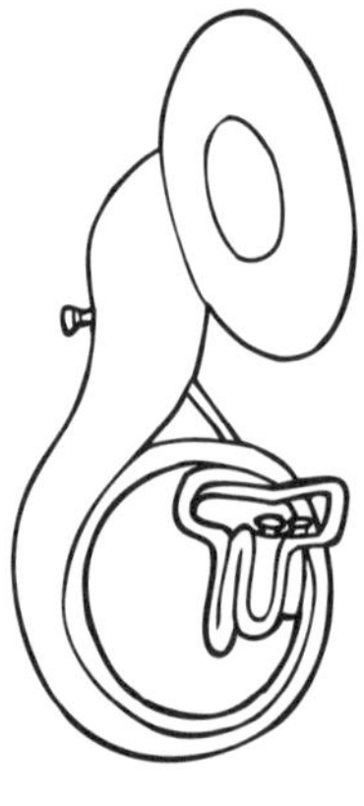

What Am I?

36 **What am I?**

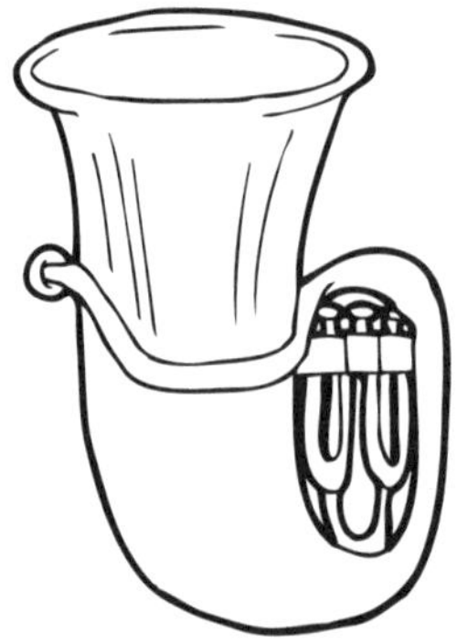

What Am I?

Instructions: Copy one set of cards for each team. Give each team a set of cards to play Showdown.

What Am I?

33 **Hints:**

1. I am a brass instrument.
2. I am the highest voice of the brass family.
3. I am played by blowing into my cup-shaped mouthpiece and pressing on valves to change pitch.
4. I make a loud sound.

What Am I?

34 **Hints:**

1. I am a brass instrument.
2. I have a low, rich voice in the brass family.
3. I am played by blowing into my cup-shaped mouthpiece and sliding one part of me in and out.
4. I make a loud sound.

What Am I?

35 **Hints:**

1. I am a brass instrument.
2. I have a low voice in the brass family.
3. I am played by blowing into my cup-shaped mouthpiece and pressing on valves to change pitch.
4. I am named after a famous composer.

What Am I?

36 **Hints:**

1. I am a brass instrument.
2. I am the lowest voice of the brass family.
3. I am played by blowing into my cup-shaped mouthpiece and pressing on valves to change pitch.
4. I am the largest member of my family.

What Am I?

Instructions: Copy one set of cards for each team. Give each team a set of cards to play Showdown.

What Am I?

37 What am I?

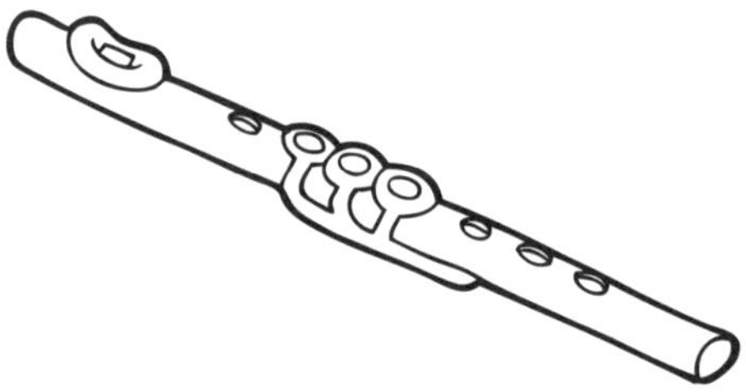

What Am I?

38 What am I?

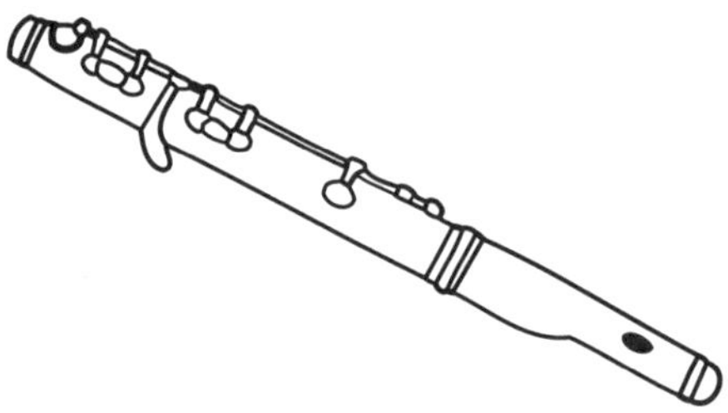

What Am I?

39 What am I?

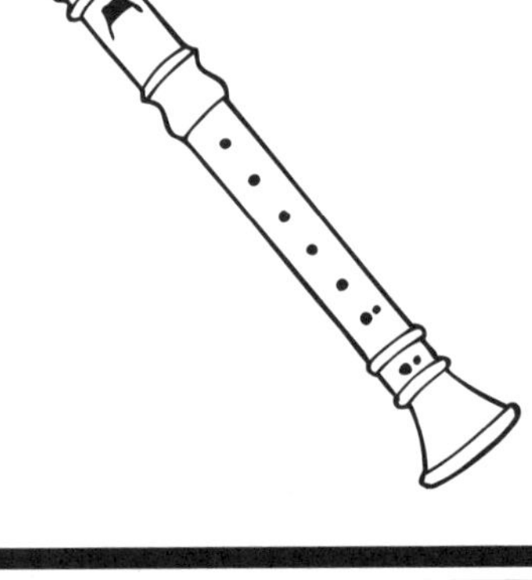

What Am I?

40 What am I?

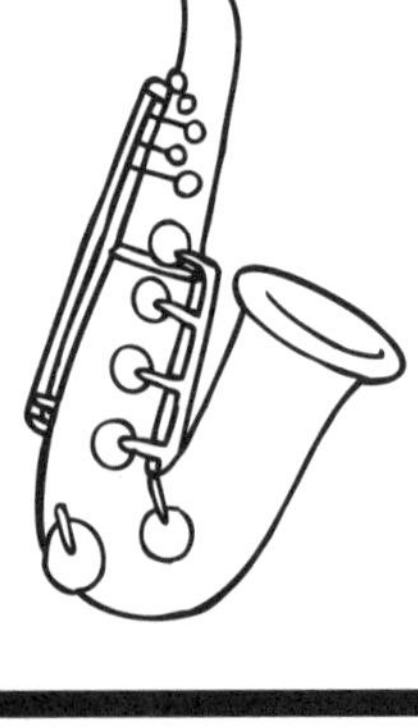

What Am I?

Instructions: Copy one set of cards for each team. Give each team a set of cards to play Showdown.

What Am I?

37

Hints:

1. I am a woodwind instrument.
2. I have a high voice.
3. I am played by blowing across the mouthpiece.
4. I am made of silver metal.
5. I am shaped like a tube.

What Am I?

38

Hints:

1. I am a woodwind instrument.
2. I have the highest voice in my family.
3. I am played by blowing across the mouthpiece.
4. I am made of silver metal or wood.
5. I am shaped like a tube.

What Am I?

39

Hints:

1. I am a member of the woodwind family.
2. I have a high voice.
3. I am played by blowing into a mouthpiece.
4. I can be made of wood or plastic.
5. I am shaped like a tube.
6. I have a quiet sound.

What Am I?

40

Hints:

1. I am a woodwind instrument.
2. I am made of brass.
3. I can be found in 4 different sizes.
4. I am played by blowing into a mouthpiece across a single reed.
5. I am shaped like a curved tube.

What Am I?

Instructions: Copy one set of cards for each team. Give each team a set of cards to play Showdown.

What Am I?

41 What am I?

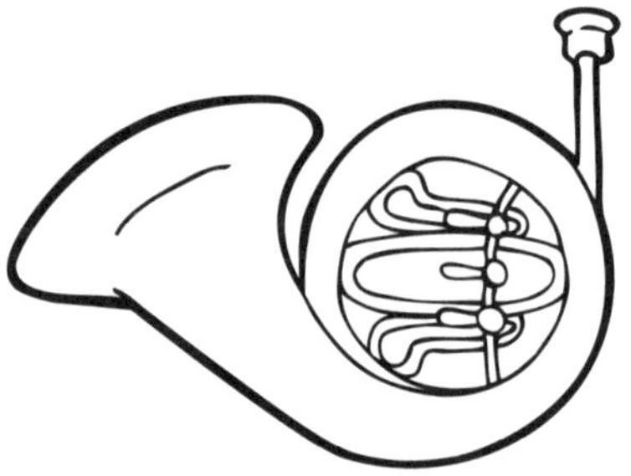

What Am I?

42 What am I?

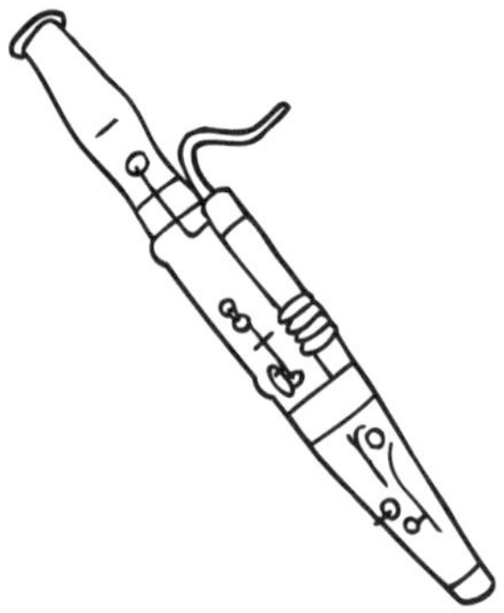

What Am I?

43 What am I?

What Am I?

44 What am I?

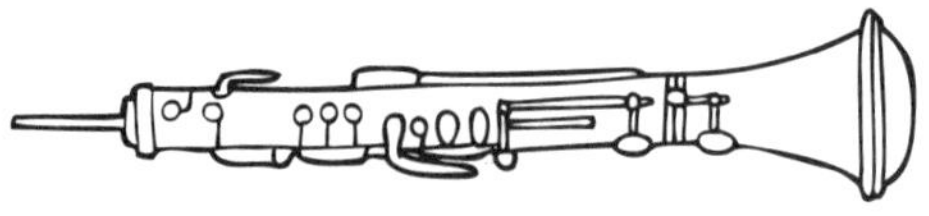

What Am I?

Instructions: Copy one set of cards for each team. Give each team a set of cards to play Showdown.

What Am I?

41

Hints:

1. I am a brass instrument.
2. I often play with the woodwind family.
3. I am played by blowing into the mouthpiece and pressing valves to change pitch.
4. I am 16-feet long if you could uncoil me!

What Am I?

42

Hints:

1. I am a woodwind instrument.
2. I have a low voice.
3. I am played by blowing into the mouthpiece across a double reed.
4. I am shaped like a tube that has been folded in half.

What Am I?

43

Hints:

1. I am a woodwind instrument.
2. I have a medium-high voice.
3. I am played by blowing into the mouthpiece across a single reed.
4. I am shaped like a tube.

What Am I?

44

Hints:

1. I am a woodwind instrument.
2. I have a medium-high voice.
3. I am played by blowing into the mouthpiece across a double reed.
4. I am shaped like a tube.
5. I give the orchestra the pitch for tuning.

What Am I?

Answer Key

1. autoharp
2. banjo
3. dulcimer
4. guitar
5. violin
6. viola
7. cello
8. double bass
9. harp
10. piano
11. chimes
12. gong
13. timpani drum
14. bass drum
15. conga drum
16. bongo drum
17. hand drum
18. snare drum
19. xylophone
20. wood block
21. maracas
22. guiro
23. Lummi sticks
24. cabasa
25. crash cymbals
26. finger cymbals
27. triangle
28. jingle bells
29. tambourine
30. sand blocks
31. cowbell
32. castanets
33. trumpet
34. trombone
35. sousaphone
36. tuba
37. flute
38. piccolo
39. recorder
40. saxophone
41. French horn
42. bassoon
43. clarinet
44. oboe

Blank Card Template

Instructions: Use this blank card template to create your own Showdown question cards.

Blank Card Template

Instructions: Use this blank card template to create your own Showdown question cards.

Section 2

Let's Talk & Write About Music

Structure 4

Timed Pair Share

Structure 4

Timed Pair Share

In pairs, students share with a partner for a predetermined time while the partner listens. Then partners switch roles.

Steps

Setup: *Students find a partner and respond to a prompt given by the teacher. Timed Pair Share enhances thinking skills and builds communication skills.*

Measures 1-12 (pg) practice ↑

1 **Teacher announces a topic, states how long each student will have to share, and provides think time.** *fingerings, pitch*

open-ended questions

The concert band has been working toward a performance, but the teacher senses that students have not been attending to private practice as diligently as they should. Near the end of the class session, the teacher announces the prompt: "*Why is practicing important?*" The teacher tells students they will have one minute to discuss this question with a partner in a Timed Pair Share. Students are given 5–7 seconds of think time (no talking, no writing—just thinking about how they will answer the question). Timed Pair Share can be done with a face or shoulder partner on the same team, or the teacher calls, "*Stand up, hand up, pair up*" for students to quickly find a talking partner.

2 **Partner A shares; Partner B listens.**

30 sec. steady beat - fingering

The teacher assigns Partner A and Partner B roles in each pair using a cue. ("*The one who has on the darkest color of clothing is Partner A.*") Partner A then has one minute to tell Partner B why it is important to practice. Partner B listens attentively.

3 **Partner B responds with a positive gambit.**

When the teacher calls "time" on Partner A's share time, Partner B then responds to give positive feedback to Partner A ("*I understand that you think practicing is important because you said…*") and then praises Partner A's effort ("*Your ideas really made me think about this!*").

4 **Partners switch roles.**

Partner B now offers thoughts about the importance of practicing to Partner A for the one-minute time limit, and Partner A will be given the opportunity to provide feedback.

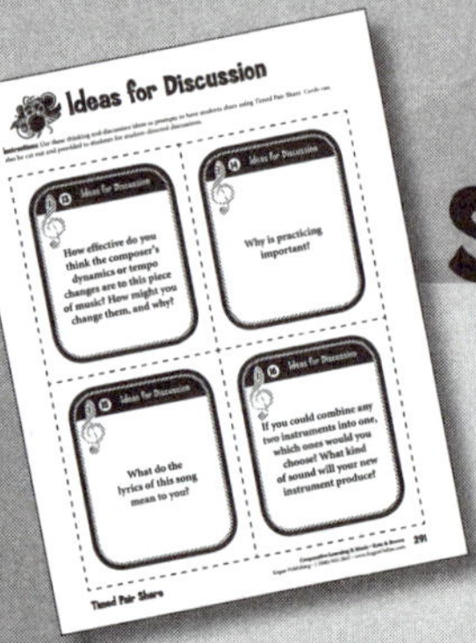

Sample Activity

The importance of practice: Pairs take turns sharing their thoughts on the discussion prompt, "*Why is practicing important? Think about the practicing done during band rehearsals, as well as individual practice outside of class time.*"

Benefits

- All students are actively involved.
- Students interact with a partner.
- Students learn and practice social skills: patience, active listening, compassion, tolerance, accepting and giving praise, and taking turns.
- Students gain practice in paraphrasing and giving feedback.

Hints

- **Model.** Teacher models both the sharing component and the various ways that positive feedback can be given.

- **Prompts.** This structure uses only open-ended questions as prompts: opinions, predictions, "wrap-up" reviews to learning sequences or class lessons, etc.

- **Management Tips.**
  - Master this structure first in a seated position before adding in the component of standing or moving around the room.
  - When seated, students turn to face the student beside or nearest to them.
  - Gp of 3 A-30 B-20 B-20

- **"StandUp-HandUp-PairUp."** Another Kagan Structure is often used to find a partner; movement energizes students and produces additional nourishment for the brain in the form of oxygen and glucose.

- **Time Limits.**
  - "Think Time" should be limited to 3–5 seconds, up to a maximum of 10 seconds, in order to keep students on task with the prompt.
  - Primary students (preK–2nd grade): When the structure is first introduced, give 10–15 seconds of talking time. Increase the time gradually, up to a maximum of 30 seconds, as students become more comfortable and proficient with the structure.
  - Intermediate elementary (3rd–5th grade) and secondary (middle and high school) students: Begin with 30 seconds, increasing the talking portion of the structure up to a maximum of two minutes per person.
  - All talking time limits should be connected to the difficulty of the specific higher-level thinking question, the students' developmental level of communication skills, and the grade level of the students.

- **Write Time.** For intermediate and secondary students, allowing them to write down their ideas prior to talking reinforces individual accountability.

- **Examples of Response Gambits.**
  Copycat response gambits ("*Tell your partner…*):
  - "*Thanks for sharing!*"
  - "*You are interesting to listen to!*"

  Complete the sentence gambits:
  - "*One thing I learned listening to you was…*"
  - "*I enjoyed listening to you because…*"
  - "*Your most interesting idea was…*"

Structure 4 Timed Pair Share (continued)

Principles

P Positive Interdependence: Students share new ideas that benefit others.

I Individual Accountability: Students are accountable when offering their own unique ideas in response to a prompt.

E Equal Participation: Equal time provides equal opportunity to talk.

S Simultaneous Interaction: 50% of the students are speaking at once.

* Open-ended / Discussion quest. (pg 288-294)

* PRACTICE ~ Enhance Performance

Timed Pair Share Activities

Note: *In Timed Pair Share, the teacher provides the discussion prompt for partners to take turns sharing their ideas. The following activities provide a variety of higher-level thinking music discussion prompts. The prompts are provided on cards so you may also give them to students for a student-led Timed Pair Share or for use with another discussion structure such as RoundRobin (see page 298).*

Ideas for Discussion 288-294

The cards in this set are for discussing higher-level thinking questions with a partner. Partners take turns thinking about their answer to a question, share with their partners, and then switch roles after giving each other feedback and praising their partner's efforts. *Recommended for upper elementary level students (3rd–6th grade) and secondary level students.*

Blank Card Templates.. 295-296

Use these blank card templates to create your own Timed Pair Share cards.

Additional Activities for Timed Pair Share Question Cards

Question cards can be used for Structure 2: Fan-N-Pick (one set of cards per team). Students experience the function of Thinking Skills during Fan-N-Pick with discussion.

Ideas for Discussion

Instructions: Use these thinking and discussion ideas as prompts to have students share using Timed Pair Share. Cards can also be cut out and provided to students for student-directed discussions.

1 Ideas for Discussion

If you could play any instrument, which one would it be and why?

2 Ideas for Discussion

A producer has asked you to write the musical score for a movie. Describe the music and instrumentation you would use and why.

3 Ideas for Discussion

The Grammy Awards has nominated you for "Best New Artist." If you win, who would you thank and why?

4 Ideas for Discussion

It is said, *Attitude reflects leadership.* Pretend you are the conductor of the symphony. Tell us what it is like getting on the podium and leading an orchestra. What are you thinking about? How do you help your musicians with stage fright?

Ideas for Discussion

Instructions: Use these thinking and discussion ideas as prompts to have students share using Timed Pair Share. Cards can also be cut out and provided to students for student-directed discussions.

5 Ideas for Discussion

Athletes prepare for competition in many ways. What do you do as a musician? How do you prepare for a performance?

6 Ideas for Discussion

The Grammy Awards has nominated you for "Outstanding Artist." In what category of music are you nominated and why?

7 Ideas for Discussion

As the music director of a new school, you have been allowed to spend $50,000 on your new music program. What kind of music program are you starting? How would you spend the money and why?

8 Ideas for Discussion

You are traveling to another country to meet students your age. You are allowed to bring only one CD (compact disc) with you. Which one would you bring and why?

Ideas for Discussion

Instructions: Use these thinking and discussion ideas as prompts to have students share using Timed Pair Share. Cards can also be cut out and provided to students for student-directed discussions.

9 Ideas for Discussion

If you were allowed to choose only one song from your iPod, which one would you recommend to your friends and why?

10 Ideas for Discussion

Besides music classes, what are other elective classes that you would sign up for and why?

11 Ideas for Discussion

The Board of Education is considering a plan to eliminate all music programs at your school. What do you say to defend the impact of music in your life?

12 Ideas for Discussion

What emotions do you think the composer of this piece was trying to convey through the music? What did you hear in the music to support your idea?

Ideas for Discussion

Instructions: Use these thinking and discussion ideas as prompts to have students share using Timed Pair Share. Cards can also be cut out and provided to students for student-directed discussions.

13 Ideas for Discussion

How effective do you think the composer's dynamics or tempo changes are to this piece of music? How might you change them, and why?

14 Ideas for Discussion

Why is practicing important?

15 Ideas for Discussion

What do the lyrics of this song mean to you?

16 Ideas for Discussion

If you could combine any two instruments into one, which ones would you choose? What kind of sound will your new instrument produce?

Ideas for Discussion

Instructions: Use these thinking and discussion ideas as prompts to have students share using Timed Pair Share. Cards can also be cut out and provided to students for student-directed discussions.

17 Ideas for Discussion

What story or picture came to your mind as you were listening to this music? What did you hear in the music that created that story or picture?

18 Ideas for Discussion

What color would you associate with this music, and why?

19 Ideas for Discussion

Who is your favorite composer, and why do you like his (or her) music?

20 Ideas for Discussion

You have been commissioned to write a fanfare for an upcoming event. What instruments will you choose to play in it, and why?

Ideas for Discussion

Instructions: Use these thinking and discussion ideas as prompts to have students share using Timed Pair Share. Cards can also be cut out and provided to students for student-directed discussions.

21 Ideas for Discussion

Based on the music excerpt you have just heard, how do you predict the composer will finish the piece?

22 Ideas for Discussion

Why is it important for the performers to watch their conductor?

23 Ideas for Discussion

Which is your favorite family of instruments from the orchestra, and what do you like about their tone color?

24 Ideas for Discussion

Compare the two versions of the piece you just heard. What was different about them? What was alike about them? Which one did you like better, and why?

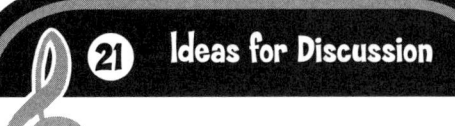

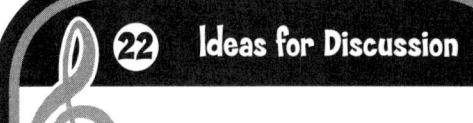

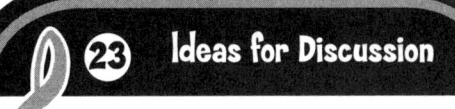

Ideas for Discussion

Instructions: Use these thinking and discussion ideas as prompts to have students share using Timed Pair Share. Cards can also be cut out and provided to students for student-directed discussions.

25 Ideas for Discussion

Who do you think is the most important member of the orchestra, and why?

26 Ideas for Discussion

Which element of music (melody, harmony, rhythm, form, texture, expression) do you think is the most important, and why?

27 Ideas for Discussion

28 Ideas for Discussion

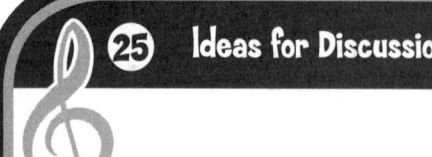

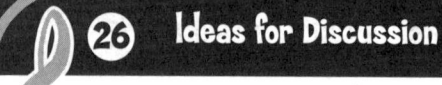

Blank Question Card Template

Instructions: Use this blank card template to create your own question cards for discussion.

Ideas for Discussion

Ideas for Discussion

Ideas for Discussion

Ideas for Discussion

Blank Question Card Template

Instructions: Use this blank card template to create your own question cards for discussion.

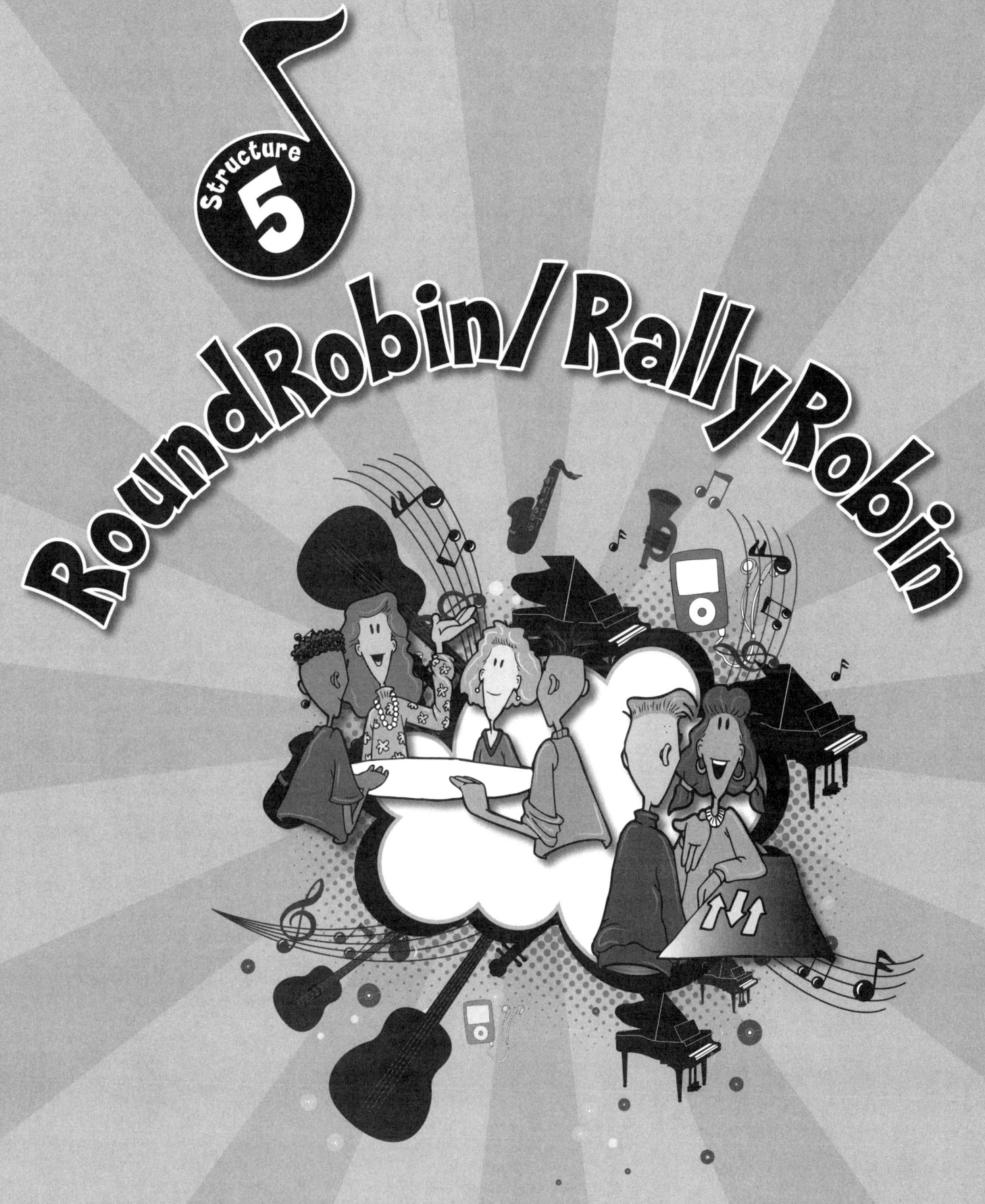

Structure 5

RoundRobin/ RallyRobin

Structure 5

RoundRobin/ RallyRobin

(4) (2)

Students take turns responding orally. In RoundRobin, students take turns in their teams. In RallyRobin, partners take turns.

Steps

1 Teacher poses a prompt to which there are multiple possible responses or solutions, and provides think time.
The teacher prepares a prompt. For example, the teacher asks students to listen to a music selection and to identify instruments they hear. After listening, the teacher allows 3–5 seconds of think time, and cues which student will start the list. For example, "*the one who got up earliest this morning.*"

- quick verbal list
- short answer responses

(singing/playing)

- Tune
- Line
- Measures
- phrases
- Scale

2 Students take turns stating responses or solutions.
In RallyRobin, each partner, in turn, lists one instrument that he or she heard in the selection. For example, Partner A states "*guitar,*" Partner B states "*drums,*" Partner A states "*fiddle,*" Partner B states "*flute,*" etc. In RoundRobin, teammates list an instrument on his or her turn. Students continue to add to the list until the teacher calls, "*Stop,*" or gives a signal (such as chiming a bell or playing a fanfare on the piano). Students thank their partners (or teammates) for sharing. RallyRobin is great for having pairs generate a list of ideas or examples. For example, "*Create a list of popular bands.*" RoundRobin is also used to create an oral list in teams. RoundRobin can also be used to have teammates share elaborated responses. For example, "*Who is your favorite band and why?*"

Sample Activity

What Did You Hear? After listening to a musical selection, partners or teammates take turns listing an instrument they heard.

Benefits

- All students are actively involved.
- Students interact with their teammates or partners.
- Students learn and practice social skills: encouraging contributions, quiet voices, responsibility, sharing, working together, active listening, and taking turns.
- Students gain new ideas or insights.

Hints

- **Model.** Model how to generate a list by doing a RallyRobin in front of the class with a student helper. Use the student helpers to model a RoundRobin for the class.
- **Prompts.** Use prompts with multiple ideas or examples so students can create a verbal list.
- **Think Time.** Allow from 3–5 seconds of time, up to a maximum of 10 seconds, for students to independently think about possible solutions. No talking or writing is allowed during think time. The think time allows the brain to process ideas. Students will create responses spontaneously as partners and teammates share ideas that trigger new ideas and as students think of more ideas and examples.
- **Write Time.** Intermediate or secondary students may also be given the option of writing their answers before sharing, especially during a RoundRobin. For example, given the prompt of "Key Signatures," the students in a high school theory class are given 10 seconds to write down as many as they can remember; then, in the RoundRobin, each member of the team, in turn, shares one from their written list.

Structure 5 RoundRobin/RallyRobin (continued)

Variations

Raindrop. The teacher includes a short "debriefing" after the structure by polling students for "raindrops" of information. For example, the teacher randomly selects 4–5 students to tell the class something their teammate or partner added to the list. The teacher can assess the accuracy of responses, as well as assess active listening.

RoundRobin Variations:

- **Single RoundRobin**—Each student responds only once to the prompt.
- **Continuous RoundRobin**—Students continue to take turns, in order, until the teacher calls, "*Stop.*"
- **Timed RoundRobin**—The teacher sets a time limit for each student response; each student shares until his or her time is up, then the next teammate shares. Timed RoundRobin works best for elaborate thinking and discussion prompts.
- **AllWrite RoundRobin**—Each student has a paper (blank); everyone writes down each response shared on their own paper.

Principles

P **Positive Interdependence:** Students need each other to participate to do these turn-taking structures. They benefit from the ideas they hear from other students.

I **Individual Accountability:** Students are responsible for offering their own unique ideas in response to the prompt.

E **Equal Participation:** All participation is equal through taking turns.

S **Simultaneous Interaction:** RallyRobin (in pairs)—50% of the students are talking; RoundRobin (in teams of 4)—25% are talking at once.

RoundRobin/RallyRobin Activities

Extension to the Lesson: RoundRobin with a Twist

Setup: *Teams are seated in small circles; each student has a plastic cup, but one cup is a different color from all the rest of the set. The teacher plays a listening selection with a steady duple-meter beat while students pass the cups simultaneously around the circle (pick-up, pass, pick-up, pass, etc.).*

When the music stops, the teacher asks a question that requires multiple responses. For example, "*Can you and your team spell the word melody?*" or "*Can you and your team chant the rhythm pattern I'm showing you?*" The student who is holding the different-colored cup begins (in the example, say "*M*" or "*ta*"), with subsequent letters or rhythm notes being passed counterclockwise until the word or pattern is finished (Continuous RoundRobin). The music and cup passing are resumed, and a different question is presented the next time the music stops.

Musical Lists

Teacher Instructions: Students take turns creating a verbal list to these prompts.

1 Create a verbal list of...

Titles or styles of music composed during a specific style period (Baroque, Classical, etc.).

2 Create a verbal list of...

Musical styles (Renaissance, Baroque, Classical, Romantic, Modern, Jazz, Folk, March, Lullaby, Gospel, Rock-n-Roll, Rap, etc.).

3 Create a verbal list of...

Style characteristics (Renaissance, Baroque, Classical, Romantic, Modern, Jazz, Folk, March, Lullaby, Gospel, Rock-n-Roll, Rap, etc.).

4 Create a verbal list of...

Major composers from the various periods of music history.

5 Create a verbal list of...

Composer facts (after studying about a particular composer).

Musical Lists

Teacher Instructions: Students take turns creating a verbal list to these prompts.

6 Create a verbal list of...

Instruments of the orchestra and the family of the instrument.

7 Create a verbal list of...

Folk instruments, instruments used for accompaniment, or instruments from other cultures.

8 Create a verbal list of...

Qualities that distinguish a person as a "musician."

9 Create a verbal list of...

Qualities of an accomplished performer.

10 Create a verbal list of...

Qualities of a good section leader.

Musical Lists

Teacher Instructions: Students take turns creating a verbal list to these prompts.

11 Create a verbal list of...

Qualities of a successful marching band.

12 Create a verbal list of...

Qualities of a good conductor.

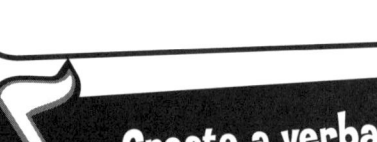

13 Create a verbal list of...

Names of dynamics and what their symbols look like.

14 Create a verbal list of...

Names of dynamics and their meanings.

15 Create a verbal list of...

Harmonic changes heard in a musical selection.

Musical Lists

Teacher Instructions: Students take turns creating a verbal list to these prompts.

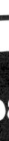

16 Create a verbal list of...

Types of harmony.

17 Create a verbal list of...

Key Signatures (naming the sharps or flats for the key selected).

18 Create a verbal list of...

Vocal ranges for both male and female members of a choir.

19 Create a verbal list of...

Jazz artists the class has studied and performed pieces by so far.

20 Create a verbal list of...

Instruments heard in a musical selection.

Musical Lists

Teacher Instructions: Students take turns creating a verbal list to these prompts.

21 Create a verbal list of...

Tempo markings and their meanings.

22 Create a verbal list of...

Classroom percussion instruments: what they are made of or how they are played.

23 Create a verbal list of...

Letter names of the staff and where notes are located on the staff.

24 Create a verbal list of...

Alphabetized instrument names (begin with "A" then partner gives "B," etc.).

25 Create a verbal list of...

Solfege notes of the pentatonic scale.

Musical Lists

Teacher Instructions: Students take turns creating a verbal list to these prompts.

26 Create a verbal list of...

Ways that a melody can move.

27 Create a verbal list of...

Note durations.

28 Create a verbal list of...

Examples of form structures.

29 Create a verbal list of...

Enharmonic tones (example: partner A says "G sharp" for partner B to respond "A flat"—then partner B says "B flat" for partner A to respond "A sharp").

30 Create a verbal list of...

Spelling vocabulary words: composers' names (one letter at a time).

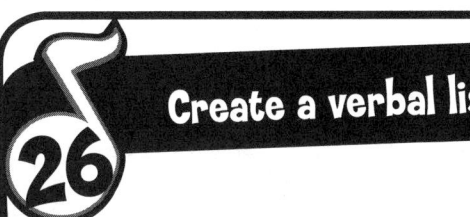

Taking Turns Performing

Teacher Instructions: Students take turns singing, clapping, or playing a musical instrument.

1 Sing or play...

Rhythm Clap (partner A claps a rhythm, partner B chants in syllables—then trade roles).

2 Sing or play...

Sing or play a song in "hocket": partners (Rally) or team members (Round) take turns playing 2 measures at a time until the song is complete.

3 Sing or play...

Sing or play a particular scale (major, minor, pentatonic): partners (Rally) or team members (Round) take turns adding to the scale until it is complete.

4 Sing or play...

Sing or play a sequence: partners (Rally) or team members (Round) perform the next pattern in a sequence.

5 Sing or play...

Sing or play a song: partners or teammates each take a turn preforming.

Structure 6

Simultaneous RoundTable

Structure 6

Simultaneous RoundTable

In teams, students each write a response on their own piece of paper. Students then pass their papers clockwise so each teammate can add to the prior responses.

Steps

Setup: Each team of four needs four papers and four pencils.

1 The teacher assigns a topic or question and provides think time.
For example, students in teams are given the worksheet "Label It!" Think time is provided for each student to preview the worksheet and consider how to begin responding (no writing during think time).

2 All four students respond, simultaneously writing, drawing, or building something with manipulatives.
In our example, each student chooses one box on the page to fill in with the name of the music symbol required. (It is not necessary for everyone to fill in the same box.)

3 The teacher signals time, or students signal to teammates when they are finished with the first problem.
When students are finished with the first symbol they have chosen to identify, each student signals silently by pretending to conduct a 3/4 meter in the air (using their pencils as batons).

4 Students pass papers or projects one person clockwise.
Each student passes the worksheet to the person on his or her left.

5 Students continue, adding to what was already completed.
Each student selects another music notation symbol to identify on the paper he or she received. When finished, students begin conducting as in Step 3.

6 Repeat structure, starting at Step 3.
Students continue to identify symbols and pass papers until all boxes have been filled in. After all have been completed, papers are returned to the original "owners." Students keep their papers to use as a test review.

Sample Activity

Label It! In a team of four, each teammate receives the same Label It! worksheet. Students label a piece of music using words in a word bank. Teammates label one item, then pass the papers for teammates to label another item. All teammates simultaneously complete the four worksheets.

Benefits

- All students are actively involved.
- Students interact with their teammates.
- Students learn and practice social skills: checking for understanding, patience, responsibility, encouraging others, and working together.
- By using different worksheets, many music concepts can be reinforced.
- Simultaneous RoundTable supports lesson concepts or skills during Checking for Understanding or lesson closure.

Hints

- **Model.** Teacher selects four students to demonstrate marking on a paper, giving a pre-arranged signal of completion (in the example given, "conducting" with their pencils), and passing.
- **Management.**
  - Students are responsible for marking their papers independently.
  - All papers pass at the same time. Do not pass papers ahead of teammates.
- **Coaching.** If a correct answer is required (as in the "Label It!" worksheet example), add coaching in order for the next student to be successful. Teach the process "tip, tip, tell, re-ask" as a coaching model.
- **Avoid Distractions.** Do not play music during the structure. Remind students to use "quiet voices" (mezzo-piano dynamic level), so all can participate without interfering with others nearby.
- **Student-Driven.** Simultaneous RoundTable is an untimed structure in order to allow each team to work at their own pace.

Structure 6 Simultaneous RoundTable (continued)

Variations

- **Pass-N-Praise.** Students compliment the student who passes them the paper for contribution. Students are instructed not to release their paper until they receive a compliment that makes them feel good.
- **Related Topic Papers.** Instead of every student using the same worksheet, Simultaneous RoundTable works well when each of the 4 papers are labeled with 4 related topics (for example: identifying instruments in the four orchestral families, writing the names of composers from the four major historical time periods of music).
- **RoundRobin.** Have students do a RoundRobin before Simultaneous RoundTable to discuss the topic. RoundRobin may also be used after the Simultaneous RoundTable to process the worksheet or project, or to discuss what students learned.

Principles

P **Positive Interdependence:** Students need each other to complete the worksheet. A student's knowledge or skill benefits his or her teammates.

I **Individual Accountability:** Each individual student is required to answer in the presence of teammates.

E **Equal Participation:** Equal opportunity is provided through turn-taking.

S **Simultaneous Interaction:** 100% of the students are actively writing on the paper.

A Note About the Activity

The Blackline Activities for Structure 6: Simultaneous RoundTable and Structure 7: RoundTable/RallyTable begin on page 318 and continue to page 328. The activities are grouped together because they work well with any of these RoundTable variations.

Structure 7

Simultaneous RoundTable/ RoundTable/RallyTable

Structure 7

Simultaneous RoundTable RoundTable/RallyTable

Students take turns generating written responses, solving problems, or making a contribution to a project. In RoundTable, students take turns in their teams. In RallyTable, partners take turns.

Steps

__Setup:__ The teacher prepares a worksheet or asks a question that requires many possible responses. One worksheet is distributed per team (RoundTable) or one worksheet per pair (RallyTable).

1 The teacher provides a task to which there are multiple possible responses, and provides think time.

In our Bar Line Relay example, the activity is done as a RoundTable in teams. Teams are given a page of un-metered music notation. The teacher gives students 3–5 seconds of think time to consider silently how the beats will be divided into measures in accordance with the time signature.

2 Students take turns passing a paper and pencil or a team project, each writing one answer or making a contribution.

The first student recognizes the time signature, counts the appropriate number of beats required, and draws the first bar line on the worksheet. The paper and pencil are then passed counterclockwise to the next teammate who continues to count beats from the latest bar line addition and adds the next bar line on the paper. The worksheet continues to rotate around the team until the last person places the double bar line at the end of the page.

RallyTable: To do the activity as RallyTable, pairs add bar lines, one at a time, until the page is completely marked with measures in the correct meter.

Sample Activity

Bar Line Relay: Before starting the structure, the teacher leads a whole-class review of dividing music notation into measures in 4/4 meter. Then, students do a RoundTable to divide the beats into measures. Each student adds a bar line, then passes the paper to the next teammate.

Benefits

- All students are actively engaged.
- Students interact with their teammates (or partners).
- Students learn and practice social skills: encouraging contributions, checking for understanding, responsibility, taking turns, and working together.
- By using different worksheets, many music concepts can be reinforced.
- RoundTable and RallyTable support lesson concepts or skills during Checking for Understanding or lesson closure.

Hints

- **Model.** Teacher models thinking strategies for answering problems from the worksheet.
- **Management.**
  - Each student is responsible for his or her own work.
  - Primary level students need assistance with paper rotation.
  - Need 1 paper per team (Round), 1 paper per pair (Rally).
  - AnswerBoards are an alternative to sharing worksheets.
- **Coaching.** If a correct answer is required (as in the "Bar Line" worksheet example), add coaching in order for the next student to be successful. Teach the process "tip, tip, tell, re-ask" as a coaching model.
- **Avoid Distractions.** Do not play music during the structure. Remind students to use "quiet voices" (mezzo-piano dynamic level), so all can participate without interfering with other teams.
- **Review First.** Before doing a worksheet, lead the class in a review of the topic or skill. You may use the answer sheets for these worksheets to present the skill or topic.

Structure 7 Simultaneous RoundTable/ RoundTable/RallyTable (continued)

Variations

- **Pass-N-Praise.** Students praise the contribution of the person passing the paper to them before writing the next addition to the list.
- **RoundTable Consensus.** Students must reach consensus before recording each answer.
- **Timed.** The teacher may add a time limit for teams or pairs to complete the task.

Principles

P **Positive Interdependence:** Students benefit from the contribution of each teammate (RoundTable) or partner (RallyTable) and need each other to complete the task.

I **Individual Accountability:** Each student is accountable to his or her team or partner for writing answers, or adding to the lists.

E **Equal Participation:** Students participate equally through turn-taking.

S **Simultaneous Interaction:** 25% (RoundTable) or 50% (RallyTable) of the students are actively contributing answers.

Simultaneous RoundTable/RoundTable/RallyTable

Activities

Note: These activities may be done using any of the following structures: Simultaneous RoundTable, RoundTable, or RallyTable.

Bar Line Relay

Instructions: Draw a bar line to divide the beats into measures in 4/4 meter, then pass the paper.

Names_______________________________ **Date** _______________

Simultaneous RoundTable/ RoundTable/RallyTable

Seating Chart for the Symphony Orchestra

Instructions: Write the name of a musical instrument in the correct place on the seating chart, then pass the paper.

Names____ **Date** ____

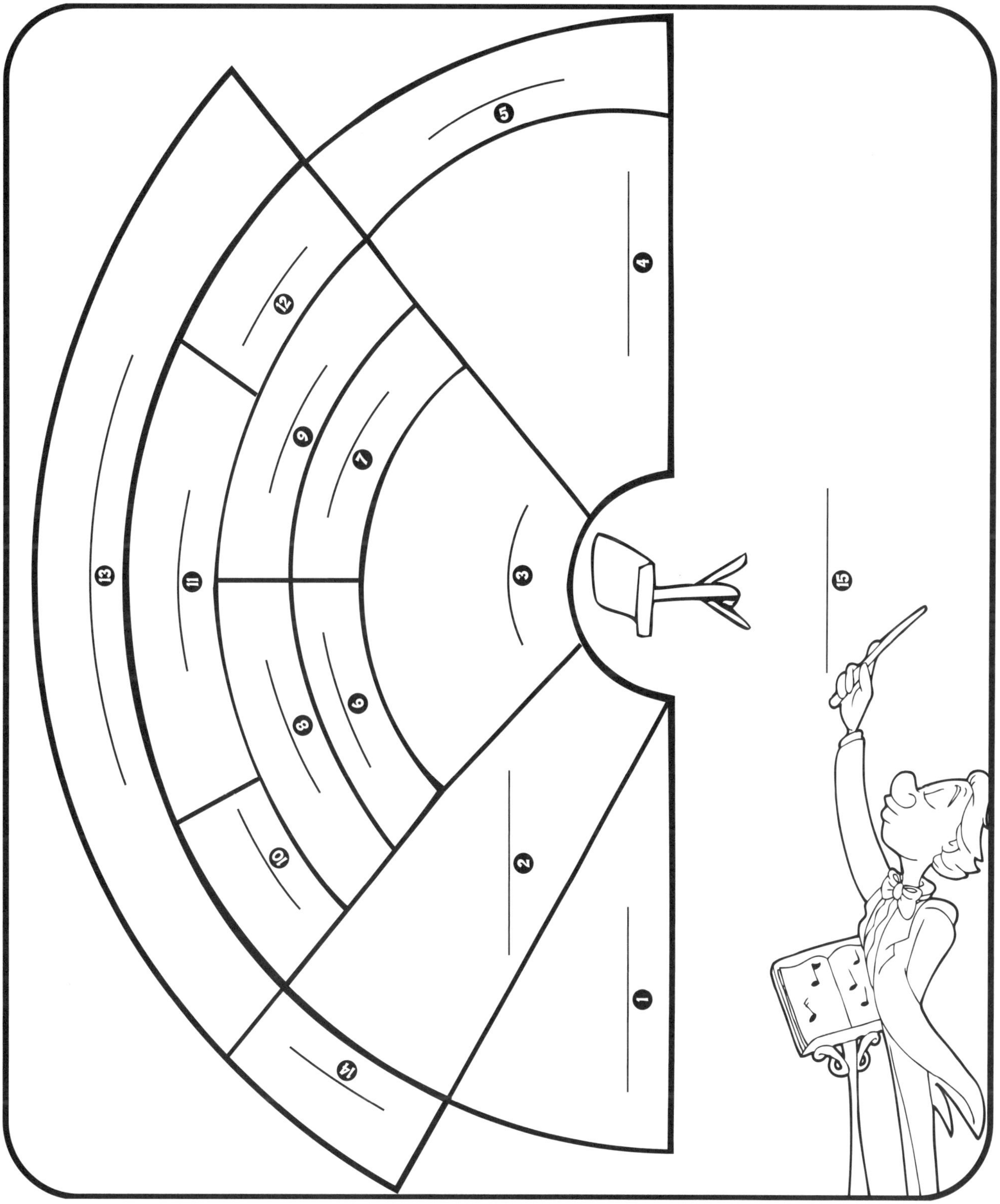

Simultaneous RoundTable/ RoundTable/RallyTable

Seating Chart for the Symphony Orchestra

Answer Key

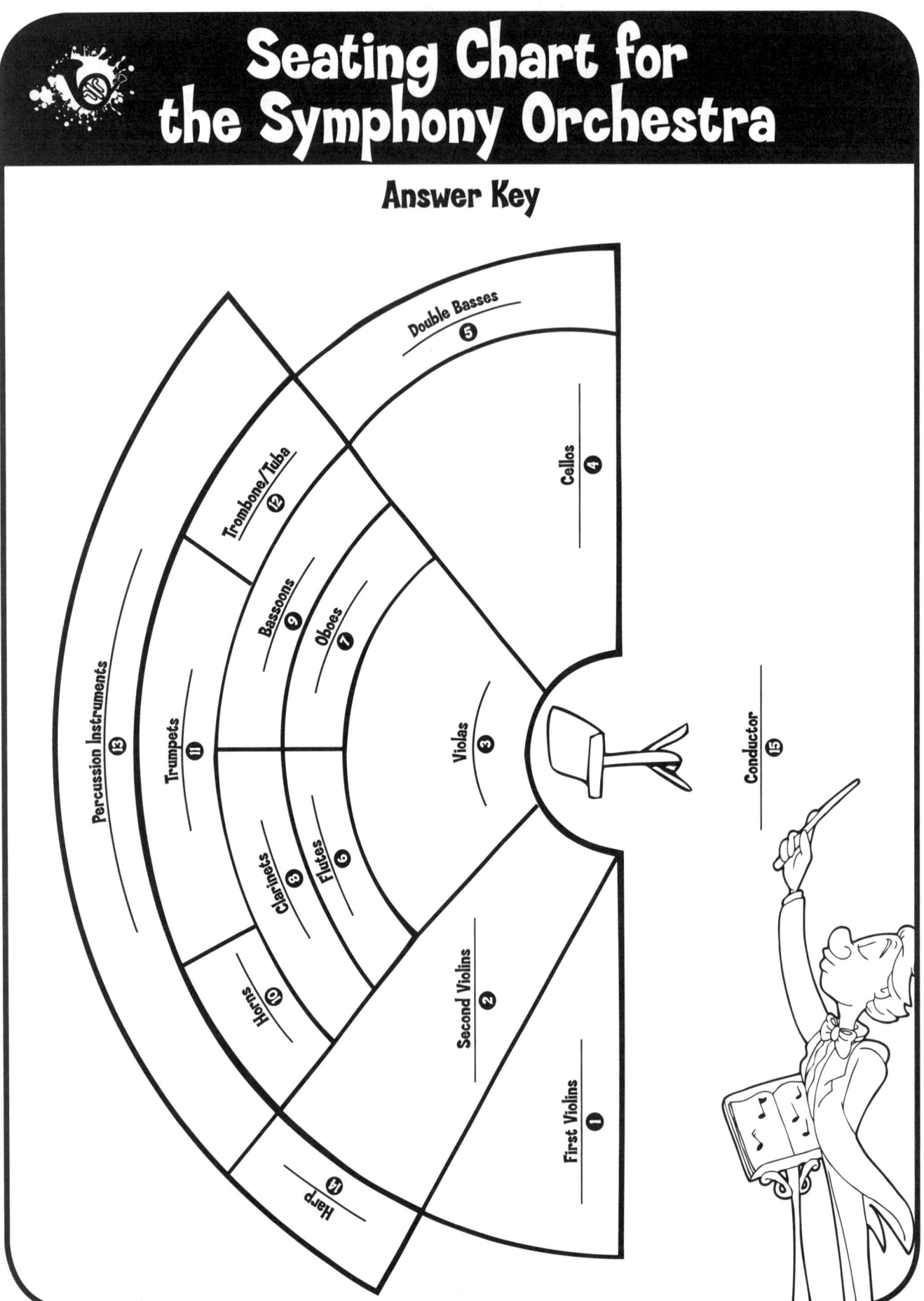

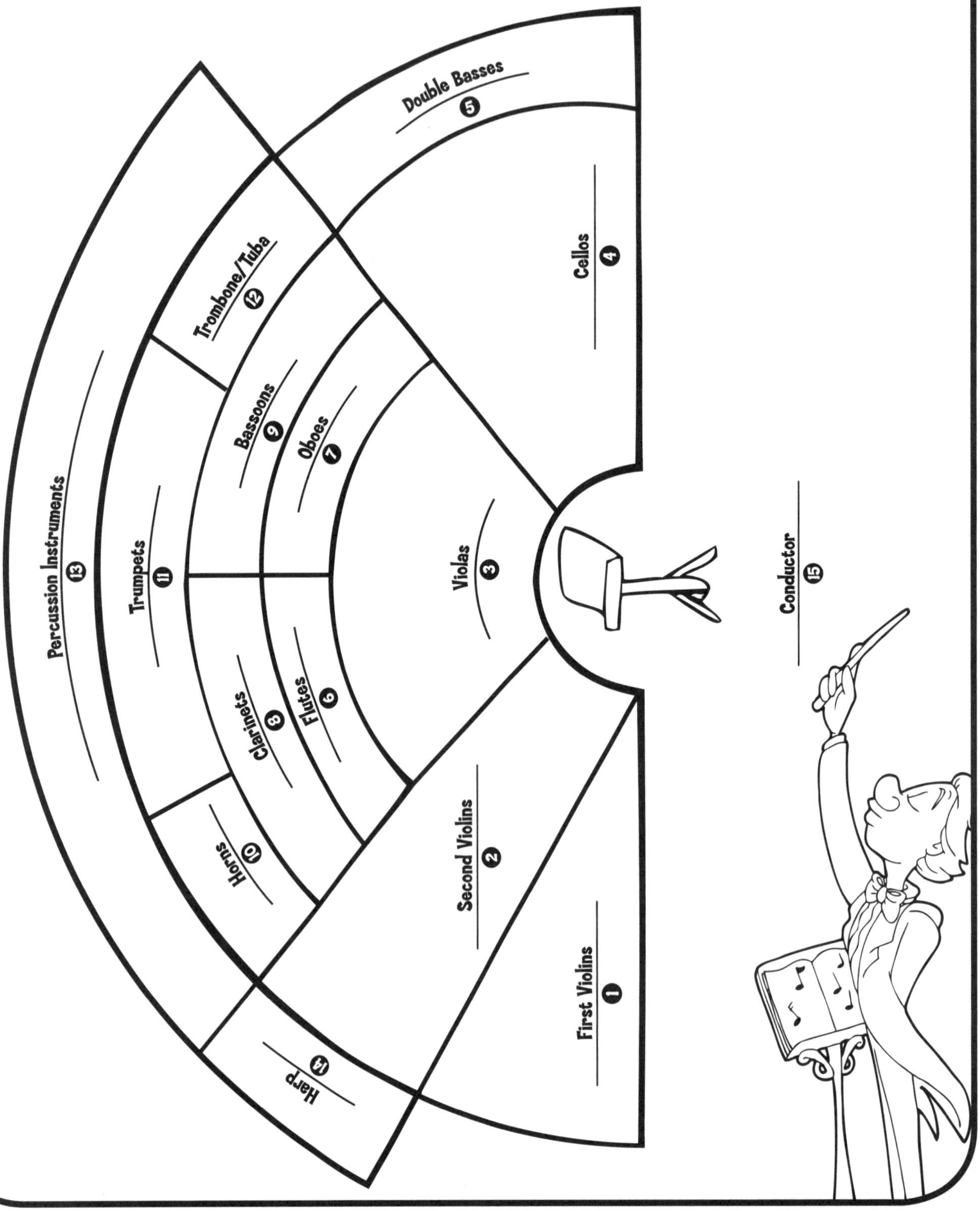

Simultaneous RoundTable/ RoundTable/RallyTable

Label It!

Instructions: Using the word bank, write the name of a note or symbol in a box, then pass the paper.

Names ______________________________ **Date** ______________________________

Word Bank

Treble Clef	Triplet	Measure	Double Bar Line
Quarter Notes	Rests	Bar Line	Syncopation
Eighth Notes	Meter Signature	Whole Note	Dotted Half Note
Staff	Half Notes	Sixteenth Notes	

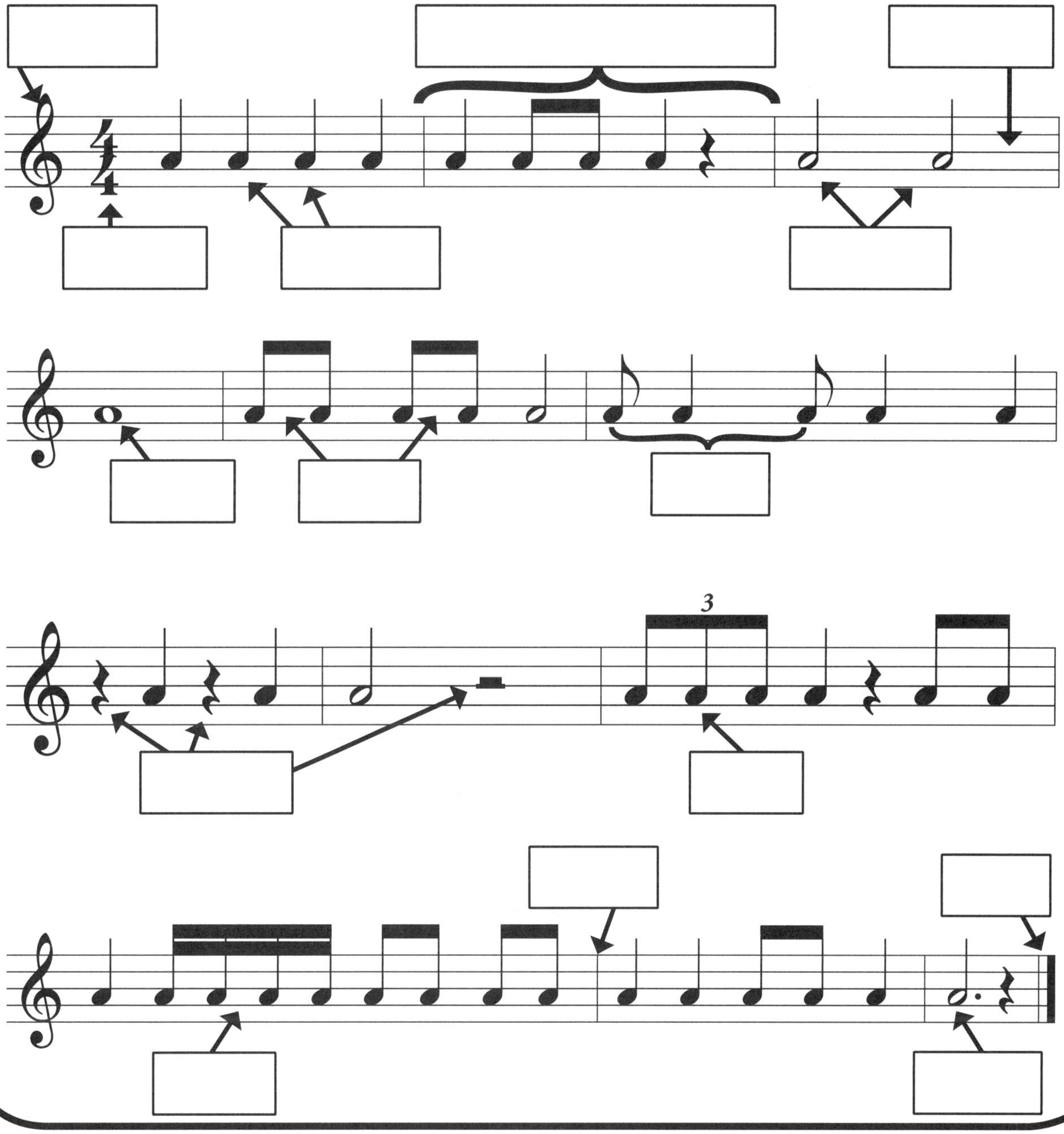

Simultaneous RoundTable/ RoundTable/RallyTable

Label It!

Answer Key

Word Bank

Treble Clef	Triplet	Measure	Double Bar Line
Quarter Notes	Rests	Bar Line	Syncopation
Eighth Notes	Meter Signature	Whole Note	Dotted Half Note
Staff	Half Notes	Sixteenth Notes	

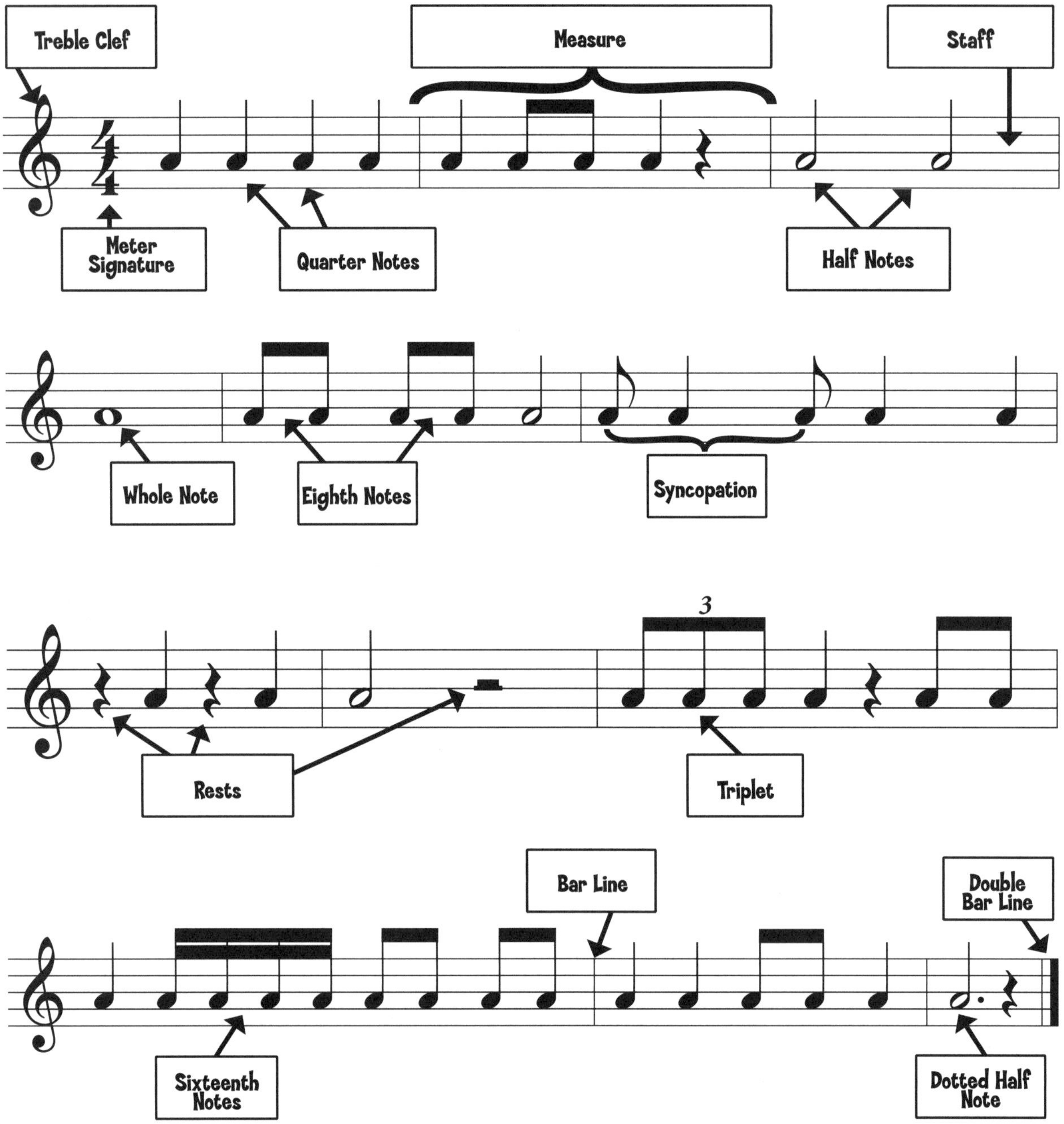

Music Cues and Symbols

Instructions: Next to each term, write a letter corresponding to the correct music cue or symbol in the Answer Bank, then pass the paper.

Names__________________________________ **Date** __________________________________

______**1.** **Bar lines**–divide the beats into measures

______**2.** **Staff**–where melody notes are written

______**3.** **Accent**–a stronger beat than the others around it

______**4.** **Fermata**–makes the note a little bit longer than normal

______**5.** **First and Second Endings**–a way to repeat, but end differently the second time

______**6.** **Repeat Signs**–tells the performer to repeat the selection exactly

______**7.** **Double Bar**–the end of the music

______**8.** **Meter Signature**–tells how many beats in each measure, and what kind of note will get one beat

Answer Bank

A. 

B. 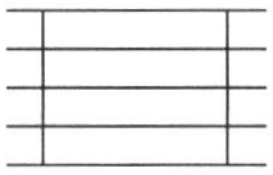

C. 

D. >

E. 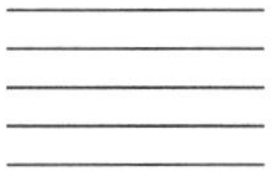

F. 

G. $\frac{2}{4}$

H. 

Music Cues and Symbols

Answer Key

1 Bar Lines

Divide the beats into measures

B

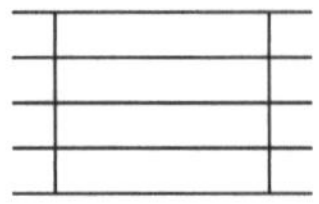

2 Staff

Where melody notes are written

E

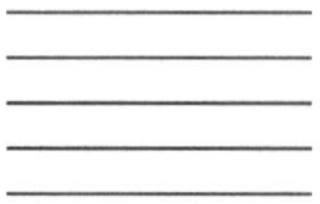

3 Accent

A stronger beat than the others around it

D

4 Fermata

Makes the note a little bit longer than normal

A

5 First & Second Endings

A way to repeat, but end differently the second time

H

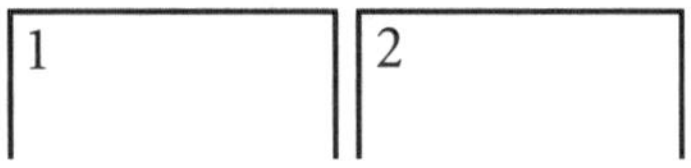

6 Repeat Signs

Makes the performer repeat the selection exactly

C

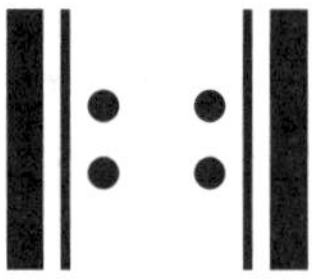

7 Double Bar

The end of the music

F

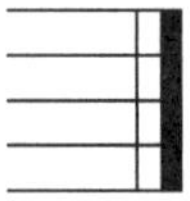

8 Meter Signature

Tells how many beats in each measure, and what kind of note will get one beat

G $\frac{2}{4}$

Simultaneous RoundTable/
RoundTable/RallyTable

Beat Math!

Instructions: Compete a line of beat math, then pass the paper.

Names______________________________ **Date** ______________________________

Example:

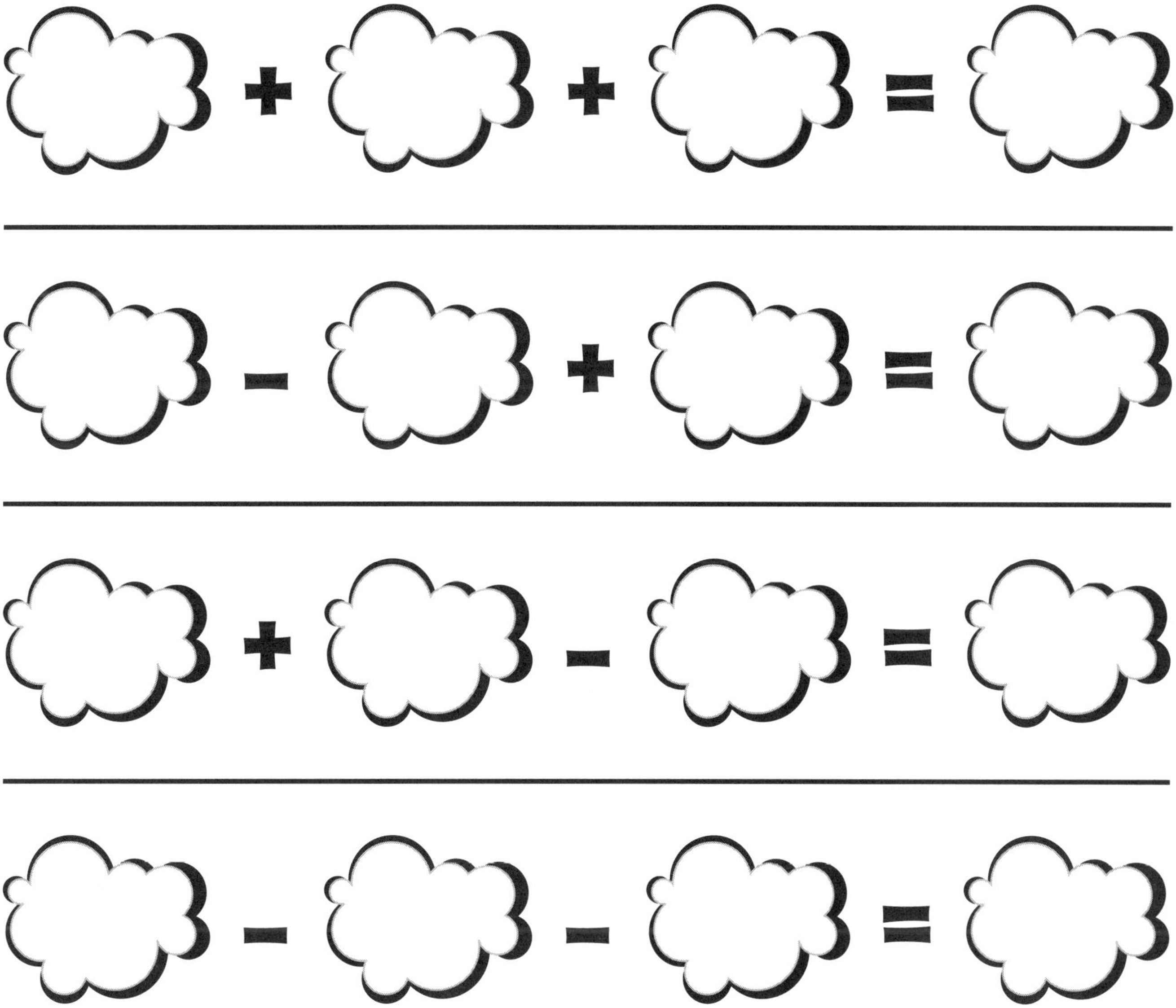

Beat Math!

Instructions: Add a beat in each cloud and a plus (+) or minus (-) symbol in each box. Complete a line of beat math, then pass the paper.

Names ______________________________ **Date** ______________________________

Simultaneous RoundTable/ RoundTable/RallyTable

Additional Activity Ideas

Set-Up: Here are a number of activity ideas for use with RoundTable, Simultaneous RoundTable, and RallyTable.

Primary Level (PreK–2nd Grade)

- Draw circles around all the pictures of instruments on a page that must be tapped (or shaken, or scraped) when they are played.
- Draw squares around all the pictures of instruments on a page that are made of metal, wood, or skin.
- Draw notes to add to a rhythm pattern.
- Draw notes on a staff to add to a composition.
- Name the notes of the treble clef staff.
- Sing one or two measures of familiar songs, or sight-read short melody patterns.
- Demonstrate a steady beat.

Upper Elementary Level (3rd–5th Grade)

- Make a list of dynamic levels.
- Make a list of instruments from each section of the orchestra.
- List the instruments from world cultures.
- Finish the Rhythm—given an incomplete measure, students add notes to finish it. (There are multiple responses possible.)
- Sing simple examples in pentatonic tonality.
- Create a rhythmic composition by adding notes one at a time.
- Create a melodic composition by adding tones on a staff one at a time.
- Draw the notation for rhythm durations.
- Draw notation for the pentatonic scale.
- Draw music notation symbols.
- Identify intervals found in notation.
- Identify melodies that move by step, leap, or repeated tones.
- Spell words by adding one letter at a time (teacher or class helper call out the vocabulary word or composer's name; all teams begin on cue).
- Make a list of emotions that music can express.
- Make a list of music history style periods.
- List the duties of a conductor.

Additional Activity Ideas

Set-Up: Here are a number of activity ideas for use with RoundTable, Simultaneous RoundTable, and RallyTable.

Secondary Level (6th–12th Grade)

- List composers or composition titles.
- List facts about a composer (style, biography, etc.).
- Draw the sharps or flats on the staff in order.
- Identify keys from key signature notation.
- Build key signatures (major or minor).
- Create a composition (rhythmic or melodic).
- Build chords by placing notes on a staff.
- Identify intervals (from notation examples).
- List the form structures in music.
- Make a list of musical styles.
- List characteristics of various musical styles.
- Perform short melodic or rhythmic examples.
- Make a comparison of musical styles (e.g., "folk" versus "jazz").
- Make a list of dances.
- List the steps to learning a new piece of music.
- List practice/rehearsal strategies.

Structure 8

Find Someone Who

Structure 8

Find Someone Who

Students circulate through the classroom, forming and reforming pairs, trying to "find someone who" knows an answer, then they become "someone who knows."

Steps

Setup: The teacher prepares a worksheet or questions for students.

1 Students mix in the class, keeping a hand raised until they find a partner that is not a teammate.
Students take paper and pencil in one hand while walking around until they each connect with a classmate who will become their first partner.

2 In pairs, Partner A asks a question from the worksheet; Partner B responds. Partner A records the answer on his or her own worksheet and expresses appreciation.
The first student, "Partner A," selects one of the questions to ask. In our Interval Identification example, Partner A asks, "*What is the interval shown in this frame?*" Partner B tells the answer, "*That is a perfect 5th.*" Partner A writes down the answer given by Partner B and thanks Partner B for the information.

3 Partner B checks and initials the answer.
Partner B checks to be sure Partner A recorded the answer exactly as Partner B had given it, then initials beside it to accept responsibility for the answer.

4 Partner B asks a question; Partner A responds. Partner B records the answer on his or her own worksheet and expresses appreciation.
Roles are now reversed; Partner B selects a different question from the worksheet, "*What interval is this frame showing?*" Partner A gives the answer, "*It is an octave.*" Partner B then writes Partner A's response and thanks Partner A.

5 Partner A checks and initials the answer.
Partner A checks to be sure Partner B recorded the answer exactly as Partner A had given it, then initials beside it to accept responsibility for the answer.

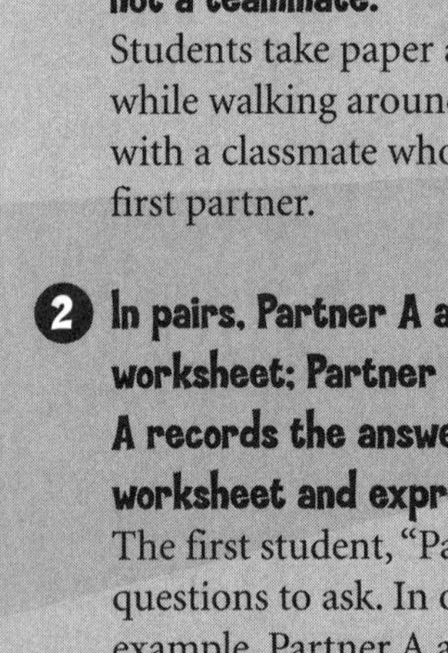

Sample Activity

Interval Identification: Each student receives a worksheet displaying various interval relationships for identification. Students pair up with various partners to identify all the intervals on the worksheet.

Steps (continued)

6 Partners shake hands, and raise a hand as they search for a new partner.
Any departing gambit may be used. There are many ways to say "*goodbye*" and "*thank you.*"

7 Students repeat steps 1-6 until their worksheets are complete.
Students continue to work at their own pace until worksheets are completed.

8 When their worksheets are complete, students sit down.
Seated students may be approached by others as a resource.

9 In teams, students compare answers.
If there is disagreement or uncertainty, they raise four hands to ask a team question. Using a RoundRobin, students take turns sharing one answer at a time.

Benefits

- All students are actively involved.
- Students interact with their classmates.
- Students learn and practice social skills: patience, responsibility, problem solving, active listening, and following directions.
- Students interview classmates to check for understanding of content.
- By using different worksheets, many music concepts can be reinforced.
- Find Someone Who supports lesson concepts or skills during Guided Practice, Checking for Understanding, or Lesson Closure.

Find Someone Who (continued)

Hints

- **Model.** The teacher chooses a student to help model the structure using one of the questions from the worksheet. A beginning process of modeling is "*I ask, you answer, I write,*" and then switch roles.
- **Management.** Watch for groups of more than two students or students not quickly pairing up.
- **Avoid Distractions.** Do not play music while the structure is progressing. Remind students to use "quiet voices" (mezzo-piano dynamic level), so all can participate without interfering with others nearby.
- **Worksheets.**
  - It is not necessary to answer the questions in order, but all questions must be completed before students sit down.
  - Remind students that they are expected to write the answers given to them on their own papers.
  - Primary level (preK–2): Use worksheets with visuals and matching as appropriate for reading and writing ability levels.

Principles

P **Positive Interdependence:** Students need each other to complete their worksheets.

I **Individual Accountability:** Students are giving answers, listening, recording, and checking answers in front of someone else.

E **Equal Participation:** Students participate equally as the role of questioner or responder is traded among partners.

S **Simultaneous Interaction:** In a "snapshot moment," 50% of the students are asking the questions while the other 50% are giving answers.

Find Someone Who Activities

Additional Activities for Find Someone Who Worksheets

Worksheets can be used with Structure 9: RallyCoach (one worksheet per pair).

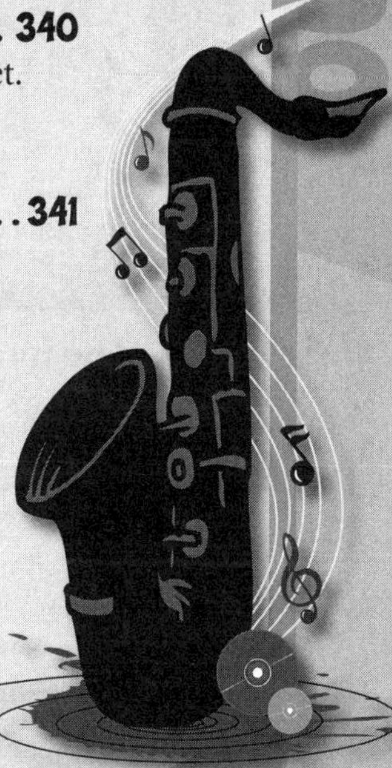

Name That Form!

Find Someone Who

Instructions: Find a partner who can answer a problem on your worksheet. Write the answer and have your partner initial it.

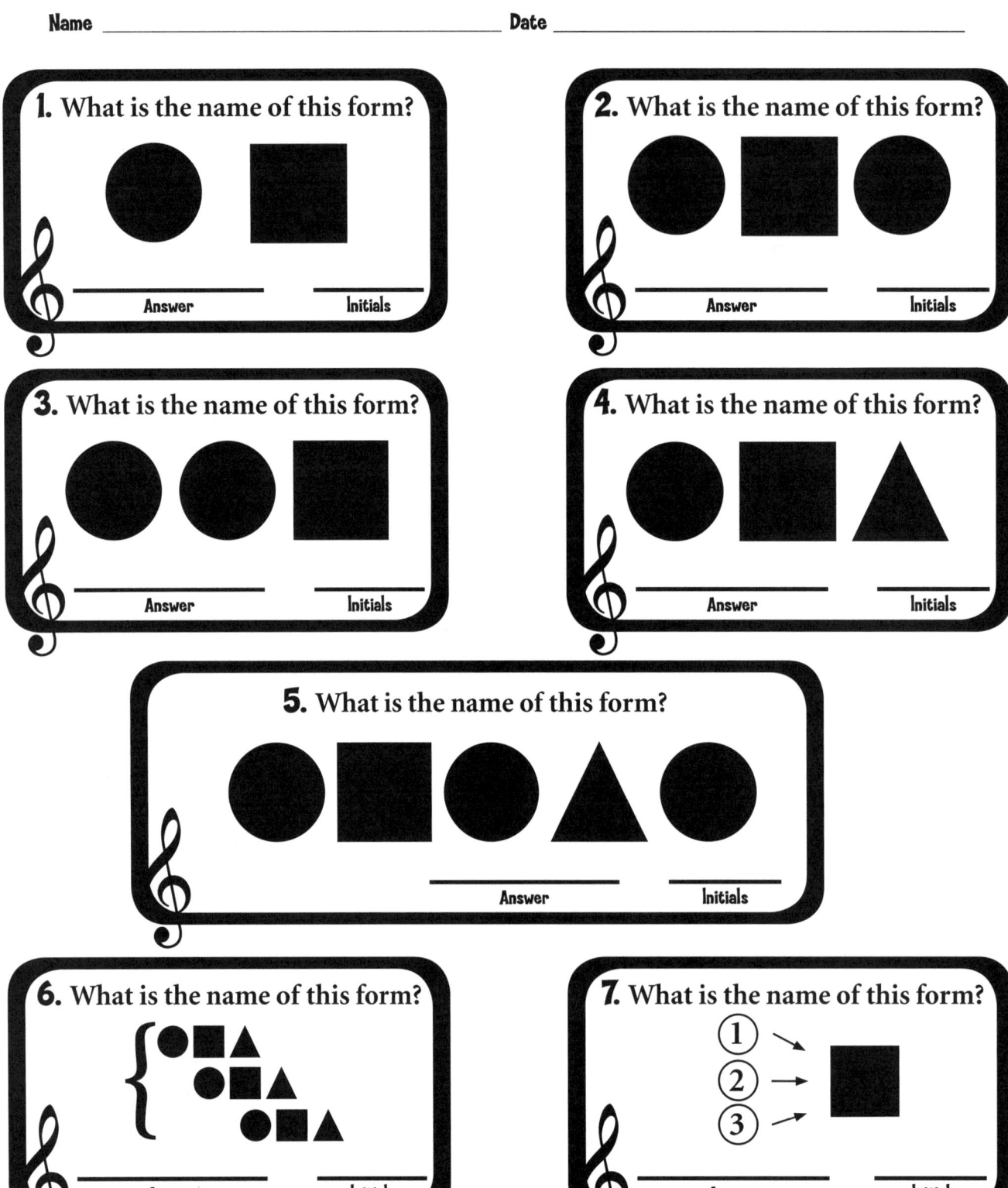

Name ______________________________ **Date** ______________________________

1. What is the name of this form?

______________ Answer ______________ Initials

2. What is the name of this form?

______________ Answer ______________ Initials

3. What is the name of this form?

______________ Answer ______________ Initials

4. What is the name of this form?

______________ Answer ______________ Initials

5. What is the name of this form?

______________ Answer ______________ Initials

6. What is the name of this form?

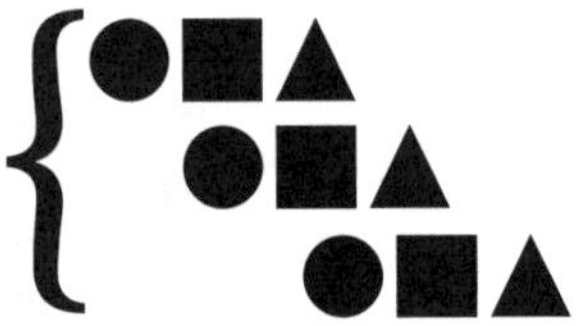

______________ Answer ______________ Initials

7. What is the name of this form?

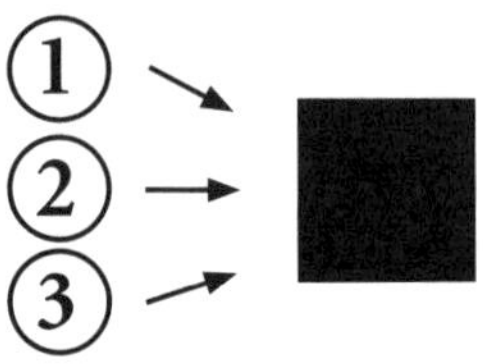

______________ Answer ______________ Initials

It's Instrumental: How It's Played

Find Someone Who

Instructions: Find a partner who can answer a problem on your worksheet. Write the answer and have your partner initial it.

Name ______________________________ **Date** ______________________________

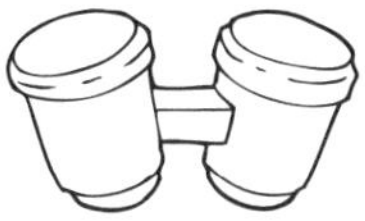

Initials

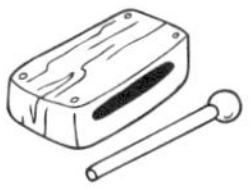

Initials

Initials

Initials

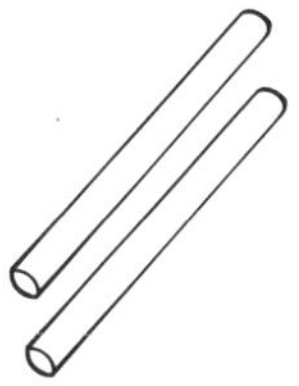

Initials

Initials

Tap It!

Scrape It!

Shake It!

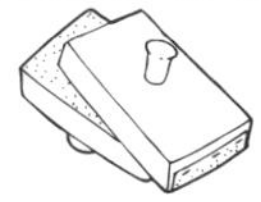

Initials

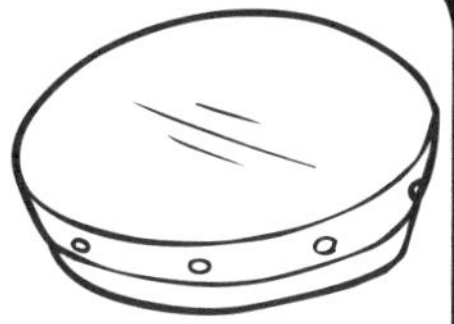

Initials

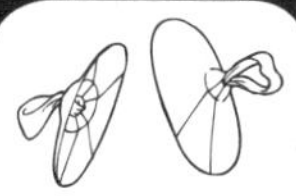

Initials

Initials

Initials

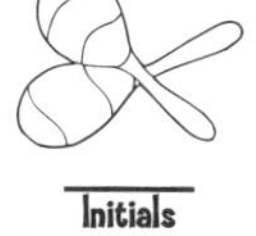

Initials

Initials

It's Instrumental: How It's Made

Find Someone Who

Instructions: Find a partner who can answer a problem on your worksheet. Write the answer and have your partner initial it.

Name ______________________ **Date** ______________________

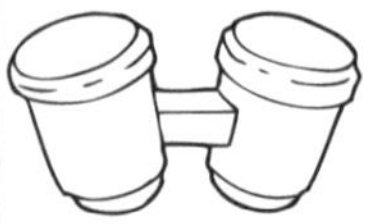

Initials

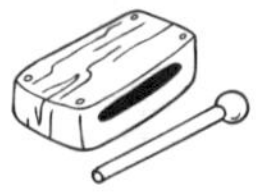

Initials

Initials

Initials

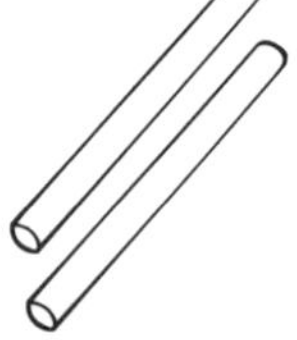

Initials

Initials

Made of Wood

Made of Metal

Made of Skin

Initials

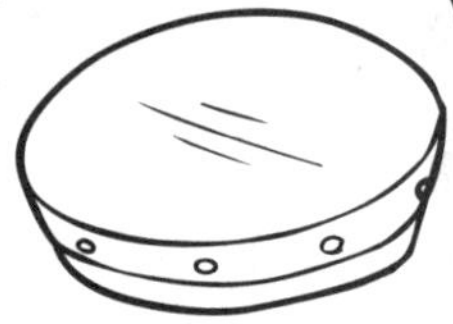

Initials

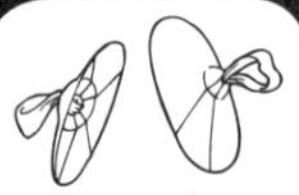

Initials

Initials

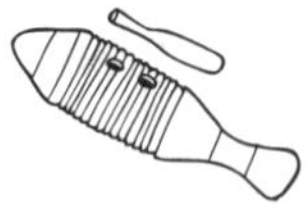

Initials

Initials

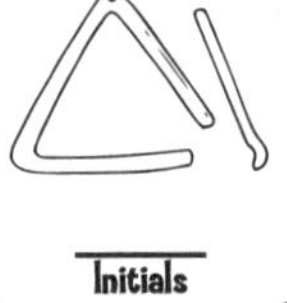

Initials

Melody: Step, Leap, Repeat?

Find Someone Who

Instructions: Find a partner who can answer a problem on your worksheet. Write the answer and have your partner initial it.

Name ______________________ **Date** ______________________

Dynamics and Tempo
Find Someone Who

Instructions: Find a partner who can answer a problem on your worksheet. Write the answer and have your partner initial it.

Name ______________________ **Date** ______________________

1
What do changes in DYNAMICS sound like?
____
____
______ Initials

2
What do changes in TEMPO sound like?
____
____
____
______ Initials

3
Which one of these symbols are **louder**? (*circle your answer*)
f *mf*
______ Initials

4
Which one of these symbols are **softer**? (*circle your answer*)
p *pp*
______ Initials

5
Which one of these tempos are **faster**? (*circle*)
Adagio Allegro
______ Initials

6
Which one of these tempos are **slower**? (*circle*)
Largo Presto
______ Initials

7
What does crescendo mean?
____
____
____
______ Initials

8
What does accelerando mean?
____
____
____
______ Initials

9
What does mezzo-piano mean?
____
____
____
______ Initials

10
What does fortissimo mean?
____
____
____
______ Initials

Interval Identification

Find Someone Who

Instructions: Find a partner who can answer a problem on your worksheet. Write the answer and have your partner initial it.

Name ______________________ **Date** ______________________

1 Name the interval

______________ Answer ☐ Initials

2 Name the interval

______________ Answer ☐ Initials

3 Name the interval

______________ Answer ☐ Initials

4 Name the interval

______________ Answer ☐ Initials

5 Name the interval

______________ Answer ☐ Initials

6 Name the interval

______________ Answer ☐ Initials

Blank Frame Template
Find Someone Who

Instructions: Use this blank frame template to create your own Find Someone Who worksheet.

Name ______________________ **Date** ______________________

______ Answer ______ Initials

______ Answer ______ Initials

______ Answer ______ Initials

______ Answer ______ Initials

______ Answer ______ Initials

______ Answer ______ Initials

______ Answer ______ Initials

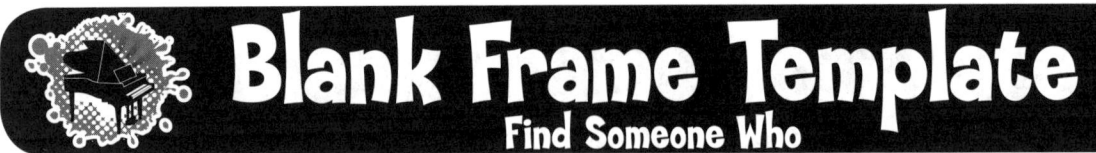

Find Someone Who

Answer Key

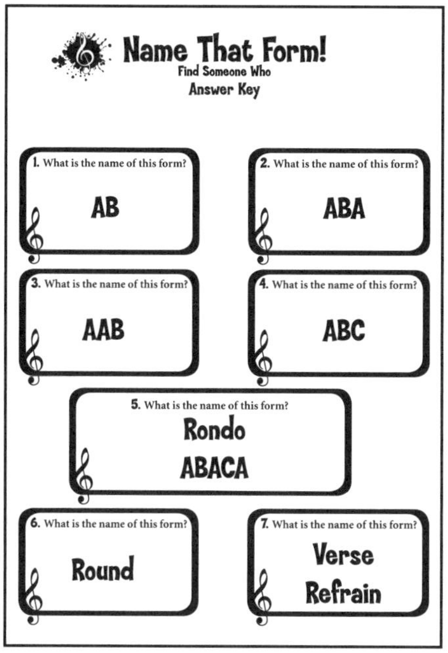

Name That Form!
pg. 334

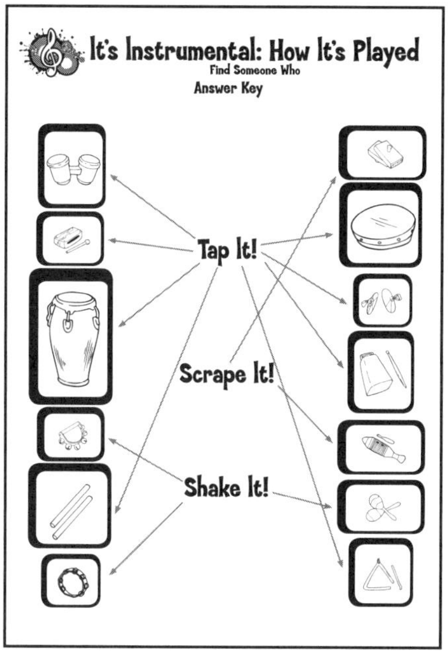

It's Instrumental: How It's Played
pg. 335

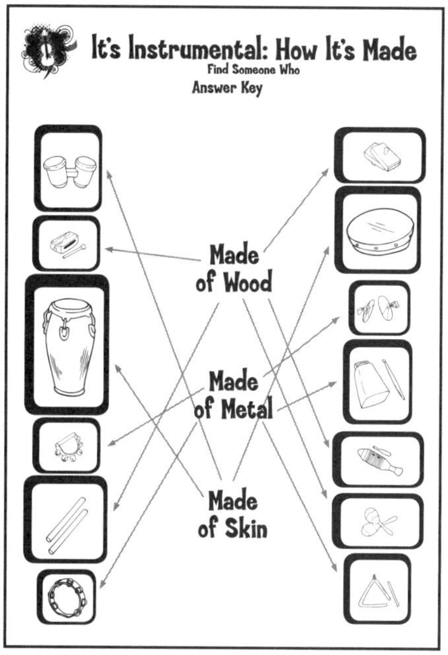

It's Instrumental: How It's Made
pg. 336

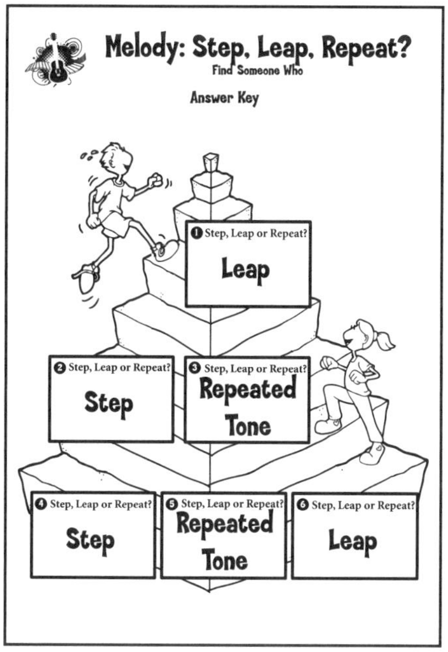

Melody: Step, Leap, Repeat?
pg. 337

Dynamics and Tempo
pg. 338

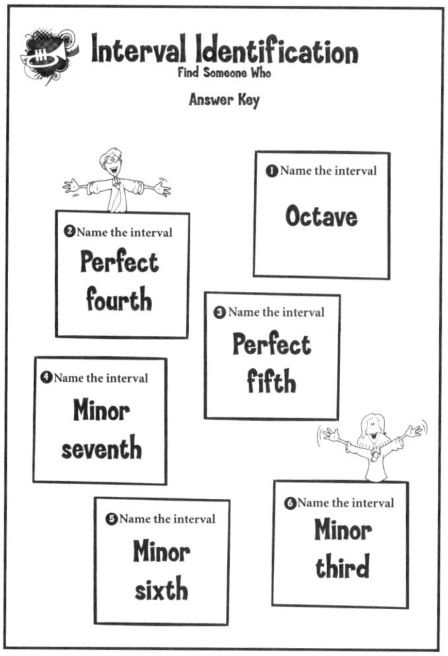

Interval Identification
pg. 339

Structure 9

RallyCoach

listening for Something specific

Structure 9

RallyCoach

Partners take turns, one solving a problem while the other coaches.

Steps

Setup: *Students are divided into pairs. Each pair needs one set of high-consensus problems and one pencil to share. RallyCoach may be used with worksheet problems, oral problems provided by the teacher (especially for primary level students), or with manipulatives/instruments.*

1 Partner A verbally solves the first problem.
In our Rhythmic Rhapsody example, Partner A selects a problem on the page to chant and clap for Partner B.

2 Partner B watches and listens, checks, coaches if necessary, and praises.
Partner B listens to Partner A's response and checks for accuracy. If Partner A performed the pattern correctly, Partner B praises. For example, "*Good job!*" or "*Great—you noticed the repeat signs!*" If Partner A did not perform the pattern correctly, Partner B coaches using tip-tip-tell. Tip 1: "*The notes that aren't colored in get 2 beats,*" or "*Be sure your clapping matches the way you say the pattern.*" After the tip, Partner B asks if Partner A doesn't know the answer, and Partner B gives tip 2. If Partner A still can't answer, Partner B performs the pattern for Partner A to listen to and then asks Partner A to echo it back—then praises Partner A for the effort.

3 Partner B verbally solves the next problem.
Partner B chooses another pattern on the page to perform for Partner A.

4 Partner A watches and listens, checks, coaches if necessary, and praises.
Partner A listens to Partner B's response, checks for accuracy, coaches, and/or praises Partner B's efforts as in Step 2.

5 Partners repeat taking turns solving successive problems.
Partners continue to chant and clap the patterns on the page, each taking turns as the performer or the coach. Patterns may be repeated; for example, a pattern that Partner A chose earlier in the course of the structure may be chosen later by Partner B.

Sample Activity

Rhythmic Rhapsody: Before starting the structure, the teacher leads a whole-class review of reading and chanting various rhythm patterns, some with and some without repeat signs in the notation. Then, pairs take turns chanting or clapping each problem while their partner coaches.

Benefits

- All students are actively involved.
- Students interact with a partner.
- Students learn and practice social skills: patience, responsibility, problem solving, active listening, providing clarification, praising, and encouraging contributions.
- Partners rely on each other, rather than on the teacher, to check for accuracy in responses to the questions.
- Teacher has the opportunity during RallyCoach for informal assessment.
- By using different worksheets or activities, many music concepts can be reinforced.
- RallyCoach supports lesson concepts or skills during Guided Practice, Checking for Understanding, or Lesson Closure.

Hints

- **Model.** The teacher chooses one student to assist in demonstrating the steps of the structure. The teacher models how Partner A solves the first problem by talking about his or her thinking. Student then models how Partner B praises Partner A.
- **Management.** If there is a group of three students, the first verbally solves the problem, the second checks or coaches the answer, and the third offers praise. Then the three roles are rotated.
- **Coaching.** Model using the "tip, tip, tell, re-ask" procedure: the coach gives one hint, if necessary gives a second hint, tells the correct answer if needed, and re-asks the question. The coach explains why that answer is correct or how to arrive at that answer, or both students develop a strategy for remembering the content.
- **Avoid Distractions.** Remind students to use "quiet voices" (mezzo-piano dynamic level), so all can participate without interfering with others nearby.

RallyCoach

Structure 9

RallyCoach (continued)

Variation

- **Pairs Check Structure.** After solving two problems (one apiece for Partners A and B), pairs wait to check their answers with another pair before continuing RallyCoach.

Principles

P **Positive Interdependence:** Partners are interdependent as they solve the worksheet problems together.

I **Individual Accountability:** An individual public performance is required. Partners solve and talk about answers with each other.

E **Equal Participation:** Students participate equally as they take turns demonstrating musical skills from the worksheet.

S **Simultaneous Interaction:** Students are actively engaged 50% of the time when solving problems or coaching.

RallyCoach Activities

Additional Activities for RallyCoach Worksheets

Worksheets can be used with Structures 8: Find Someone Who (one worksheet per person).

RallyCoach

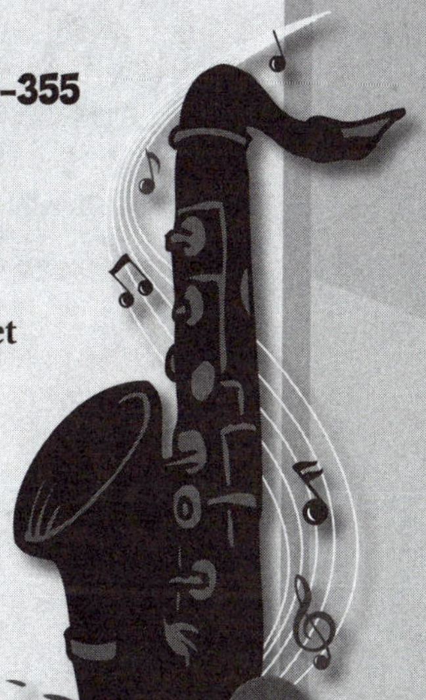

Rhythmic Rhapsody

Instructions: Pair up and take turns chanting and clapping each rhythm. Coach and support your partner on his or her turn.

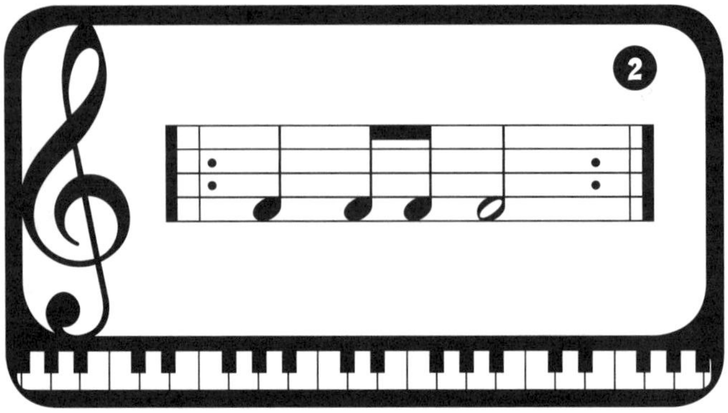

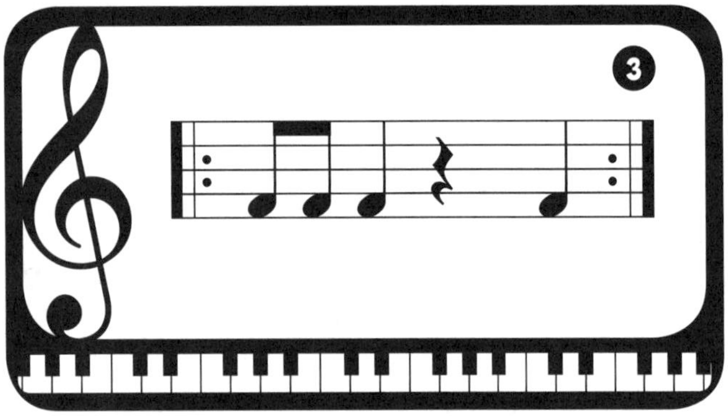

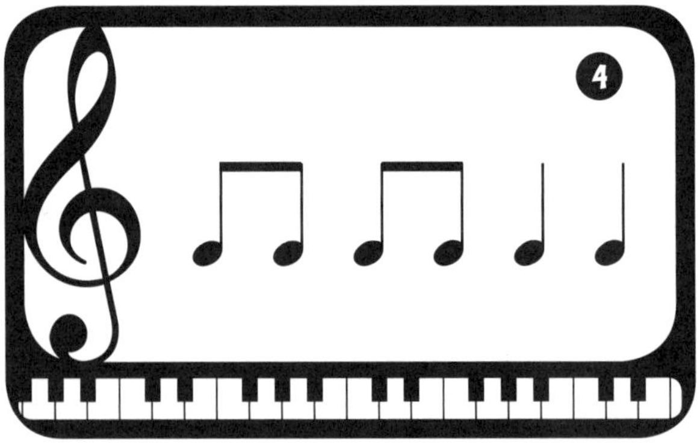

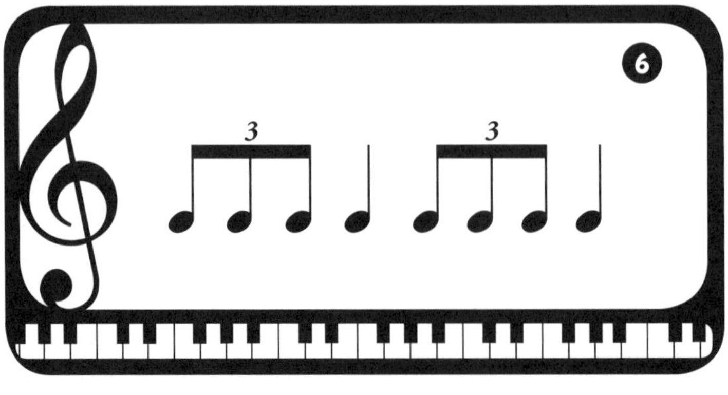

Basically Baroque

Instructions: Pair up and take turns answering each problem. Coach and support your partner on his or her turn.

Names ______________________ **Date** ______________________

1. Name three famous composers of the Baroque period of music history.

2. What are "terraced dynamics"?

3. What is "ornamentation"?

4. Name some of the Form Structures used by Baroque composers.

5. What is "improvisation"?

6. What was one of the most important musical elements of the Baroque period?

7. What are the dates of the Baroque period of music history?

8. Why were the instrumental groups of the Baroque period called "chamber ensembles"?

9. Who composed the famous "Hallelujah Chorus" as part of his oratorio *The Messiah*?

10. What is the term for the practice of writing music to express mood or emotion during the Baroque period?

11. Which keyboard instruments were popular during the Baroque period?

12. Which two kinds of music became more equal in importance during the Baroque period?

13. Which two instrument families shared equal importance with the strings during the Baroque period of music history?

14. Which Baroque composer is often considered to be the greatest composer of all time?

15. Which institution was greatly responsible for much of the music written during this time?

Clearly Classical

Instructions: Pair up and take turns answering each problem. Coach and support your partner on his or her turn.

Names ______________________ **Date** ______________________

1. Name three famous composers of the Classical period of music history.

____

____

2. Which element of music composition was the most important during this time period?

____

____

3. What is "symmetry" in music?

____

____

4. Name some of the Form Structures used by Classical composers.

____

____

5. Which keyboard instrument was invented during the Classical period?

____

____

6. Which musical element served merely to move the melody along during the Classical period?

____

____

7. What are the dates of the Classical period of music history?

____

____

____

8. What was different about the dynamics in the Classical period, compared to what was commonly heard during the Baroque period?

____

____

9. Which Classical composer was considered a "child prodigy"?

____

____

10. Which Classical composer was known for reworking his compositions many times until he was satisfied?

____

____

11. What is the approximate size of the Classical period orchestra (number of performers)?

____

____

12. What does a set of "balanced phrases" sound like?

____

____

13. Which instrument family usually had the melody in Classical orchestral compositions?

____

____

14. What is the Form Structure of a symphony?

____

____

Radically Romantic

Instructions: Pair up and take turns answering each problem. Coach and support your partner on his or her turn.

Names ______________________ **Date** ______________________

1. Name some famous composers of the Romantic period of music history.
____
____

2. Which element of music composition was the most important during this time period?
____
____

3. What does "program music" mean?
____
____

4. What was interesting about the phrase structure of Romantic compositions?
____
____

5. What did Romantic composers often try to convey in their compositions?
____
____

6. What was one of the least important musical elements of the Romantic period?
____
____

7. What are the dates of the Romantic period of music history?
____
____

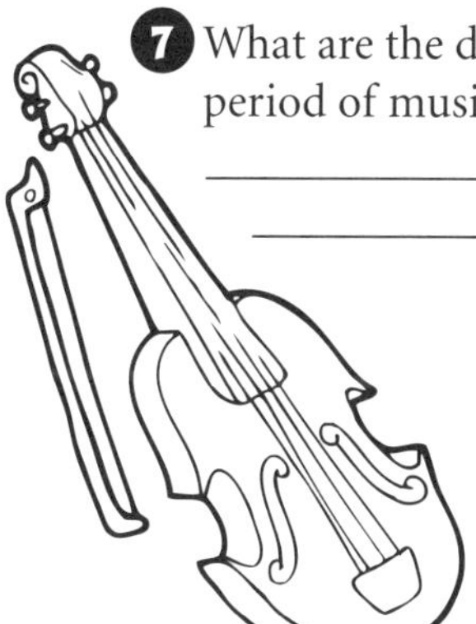

8. What was different about the dynamics during the Romantic period, compared to dynamics during the Classical period?
____
____

9. What are some of the Form Structures often found in Romantic style music?
____
____

10. Which Romantic Russian composer was known for writing ballet music?
____
____

11. What is "Nationalism" in music?
____
____

12. Which Romantic French composer wrote almost exclusively for the piano?
____
____

13. What is a "cadenza"?
____
____

14. What happened to the size of orchestras and choruses during the Romantic period?
____
____

Marvelously Modern

Instructions: Pair up and take turns answering each problem. Coach and support your partner on his or her turn.

Names ______________________ **Date** ______________________

1. Name some famous composers of the Modern (Contemporary) period of music history.

2. What does "atonal" mean?

3. Which musical element is the most varied during the Modern style period?

4. Which orchestral tone colors have become more important during the Modern period?

5. Which orchestral tone colors have become less important during the Modern period?

6. What are the dates of the Modern (Contemporary) period of music history?

7. What has been the biggest influence on the music written during the Modern style period?

8. What are some of the Form Structures often found in Modern (Contemporary) style music?

9. What is a "synthesizer"?

10. What does "impressionism" in music mean?

11. What one word can best describe Modern (Contemporary) music?

12. What happened to the size of performing ensembles during the Modern period?

13. Which form of "popular" music is often found in "serious" Modern compositions?

Blank Banner Template

Instructions: Use this worksheet frame to create your own RallyCoach worksheet.

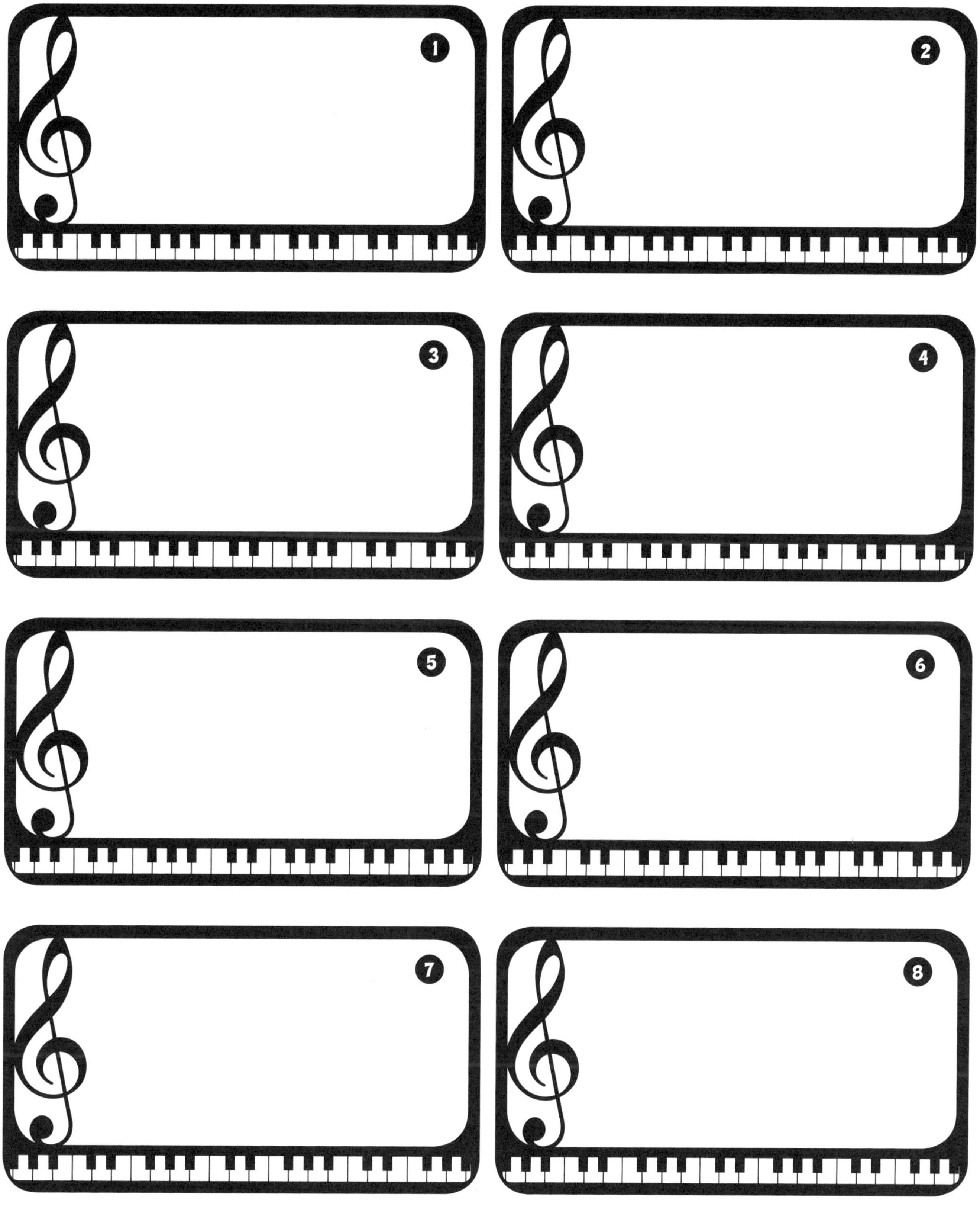

RallyCoach
Answer Key

Basically Baroque pg. 349

1. • Johann Sebastian Bach
   • George Frideric Handel
   • Antonio Vivaldi
2. When there are sudden changes from loud to soft in the music, or changes that take place by "stepping up" (soft—medium—loud) or "stepping down" (loud—medium—soft)
3. Decorating the melody with trills, mordents, grace notes
4. Concerto grosso, dance suite, opera, mass, fugue
5. When the soloist creates the music as it is being performed ("in the moment")
6. Rhythm, improvisation, major-minor system of tonality
7. 1600–1750
8. Music was performed by small groups of musicians in patrons' homes or smaller "chambers" in palaces
9. George Frideric Handel
10. The Doctrine of Musical "Affections"
11. Harpsichord, organ, and clavier
12. Vocal and instrumental
13. • Woodwinds
    • Brass
14. Johann Sebastian Bach
15. The church

Clearly Classical pg. 350

1. • Franz Joseph Haydn
   • Ludwig van Beethoven
   • Wolfgang Amadeus Mozart
2. Melody
3. Balancing the sections of a piece as in "ABA," or the pitch patterns and tonalities as in "minor-major-minor," to show congruence on either side of a contrasting middle
4. • Symphony
   • Opera
   • String quartet
   • Sonata
   • Rondo
   • Concerto
5. The piano
6. Rhythm
7. 1750–1825
8. A shift to gradually changing from soft to loud, rather than sudden changes
9. Wolfgang Amadeus Mozart
10. Ludwig van Beethoven
11. 35–40
12. Each will be the same number of beats in length
13. Strings
14. 3 or 4 movements, usually in the order of fast-slow-fast (fast-slow-fast-fast for a symphony in 4 movements)

RallyCoach
Answer Key

Radically Romantic pg. 351

1. • Franz Schubert
   • Peter Tchaikowsky
   • Camille Saint-Saëns
   • Richard Wagner
   • Johann Strauss Jr.
   • Georges Bizet
   • Frederic Chopin
   • Johannes Brahms
   (and more)
2. Expression (melodies, harmonies, and tone colors used collectively to convey emotion)
3. Music that exists to tell a story
4. Phrases were often long or extended, and of uneven lengths within a composition
5. Emotions or stories
6. Rhythm
7. 1825–1910
8. Dynamic changes were often sudden and dramatic, rather than the gradual changes of the Classical time period
9. • Opera
   • Program music
   • Tone poem
   • Overture
10. Peter Tchaikowsky
11. Music that uses themes or sounds that represent the composer's native country
12. Frederic Chopin
13. An extended solo section, often improvised, where the performer displays his or her virtuosity during a concerto
14. They became quite large, often numbering more than 100 performers

Marvelously Modern pg. 352

1. • George Gershwin
   • Aaron Copland
   • Igor Stravinsky
   • Carl Webern
   • John Cage
   • Sergei Prokofiev
   • Charles Ives
   • Benjamin Britten
   • Claude Debussy
   • Arnold Schoenberg
   (and more)
2. Music where the melody and harmony are without a home key
3. Rhythm
4. Percussion
5. Strings
6. 1900–present day
7. Electronics
8. • Ballet
   • Concerto
   • Chance music
   • Opera
   • Suite
9. An electronic instrument capable of producing sounds by generating electrical signals of different frequencies
10. A focus on sound through "suggestion" or "atmosphere," rather than an emotion or a story, with emphasis on the particular tone quality or timbre of various individual instruments
11. Experimental
12. They became much smaller than those of the previous time period
13. Jazz and blues

Section 3

More Music Resources

Staff Template

Treble Clef Staff Template

Bass Clef Staff Template

Treble Clef Staff Templates

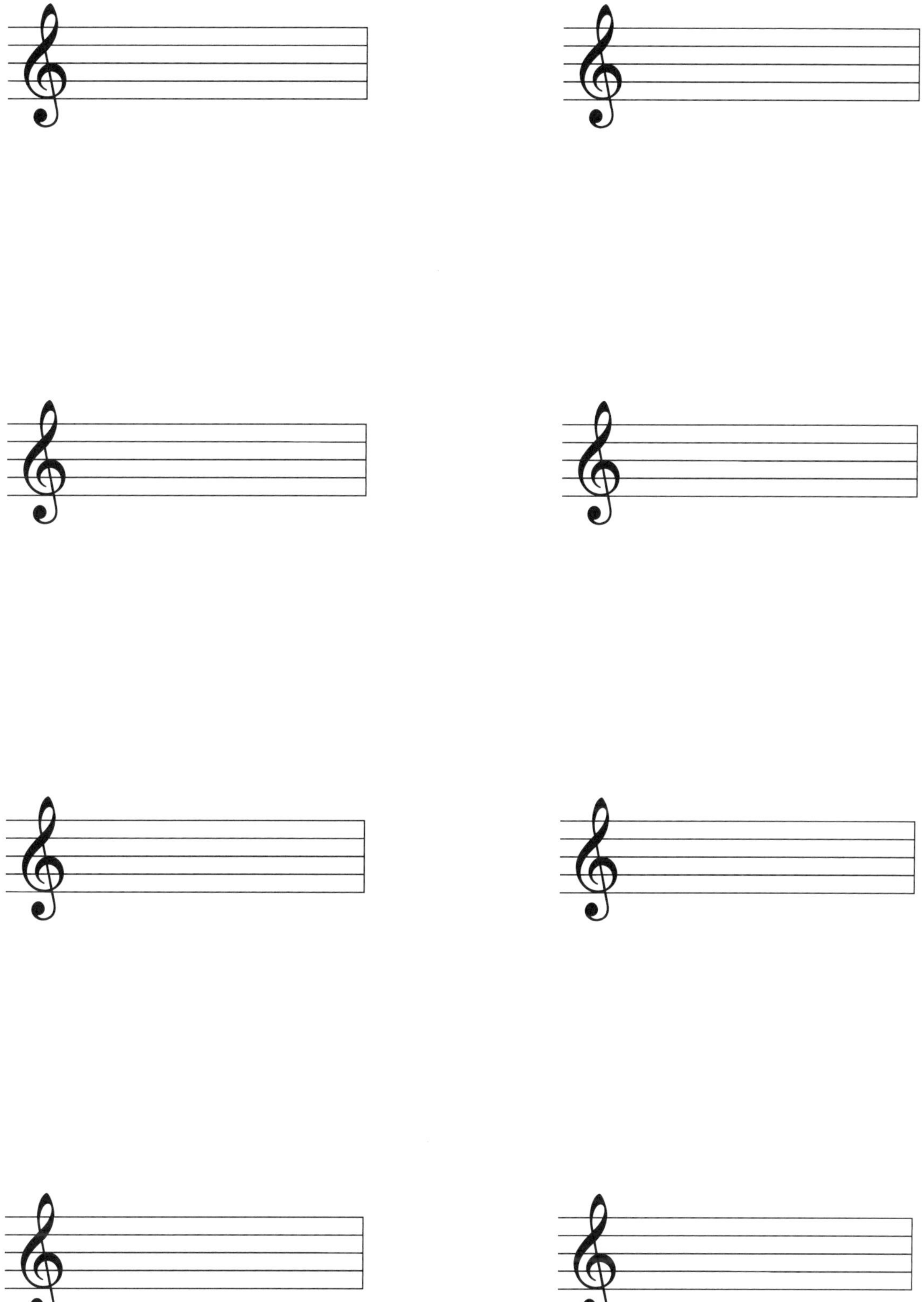

Bass Clef Staff Templates

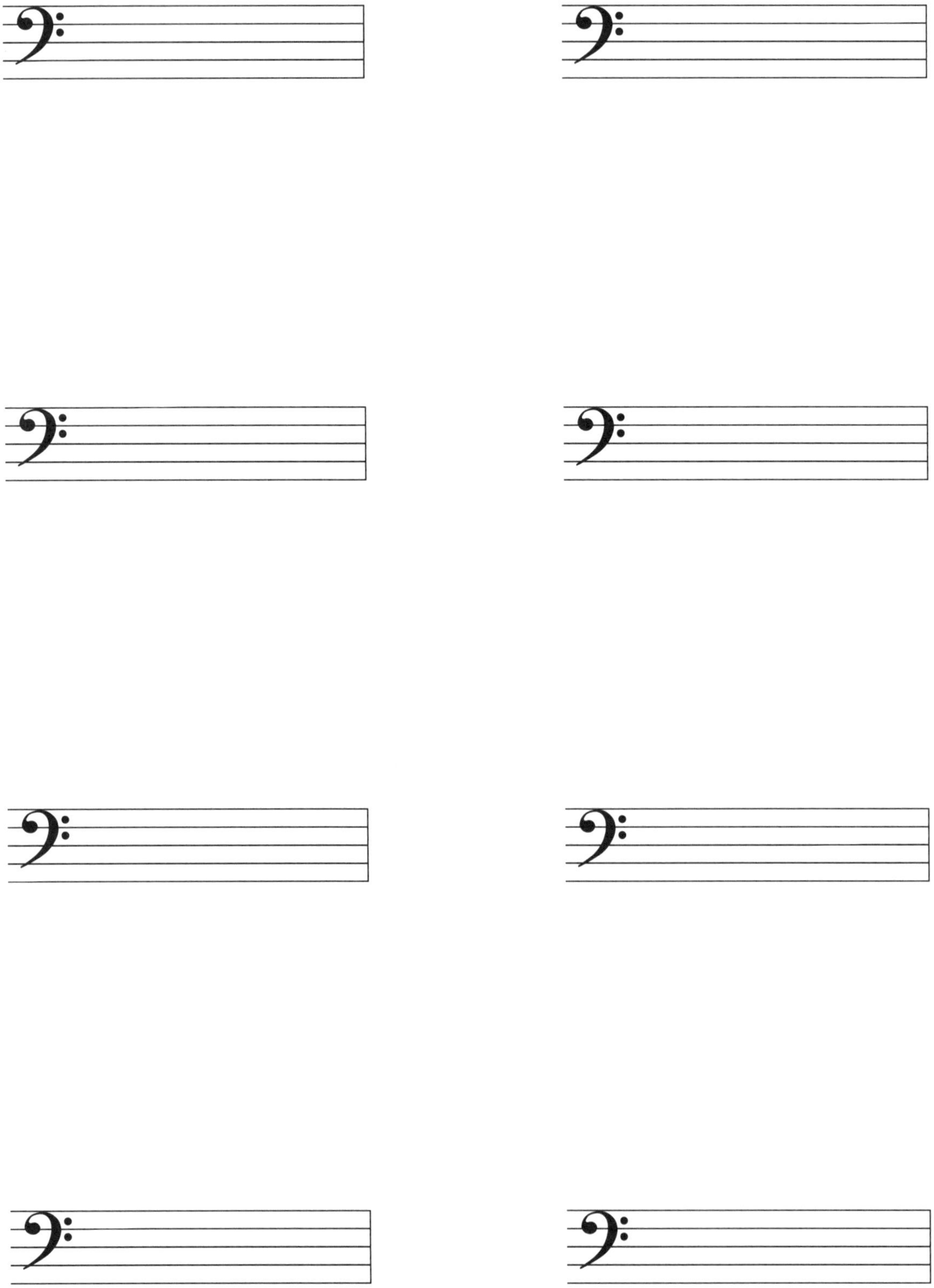

Bracket Staff Templates

Notes Page

Notes Page

Notes Page

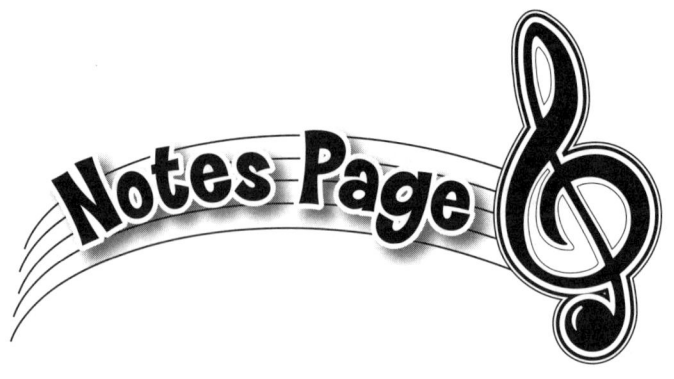

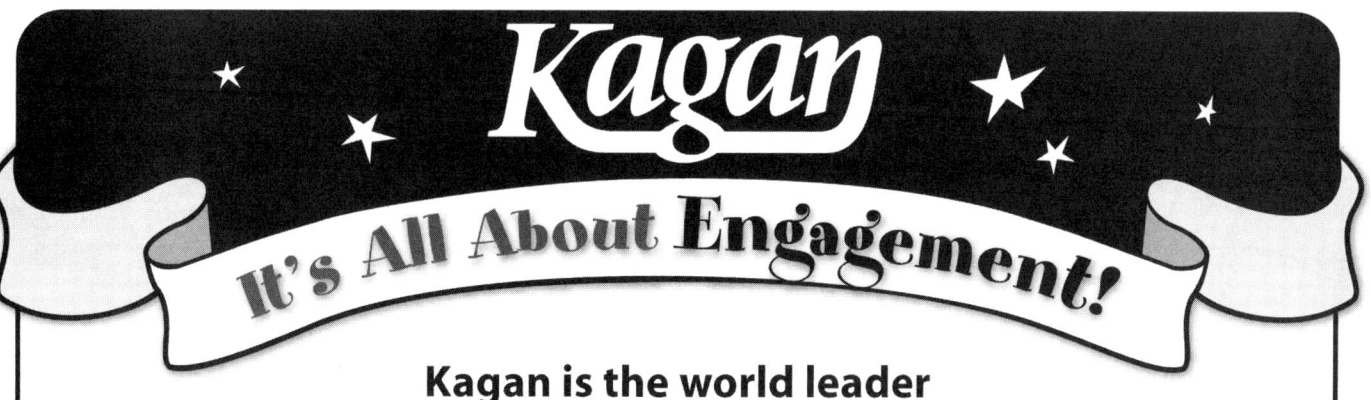

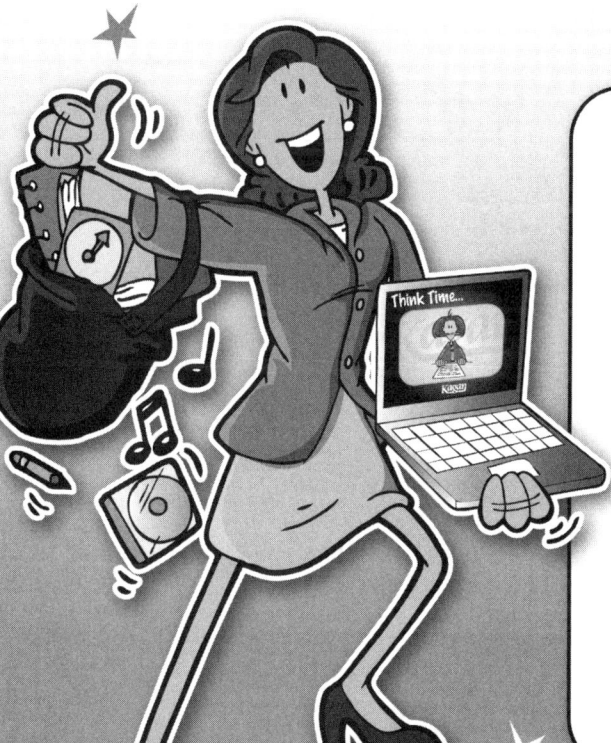

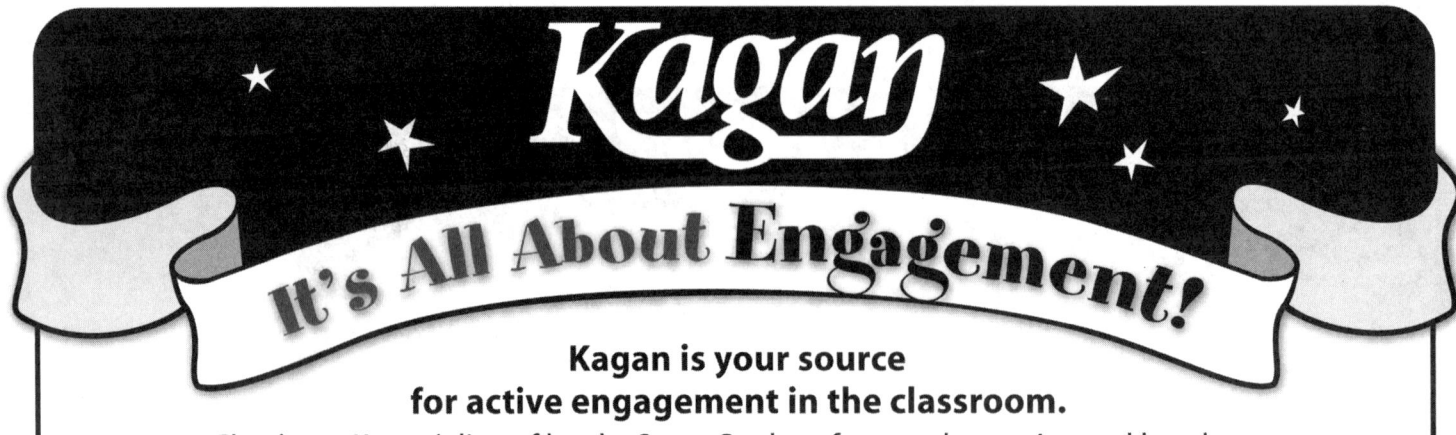

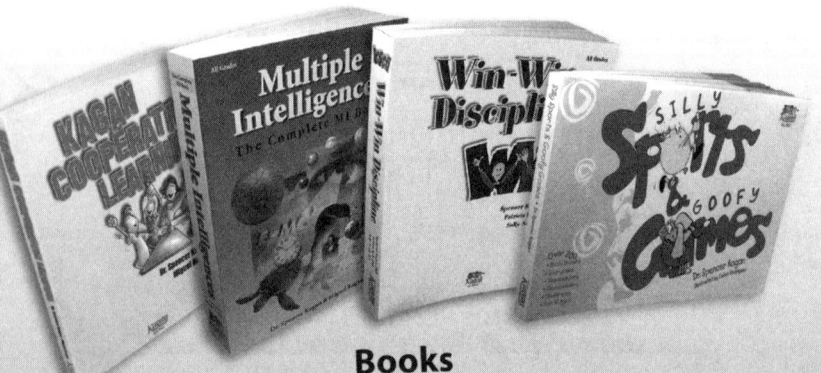

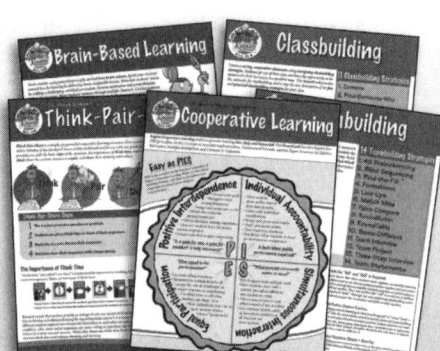

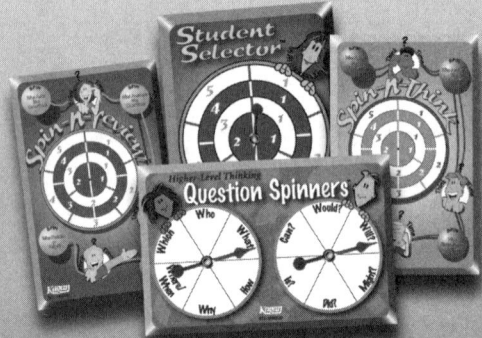

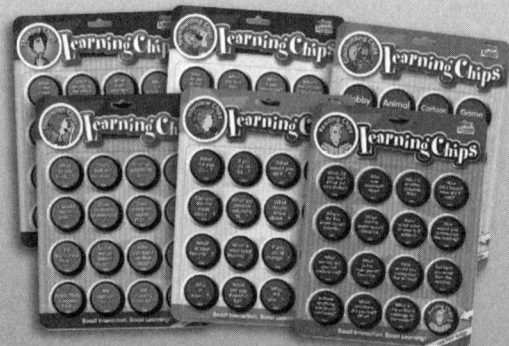

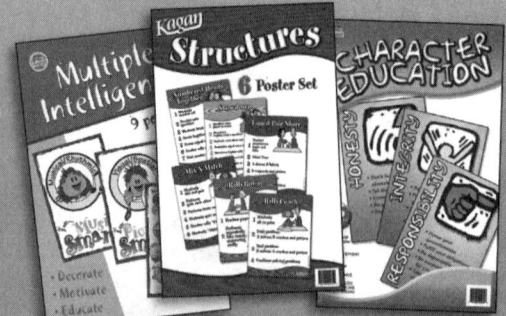

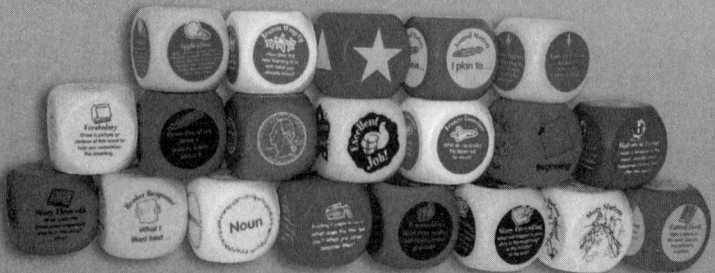